WINSTON CHURCHILL
The Wilderness Years

WINSTON CHURCHILL
The Wilderness Years

Martin Gilbert

'War is horrible, but slavery is worse.'
WINSTON CHURCHILL
7 January 1939

Houghton Mifflin Company Boston   1982

First American Edition 1982

Library of Congress Cataloging in Publication Data

Gilbert, Martin, date
  Winston Churchill, the wilderness years.

  Bibliography: p.
  Includes index.
  1. Churchill, Winston, Sir, 1874–1965. 2. Great
Britain—Politics and government—1910–1936. 3. Great
Britain—Politics and government—1936–1945. 4. Prime
ministers—Great Britain—Biography. I. Title.
DA566.9.C5G463   1982   941.082′092′4[B]   82–9279
ISBN 0–395–31869–6   AACR2

This book was designed and produced by
The Rainbird Publishing Group Limited
40 Park Street, London W1Y 4DE

Frontispiece: Churchill at Chartwell, a photograph taken
in the spring of 1939 (*BBC Hulton Picture Library*)

Printed in the United States of America

Contents

Author's acknowledgments

For more than twenty years I have been doing historical research on the personalities and episodes that appear in this book. I have also published several books using this research, beginning with a detailed study of appeasement, and including both the biography of the British Ambassador to Berlin when Hitler came to power, and several collections of documents and essays on the interwar years. From the outset, and for several years before I became Churchill's biographer, Churchill himself was a central figure in these researches, playing as he did so prominent, if controversial, a part in the national and foreign policy debate of the thirties. This book is based upon my work during these twenty years.

In 1968 I began work on the Churchill biography itself. Readers who are interested in the detailed academic story of Churchill's wilderness years may consult the fifth volume of the official biography of Sir Winston Churchill, published by William Heinemann Limited, and also the biography's three 'companion' volumes of documents. These document volumes, each of which contains more than 1,400 pages of previously unpublished material, are entitled respectively 'The Exchequer Years, 1924–1929', 'The Wilderness Years, 1929–1935' and 'The Coming of War, 1936–1939'.

Anyone wishing to follow up Churchill's political or personal life during these years may consult the above volumes, which are fully annotated for the general reader, the student and the scholar.

I have drawn further material for this volume from several sources, including: Hansard (for Parliamentary debates); the Public Record Office, London (for material on the Government's defence and foreign policy); the British Library (for Churchill's own published books and articles); the BBC Written Archives Centre (for the texts of Churchill's broadcasts during the thirties); and the Churchill papers. I am grateful to all copyright holders, and to all those who gave me their recollections of the period, for permission to quote their materials and recollections here; these sources are listed on page 269.

For help in preparing this book, I wish to thank Sue Rampton, for her valiant typing efforts; Erica Hunningher, for her considerable editorial skills; and my wife Susie, for her work with me on this subject over many years, and for her advice and guidance at every stage of the writing of this book. Without her substantial efforts, it would not have been written.

Merton College
Oxford
10 May 1981

Illustrations acknowledgments

The author and producers of this book are grateful to all those picture agencies, photographic archives and individuals listed below for permission to reproduce the photographs and cartoons used in this book.

Every effort has been made to trace the source of illustrations; in the five cases where it has not been possible, the author and producers wish to apologize; and if any owner of copyright who has remained untraced will communicate with the producers, full acknowledgment will be made in future editions of the book.

Torr Anderson Collection: 187 (*below*)
BBC Hulton Picture Library: frontispiece, 81 (*above*), 86 (*both*), 89 (*above*), 94 (*below*), 195 (*below*)
Lord Baldwin: 81 (*below*)
Bowyer Collection: 197 (*above*)
Broadwater Collection: 82, 83 (*above*), 97, 98
Bulletin and Scots Pictorial: 101 (*below*)
Central Press Agency: 87 (*both*), 89 (*below*), 90 (*below*), 91, 99 (*below*), 100 (*both*), 101 (*above*), 185, 190 (*both*), 191, 192 (*below*), 193 (*below*), 199 (*above*), 200 (*both*), 205, 206 (*above*), 208
Sybil, Lady Cholmondely: 102
Howard Coster: 93 (*above right*)
Major P. H. Courtenay: 94 (*above*)
Daily Mail: 103
Daily Mirror: 206 (*below*)
Daily Record and Mail: 99 (*above*), 187 (*above*)
Sir William Deakin: 204 (*below*)

Evening Standard (Low Trustees): 93 (*above left*)
Fox Photos Limited: 93 (*below*), 201, 203 (*above right*)
Harvey Collection: 88
Harrods: 197 (*below*)
Keystone Press Agency Limited: 85 (*below*), 90 (*above*), 92, 193 (*above*), 195 (*above*)
Paul Maze Collection: 194, 196, 207
Picture Post: 204 (*above*)
Paul Popper Limited: 202
Press Association: 83 (*below*)
Punch: 95 (*below*), 104, 203 (*above left*)
Source unknown: 84, 85 (*above*), 95 (*above*), 189, 192 (*above*)
Tatler and Bystander: 96, 188, 198
Tribune: 203 (*below*)
Viscountess Waverley Collection: 186
Yorkshire Observer: 199 (*below*)

The pinnacle of success

The year 1928 marked a high point in Churchill's career. As Chancellor of the Exchequer he had already introduced four Budgets. The Conservative Party, from which he had been estranged for more than a quarter of a century, but which he had rejoined in 1924, now held him in high esteem. The Conservative Prime Minister, Stanley Baldwin, frequently sought his advice. His speeches in the House of Commons were witty, well-argued and widely praised. After nearly thirty years in British politics he was a well-known and well-liked figure, despite past controversies. At the age of fifty-three he had reached a pinnacle of national recognition, and of personal contentment.

As an administrator Churchill had already held, by 1928, a series of Minister-ial posts in which his zest for work and his interest in constructive legislation had made him a popular chief. Since first entering the Cabinet twenty years before, he had held office as President of the Board of Trade, Home Secretary, First Lord of the Admiralty, Minister of Munitions, Secretary of State for War and Air, Colonial Secretary, and now Chancellor of the Exchequer. This list itself was a formidable one. So too was the range of legislation for which he had been responsible, and which he had piloted through Parliament.

Three Prime Ministers, Asquith, Lloyd George and Baldwin, had each in their turn found Churchill an energetic, frank and constructive colleague, always willing to defend the Government in public against attack, a brilliant debater on controversial issues, a font of stimulating ideas in Cabinet and of wise counsel in private. Each of these three Prime Ministers had given Chur-chill senior Cabinet office, and had asked him to undertake major respon-sibilities outside the normal range of ministerial duties. Each had made use of Churchill's strength of character and resolution, turning to him in times of crisis.

Churchill had responded with alacrity to these approaches and appeals. As a member of the War Council in the early months of the First World War he had been a pillar of resolve in Asquith's often confused Cabinet. At the time of the German breakthrough on the western front in the spring of 1918 he had been a force for perseverance in Lloyd George's Government, and was sent by Lloyd George personally to report on the morale of the armies and the prospect for victory. In the aftermath of the General Strike of 1926, he had conducted conciliatory negotiations with the miners, surprising many of the members of Baldwin's Cabinet by his resourcefulness, his patience, and his desire for a magnanimous settlement.

In Foreign Affairs, Churchill had consistently sought the reconciliation of

9

former enemies and the appeasement of international hatreds. In time of war he had been a force for optimism, perseverance, and faith in the justice and triumph of Britain's cause. Yet with his first-hand experience of war as a young soldier, and on the western front in 1916, he had known and was still affected by what he himself had called the 'vile and utter folly and barbarism' of the battlefield. These feelings were expressed again and again in his own writings. By 1928 his multi-volume history of the First World War was almost completed. In it, he had already castigated the Passchendaele offensive as an unnecessary waste of life: a view which he had also held and expressed both before and during the offensive itself.

Yet despite his long experience and wide ranging achievements, Churchill's career had been punctuated by criticism, hostility and disappointment. His dynamic personality and outspokeness had gained him many enemies. For every quality he possessed, these enemies alleged equally strong defects. He was frequently accused of lack of judgment. Critics pointed to a series of episodes to uphold these accusations, among them 'Tonypandy', 'Antwerp', 'the Dardanelles', the Allied intervention against Bolshevik Russia, and even the publication of a Government newspaper during the General Strike. These accusations were emotive, and widely believed as a matter of faith, rather than of fact or of evidence. Much of this criticism arose because Churchill had taken personal responsibility for failures which were not his alone, and had refused to shirk decisions which might harm him politically. Nor could these accusations be answered fully at the time, either by Churchill himself or by his supporters, for the answers depended on the use of secret documents, many of which only became public in the decade after Churchill's death.

Despite all Churchill's successes by 1928, and despite his own confidence in his abilities, there lurked substantial public suspicion that he could never be Prime Minister. After all, what political Party would accept him as its leader?

Twice, Churchill had fallen from political grace. First, in 1915 when the Conservatives had refused to join Asquith's wartime coalition unless Churchill were removed from the Admiralty. Then, in 1922 he had been defeated at the General Election and was out of Parliament for two years. For those who believed that there was some 'fatal flaw' in his character, these two events were pointers to his vulnerability.

Churchill's abilities, combined with his open, energetic and assertive personality, inspired jealousy as well as trust and affection. Even those who most admired and supported him, could at times give way to a sense of doubt. 'It is a pity, isn't it', Asquith wrote to a friend in March 1915, 'that Winston hasn't a better sense of proportion, and also a larger endowment of the instinct of loyalty. He will never get to the top in English politics, with all his wonderful gifts; to speak with the tongue of men and angels, and to spend laborious days and nights in administration, is no good, if a man does not inspire trust.' Yet six days later Asquith himself was writing, to the same friend, 'Winston is really loyal to me. I am sure, and I have never doubted that he is.'

The First World War left Churchill a wiser man and a more mature politician. His energy was unabated and his administrative abilities more widely acknowledged. So also was his ability to inspire by speech and example. By the time he had become Chancellor of the Exchequer, even former critics spoke of the emergence of a new man. 'The remarkable thing about him', one Conservative Member of Parliament, Lord Winterton, wrote in June 1927, 'is the way in which he has suddenly acquired, quite late in his Parliamentary life, an immense fund of tact, patience, good humour and banter on almost all occasions; no one used to "suffer fools ungladly" more fully than Winston, now he is friendly and accessible to everyone, both in the House, and in the lobbies, with the result that he has become what he never was before the war, very popular in the House generally – a great accretion to his already formidable Parliamentary power.'

Even Neville Chamberlain, Churchill's chief rival in the Cabinet, looked on him with passionate mixed feelings, and could write of him in August 1928, in a private letter: 'One doesn't often come across a real man of genius or, perhaps, appreciate him when one does. Winston is such a man. . . .'

Chamberlain and Churchill were to be rivals, critics and enemies for the whole of the next decade. 'There is too deep a difference between our natures', Chamberlain wrote in this same letter, 'for me to feel at home with him or to regard him with affection. He is a brilliant wayward child who compels admiration but who wears out his guardians with the constant strain he puts upon them.' Similar feelings had bedevilled Churchill's relations with his three most powerful patrons, Asquith, Lloyd George and Baldwin. Each had turned to him, and given him high office. But each had also expressed qualms about him, for they feared his courage, decisiveness and honesty, as did many of those backbench Members of Parliament on whose support they depended. 'Winston's position is curious,' Baldwin had written to a friend in September 1927. 'Our people like him. They love listening to him in the House, look on him as a star turn, and settle down in the stalls with anticipatory grins. But for leadership, they would turn him down every time.'

Churchill was aware of these adverse feelings, and worked hard to overcome them. His fourth Budget, which he introduced in the House of Commons in April 1928, was a masterpiece, winning him much praise from those who had hitherto withheld it. In it he unveiled a plan, the complete details of which he had worked out with his advisers, and pushed through the Cabinet, aimed at stimulating industrial production and reducing unemployment, by relieving British industry of the burden of Rates.

The idea of 'de-rating' had first been put to Churchill early in his Chancellorship, by a young and reforming Conservative MP, Harold Macmillan. It had taken more than a year of arduous preparation to work out the scheme in detail, and make it acceptable to the Cabinet. Always alert to new ideas and guidance, Churchill had shown the final plans to Macmillan, and been encouraged by Macmillan's detailed scrutiny and enthusiasm.

11

In his Budget speech of April 1928, Churchill presented 'de-rating' to the nation. The whole of his speech, so Stanley Baldwin informed King George V, would be recognized by the public 'as being the most remarkable achievement in Mr Churchill's career', while a former Conservative Prime Minister, Lord Balfour – once one of Churchill's severest critics – wrote to him on the following day: 'It is a great moment in the history of British finance and of the Unionist Party – of your personal fame I will say nothing.'

That same Unionist Party – the Conservative and Unionist Party as it was formally known – had, however, years of grievance to overcome. Many of these 'old-time' Conservatives could never forgive Churchill's 'betrayal' of their Party in 1904, when he had not only left them to join the Liberals, but had used all his youthful oratorical skills both to attack them with skill and invective and to become a leading champion of one of their chief hatreds, Free Trade. A decade later he had become an outspoken supporter of another Conservative hatred, Irish Home Rule, and in 1921 he had played an important part not only in the negotiations for the Irish Treaty but also in the Parliamentary debates in which the Treaty was expounded, and in the subsequent negotiations with the southern Irish leaders – the former gunmen – for its implementation. By 1928, six years had already passed since the Irish Treaty but many Conservatives still regarded it as a grave blow to the unity of the United Kingdom, and were critical of Churchill as one of its principal architects.

The dislike, amounting at times to hatred, which Home Rule and Free Trade had roused against Churchill since before the First World War, had never died. It surfaced again during the course of 1928 when a group of Conservative backbenchers tried to move their Party towards Protection. Churchill challenged the Party's trend towards protective tariffs, but did not allow the hostility he had aroused to upset him. 'Really I feel very independent of them all', he told his wife in the autumn of 1928, and he returned for a while to his literary work, a further volume of his war memoirs, in which he told the story of the Treaty of Versailles and of the immediate postwar years, including his part in the intervention against Bolshevik Russia, and in the Irish Treaty.

Churchill's sense of personal contentment in 1928 centred on his country house, Chartwell. Bought six years before, it had quickly become the focal point of his family life, the scene of work and writing, of bricklaying and painting. From the terraces, he could look across the lawns to the swimming pool he himself had built, to the lake, and to the artificial island which had been excavated from the bank with the aid of a great mechanical digger. From the upper gardens, and from the windows of the house, fine panoramas unfolded; on the west, across a small country road, to a spectacular bank of rhododendrons opposite, and from the garden side, southwards across the rolling valleys of Kent, to the distant hills of the South Downs.

Churchill's wife Clementine, despite her original dislike of the house, supervised the comfortable domestic arrangements, and ensured that there was a large enough staff to meet the family's many needs, and the constant flow of weekend visitors. She often needed periods of recuperation away from the domestic responsibilities at Chartwell and did not always accompany Churchill on his travels. Whenever they were apart she wrote letters filled with advice which he valued. His letters to her were kaleidoscopes of news and opinion, reflection and humour, filled with personal tenderness.

It distressed Churchill enormously when his wife was tense and worried. Sometimes she expressed her anxiety about their financial affairs, sometimes about Chartwell. Whenever they were apart, he sought to comfort her in long and affectionate letters, gently and sympathetically telling her not to worry about household matters: 'let them crash if they will,' he wrote, 'Servants exist to save one trouble, and should never be allowed to disturb one's inner peace.'

By 1928, the older children were away at boarding school. Randolph was at Eton, their daughters Diana and Sarah were also only home for the holidays, Mary, their youngest daughter, just five years old, was the only child still permanently at home. In the holidays the house resounded with their bustle and laughter. There were quarrels too, for each of them was a strong character. But the storm clouds which these quarrels provoked could blow over in an instant as Churchill's own impish sense of humour cajoled and won over the disputants. Once, amid a ferocious quarrel over some topic long since forgotten, Churchill reduced the whole family to mirthful convulsions with a mock-serious stentorian outburst: 'Randolph, do not interrupt me – while I'm interrupting.'

At weekends Treasury officials came down to Chartwell to discuss the next moves in the Government's economic policy. A research assistant, seconded from the Foreign Office, helped to prepare the materials needed for the new book. Bricklayers were busy building a small cottage for Mary, and for several hours each day Churchill amused himself by helping them. One frequent visitor was an Oxford don, Professor Lindemann, who intrigued Churchill by his graphic descriptions of the world of science and physics.

Lindemann, known by the Churchills as 'Prof', held a particular fascination for Churchill. There was no scientific question which Prof could not answer, or at least appear to answer. Sometimes, at dinner, he would be asked to explain a complex theory within a specific time, say five minutes. Out would come Churchill's watch, and the explanation would begin. Two minutes, three, then four would pass. The final sixty seconds would tick to a close. Then, only seconds from the end, the explanation would be over. Led by Churchill himself, the whole table, family and other guests, would burst into applause.

Prof was witty, wise, and devoted. Often he would drive over from Oxford, a long three hours on winding roads, for a weekend, sometimes as the only guest. No Christmas or New Year passed without Prof being there: often, other than family and cousins, he was the only outsider present. But he was always welcome. Churchill, while teasing him about his antipathy to alcohol, and arguing with him volubly over many issues, delighted in his company, valued his knowledge, and frequently sought his advice.

Friends, colleagues and relations, artists, writers and politicians made the Chartwell weekends vibrate with conversation and laughter. Above all it was Churchill's own personality which gave the weekends their memorable quality for all who took part in them. 'It is a marvel how much time he gives to his guests,' one visitor noted in September 1928, 'talking sometimes for an hour after lunch and much longer after dinner. He is an exceedingly kind and generous host, providing unlimited champagne, cigars and brandy.'

Churchill's conversation was always witty and absorbing. With ease he could draw on his wide historical reading, on his knowledge of men and events, and on his personal experiences of war and politics going back to the reign of Queen Victoria and his own part in the cavalry charge at Omdurman. 'When he becomes engrossed in his subject', the young visitor noted, 'he strides up and down the room with his head thrust forward and his thumbs in the armholes of his waistcoat, as if he were trying to keep pace with his own eloquence. If he shows signs of slowing down, all you have to do is to make some moderately intelligent observation, and off he goes again.'

Churchill's capacity for work amazed those who saw it at first hand. The four or more hours after dinner, from ten or eleven in the evening until two or even three in the morning, were particularly busy ones, with long official memoranda, or chapters of the new book, being tested on Treasury officials or research assistants, and then dictated to one of the secretaries who worked special night shifts.

Those who were caught up in this fever of work found it tiring, but exhilarating. Churchill was a hard taskmaster, but a kind one, and those who worked with him most closely became all the more devoted to him. Both in good times and in bad, he generated enthusiasm and productive energy on a formidable scale.

In the autumn of 1928 there seemed no reason to believe that the good times would end, or that either the bitterness of his isolation of 1915, or the frustrations which had followed his Parliamentary defeat in 1922, would ever return.

Chapter One

Political strife

In the last week of September 1928, as the summer holidays drew to their close, Churchill was at Balmoral for four days' stag hunting and grouse shooting with King George V. Determined to continue work on his war memoirs, he took with him both his secretary, and the documents relating to the chapter he was working on: the Treaty of Versailles.

In a letter from Balmoral, Churchill gave his wife a survey of the royal scene. The King, he wrote, was 'well – but ageing'. He no longer stalked deer, but went out on the hill where the deer were 'moved about for him', in the hope that 'some loyal stag will do his duty'.

While Churchill was at Balmoral, Stanley Baldwin returned from his annual summer holiday at Aix-les-Bains. As in previous years, while the Prime Minister was away in his favourite French mountain resort, political activity in England was suspended. But as soon as Baldwin returned, political speculation mounted rapidly, centring around the question of the date for the next General Election.

In a year's time – in November 1929 – the Conservative Government would reach the end of its five-year span. An election in the spring or summer of 1929 was thought most likely.

As the election approached, Churchill's writing centred on the last volume of his war memoirs. 'He tells me', a friend noted, 'that he does a certain amount of work in bed in the morning, spends only twenty minutes in dressing, and keeps two hours free every night for dictating his books.' Among those who helped Churchill with material for the chapters on the Russian revolution of 1917 was Major Desmond Morton. Morton and Churchill had known each other for more than a decade: they had first met on the western front during the First World War.

After the war Morton had been drawn into intelligence work while Churchill was Secretary of State for War in 1919. He had become an expert in the military and economic preparations first of Soviet Russia, and later of Germany. In January 1929, while helping Churchill to assemble historical facts, Morton was appointed to a senior intelligence post, as Head of the Industrial Intelligence Centre of the Committee of Imperial Defence, a position he held until the outbreak of the Second World War. His official instructions were to 'discover and report the plans for manufacture of armaments and war stores in foreign countries'.

As Chancellor of the Exchequer, Churchill knew of Morton's new appointment. Morton's country cottage was only a fifteen-minute walk across the fields from Chartwell and they would often meet to discuss matters of State policy together.

Their most frequent topic for discussion was the balance of power in Europe, for they shared the concern that Germany was aiming at rearmament. Under the Treaty of Versailles, signed just ten years before, Germany had been stripped of her armaments, and forbidden to build up a navy, an air force or an army. These clauses of the Treaty were explicit and binding; the German Imperial Navy itself lay rusting under the water of Scapa Flow, off the coast of Scotland, where it had been scuttled at the end of the First World War.

Although Churchill did not doubt Germany's existing weakness, he was convinced of her ability to revive, and to challenge not only the Treaty of Versailles, but the very European frontiers which the Treaty had established. He had therefore consistently opposed European efforts for disarmament towards which the powers were obliged to work under the post-war settlement. In particular, for four years he had opposed international efforts to persuade France to disarm. His reasoning was clear: the existence of a forcibly disarmed France and an aggrieved, rearming Germany would lead sooner or later to war between the two.

Despite the imminence of the election, the problems of long-term defence policy continued to press upon the Government. Now the United States had begun to urge a general disarmament. Churchill was active in Cabinet in opposing what he described to his colleagues as 'these stupid disarmament manoeuvres', even if such pressure originated in the United States. Churchill believed that France must maintain an army 'strong enough to overpower a German invasion', so long as Germany's grievances resulting from the Treaty of Versailles were still unsatisfied. This was even more necessary since the United States had withdrawn from the League of Nations and gone back on its post-war promise to help France in the event of a German attack. A strong French army, Churchill argued, would protect Britain from the 'most probable danger' of being forced to intervene in Europe.

As for British rearmament, this, Churchill urged the Cabinet, should be based upon a careful study of the most recent foreign, and above all German techniques of armaments manufacture, details of which Morton and Churchill studied together.

Churchill spent Christmas 1928 at Chartwell, where work on his book kept him busy throughout the holiday period and into the New Year. As each chapter was typed it was sent out for comment to several Cabinet colleagues, experts and friends. On New Year's eve Professor Lindemann arrived with further reflections and encouragement.

Over Christmas Lindemann was plunged into a Churchill family discussion over Randolph's desire not to return to Eton but to go straight to Oxford University. It was the middle of the academic year, and Randolph had not yet sat the autumn entrance examination. But Lindemann, himself an Oxford Professor, had managed to procure a place for Randolph at Christ Church, his own college, and while at Chartwell he argued in favour of Randolph taking it. Churchill was reluctant to see his son break off his school career too early, but after a somewhat accrimonious discussion he agreed to let Randolph try his luck.

In the first weeks of the New Year Churchill's literary work intensified. He was anxious to finish his book before the election campaign began, and continued to send his chapters to friends for comment and criticism. Among those to whom he wrote, and who sent Churchill comments and material, was his former second-in-command in Flanders, Sir Archibald Sinclair, who had been Churchill's principal private secretary both at the War Office in 1919 and 1920, and at the Colonial Office in 1921 and 1922. More critical comments arrived during January 1929 from Desmond Morton, from Lord Beaverbrook – who had been Minister of Information in 1918 – and from a senior member of the Foreign Office, Robert Vansittart, another personal friend.

These men helped Churchill willingly. He accepted their criticisms, and added the documentary material which they sent him to his account of the events of a decade before. Chartwell was filled with the sights and sounds of literary activity: secretaries typing and retyping the chapters as they were written and rewritten, and Churchill pacing up and down his study, late into the night and on into the early hours of the morning, dictating, pausing to mould a sentence or to polish a phrase, stopping to consult a reference book or to pore over a map.

The publication of the new, and fifth, volume of his war memoirs provided Churchill with a moment of personal satisfaction. The book was called *The World Crisis: The Aftermath*, and Churchill sent out, at his own expense, more than a hundred personal copies. One copy went to his Labour Party opposite number, Philip Snowden, one of his fiercest and most persistent opponents in Parliament. 'I shall treasure it', Snowden wrote, 'not only for its own worth, but as a memento of the friendly personal relations which can and do exist between keen political opponents.'

Not only the personal, but also the public comments, showed the extent to which Churchill had succeeded as an author and historian. 'With what feelings does one lay down Mr Churchill's two-thousandth page?' J. M. Keynes wrote in the *New Republic*. 'Gratitude to one who can write with so much eloquence and feeling of things which are part of the lives of all of us of the war generation, but which he saw and knew much closer and clearer. Admiration for his energies of mind and his intense absorption of intellectual interest and elemental emotion in what is for the moment the matter in hand – which is his best quality. A little envy, perhaps, for his undoubting conviction that frontiers, races, patriotisms, even wars if need be are ultimate verities for mankind, which lends for him a kind of dignity and even nobility to events, which for others are only a nightmare interlude, something to be permanently avoided.'

As the date for the General Election drew nearer Churchill began to worry about its outcome. Lord Beaverbrook told a friend, 'Churchill is plunged in despair', believing electoral defeat to be inevitable. Beaverbrook added, however, that of all the prominent men he knew, Churchill was the worst judge in these matters.

Early in January 1929, almost five months before election day, Churchill advised the Prime Minister that everything possible should be done to confront the electors with a direct choice between Socialism on the one hand, and what he called 'modern Conservatism' on the other. Votes for Conservatism, Churchill believed, would be cast by all who believed in national cooperation, and the continuity of national policy. This was the trend all over the world. 'Women', he told Baldwin, 'can feel these tide movements by instinct.'

Churchill's contribution to the actual election campaign began in mid-February when he spoke in London at a meeting organized by the Anti-Socialist and Anti-Communist Union. His message was clear: the Labour Party in power would bring subversion in the factories and in the armed forces and would probably lead to a second 'general strike'. Here was Churchill's election cry: anti-socialism. He feared a façade of respectable Labour Cabinet ministers becoming the tools of an evil conspiracy; and he was determined to ring what he called the 'alarm bells'.

During the campaign Churchill's political future was the topic of some discussion among his fellow Cabinet Ministers. Much of this speculation took place behind his back and not all of it was complimentary. Some of his more senior Cabinet colleagues, especially Neville Chamberlain, were keen that Churchill should be removed from the Exchequer. One Minister suggested Churchill might make an excellent Foreign Secretary. Neville Chamberlain disagreed. But he was also afraid that Churchill might, if he remained Chancellor, become Baldwin's obvious successor as Prime Minister, and he expressed these fears in private conversation, and in his diary. Baldwin himself considered Churchill as a possible Secretary of State for India, remembering as he did Churchill's successful efforts for conciliation both towards the defeated Boers in South Africa in 1906, when Churchill was Under Secretary of State for the Colonies, and again in 1921 towards the southern Irish, when Churchill was Colonial Secretary. Even the Viceroy of India, Lord Irwin – later Lord Halifax – agreed, but went on to express his doubts as to whether Churchill might not prove 'out of sympathy' with Indian political aspirations, and even 'rather disposed to despise' them.

Baldwin rejected these arguments, and asked Churchill to become Secretary of State for India. An important measure of Indian constitutional reform was imminent. A leading Liberal politician and lawyer, Sir John Simon, had already been sent to India by Baldwin, at the head of a Royal Commission, to make suggestions for further steps towards Indian self-government. Baldwin wanted Churchill to be in charge of the subsequent reform, as he believed that it would be in general harmony with Churchill's sentiments, and with his past constructive record, to direct a third great measure of self-government within the Empire.

Churchill declined Baldwin's invitation. 'I was not attracted by this plan,' he later recalled. 'My friendship with Lord Birkenhead, then at the India Office, had kept me in close touch with the movement of Indian affairs, and I shared his deep misgivings about that vast sub-continent.'

Meanwhile, with election speculation in the air, Conservative hostility to Churchill was growing. In particular, mischief was being made about a meeting between Churchill and Lloyd George, at which Lloyd George had put the Liberal Party's conditions for supporting a future Conservative Government.

Baldwin ignored the anti-Churchill talk, however, and decided not to move him from the Exchequer. On 15 April 1929 Churchill presented his fifth Budget: he abolished the duty on tea, removed railway passenger duty, ended the betting tax, reduced the duty on motorcycles and bicycles, imposed new duties on brewers, distillers and tobacco manufacturers, and announced an increase in Government spending on the telephone service, especially in rural areas.

On the following day Baldwin wrote to Churchill in a personal handwritten note: 'I have never heard you speak better, and that's saying a great deal.' Baldwin added: 'I hate the word "brilliant": it has been worked to death and is too suggestive of brilliantine: but, if I may use it in its pristine virginity, so to speak, it is the right one. I congratulate you with both hands.'

After the Budget, in a special election broadcast on April 30 to an audience of more than a million, Churchill set out the Conservative Government's achievements: 'Peace abroad; steady stable government at home; clean, honest, impartial administration; good will in industry between masters and men; public and private thrift.' All these benefits could be lost, he warned, if the election went against the Tories. 'Avoid chops and changes of policy', he told his listeners, 'avoid thimble-riggers and three-card trick men; avoid all needless borrowings; and above all avoid, as you would the smallpox, class warfare and violent political strife.'

Churchill was also able, during the campaign, to remind the electorate of the domestic achievements of his five years as Chancellor of the Exchequer. Since the passing of one of his very first pieces of legislation in 1925, well over a million people had become entitled to State benefits, including 236,800 widows, 344,800 children, 227,000 people over seventy, and 450,000 people between the ages of sixty-five and seventy. It was a formidable achievement.

Two days before the Poll, Churchill sought to rally his constituents at Epping, telling them: 'Victory is in the air. We are on the eve of a decisive manifestation of the steadfastness and perseverence of the nation.'

The British people went to the Polls on 30 May 1929. That night Churchill went to 10 Downing Street, where the Prime Minister was reading the results as they came in over a tape machine. One of those present recorded the unfolding scene in his diary: Baldwin, sitting at one desk, with narrow slips of paper on which he 'inscribed the three lists as they arrived'; at another desk,

'Winston doing similar lists in red ink, sipping whisky and soda, getting redder and redder, rising and going out often to glare at the machine himself, hunching his shoulders, bowing his head like a bull about to charge.' As Labour gain after Labour gain was announced, those present watched as 'Winston became more and more flushed with anger, left his seat and confronted the machine in the passage; with his shoulders hunched he glared at the figures, tore the sheets and behaved as though if any more Labour gains came along he would smash the whole apparatus. His ejaculations to the surrounding staff were quite unprintable.'

The Conservatives won only 260 seats, as against Labour's 288. Churchill was re-elected. Stanley Baldwin resigned, and Ramsay MacDonald became Prime Minister for the second time, at the head of a Labour Government. The Liberals announced that they would not use their balancing votes to topple MacDonald. The Conservatives were now in opposition.

The Party Churchill had rejoined only four years before was now out of office. The Liberals, in whose ranks he had once been so influential and popular a figure, now held the balance of political power. Once again, but only for the third time since 1908, he was without Ministerial office.

The five difficult but happy years at the Exchequer had marked a high point of Churchill's influence and achievement. Now, free of the daily pressure of departmental and Cabinet affairs, he embarked on a period of writing, reflection, relaxation and travel. In July 1929, less than two months after the General Election, he began work on a massive, long-term task, a full-scale biography of his famous ancestor, John Churchill, victor of the battle of Blenheim and later First Duke of Marlborough. It was work which was to absorb many of his energies for the next five years, keep him up long into the night, and lead to four enormous and magnificent books. His aim, as he explained to his cousin 'Sunny', the Ninth Duke of Marlborough, was 'to tell this famous tale from a modern point of view', and he had no doubt that he could do so, and do so successfully.

Churchill began work in the archive at Blenheim, amid the hundreds of letters and documents of his ancestor's life. It was here at Blenheim, nearly a quarter of a century before, that he had written his other biography, a two-volume life of his father. Sunny had been Churchill's friend throughout those years, despite their differences in temperament, Sunny irascible and morose, Churchill good humoured and philosophical. Again and again Churchill revived his cousin's flagging spirits, and sought to reconcile him to the modern world of social reform and growing equality of opportunity. Sunny resented these changes. Churchill urged him to accept them.

Travel plans also filled Churchill's unexpected leisure time. He decided to go to Canada and the United States, and to show his son Randolph 'these mighty lands'. To one of his American hosts he wrote that he was anxious to discuss the future of the world, 'even if we cannot decide it'. As for himself, he wrote, during the trip he would have 'no political mission and no axe to grind'.

Before leaving Britain for his transatlantic travels, Churchill made two efforts to influence the future direction of British Conservatism. Both efforts failed. And both, in failing were to divide him still further from the emerging leadership.

The first undertaking was to seek a Conservative reconciliation with the Liberals. To do so, Churchill urged his fellow Conservatives not to return to the policies of Tariffs and Protection which had marked their pre-war breach with Liberalism and had driven him into the Liberal Party twenty-five years before. There were, he pointed out to Baldwin, eight million Tory voters, and eight million Labour voters. The five million Liberals held the balance. 'Where will these five million go?' If the Tories returned to Protection or allowed their traditional 'anti-Liberal resentments' to have sway, a Liberal–Labour grouping was inevitable. Such a development, Churchill warned Baldwin, would reduce Conservatism to nothing but 'a Conservative Right hopelessly excluded from power', for many years to come.

Baldwin was tempted by Churchill's vision of a Liberal–Conservative alliance. Indeed, he went so far as to authorize Churchill to talk again privately to Lloyd George, a man whose past history and reputation were anathema to millions of Tories, and above all, on personal grounds, to Neville Chamberlain, who had served under Lloyd George in the First World War, and had come almost to loathe him.

Churchill saw Lloyd George in utmost secrecy, and suggested a pact based on Liberal–Conservative agreement on specific issues, as they might arise in the House of Commons. But within a week Neville Chamberlain had alienated the Liberals by publicly declaring his support for Tariffs, and for protective taxes to enable Empire goods, especially from Canada and Australia, to enter Britain more cheaply than foreign goods. Such schemes were the death-knell of any would-be Conservative alliance with any sector of the Liberal Party.

Churchill's Liberal background, experience and outlook were becoming increasingly out of place in the defeated Tory party. If Neville Chamberlain were made leader of the Conservative Party, 'or anyone else of that kind', Churchill confided to his wife, 'I clear out of politics'. Only one goal still attracted him, he told her, the Premiership itself. If that were barred, he added, 'I should quit the dreary field for pastures new'.

Churchill's second struggle with the Conservative leadership soon emerged. The divergence arose from his strongly held views on Empire. He believed that one of Britain's greatest achievements was what he described as the 'rescue of India' from centuries of tyrannical government and civil war, and the sub-continent's progress towards civilization. With Labour now in power, Churchill feared that the fabric of the Empire would be weakened, possibly even destroyed, and that Baldwin would not oppose the Labour Government's attempts to whittle away the basis of Britain's achievement in Imperial policy.

Not only British rule in India, but British control over Egypt, seemed proof to Churchill of the benefits and merits of Imperialism: as viewed 'not from the perspective of conquest and exploitation, but from the knowledge and encouragement of constructive effort'. But as Churchill had feared, the new Labour Government soon recalled the British High Commissioner in Cairo, Lord Lloyd, and announced its plan to remove all British troops from Egypt except for those in the Suez Canal zone.

Churchill reacted 'vehemently', as he later recalled, against the 'rough and sudden gesture' of Lord Lloyd's recall, and tried to rally Conservative opinion against MacDonald. His effort failed, and failed dismally. As he rose in the House of Commons from his seat on the Front Opposition Bench, and began to chastize the Labour Government's actions, he noted that Baldwin sat on the bench at his side 'silent and disapproving'. He saw at once that the Conservative Party had been instructed by the Whips not to criticize MacDonald's policy.

Yet Churchill persevered, rebuking MacDonald for damaging Britain's prestige throughout the East by the decision to withdraw troops from Egypt. 'The whole quality of Egyptian administration will deteriorate', he warned. Other European powers would demand or intrigue 'to fill the gap made by British abdication'.

As Churchill spoke, he sensed his isolation. 'Murmurs and even cries of dissent from the Conservative benches', he later recalled, 'were added to the hostile Government interruptions, and it was evident I was almost alone in the House.'

Soon after this Parliamentary humiliation, Churchill left for Canada and the United States, writing to Lord Beaverbrook that it was 'fun' to get away from the worries and responsibilities he felt for the increasingly 'tiresome' developments at home. Travelling with Churchill were his son Randolph, his brother Jack, and Jack's son Johnny. At the age of eighteen, Randolph, no longer away for months at a time at boarding school, was becoming a real companion to his father. Father and son were finding much in common.

The vast open spaces of the Canadian countryside impressed Churchill, with their untrodden forests, 'Scottish' burns and vast lakes full of fish. Churchill reported to his wife that Randolph was tempted to 'renounce society and ambition', buy a small patch of land and settle down.

'Champagne and the warmest of welcomes' greeted Churchill wherever he was recognized. As he travelled westwards, Churchill was delighted when men whom he had not seen since the turn of the century came up 'in twos and threes' at every place to shake hands with him. One day, as he told his wife, a former Sergeant of Engineers, who had helped him in 1898 to make his plans for the battle of Omdurman, stopped him in the street and gave him 'an excellent box of cigars'. Churchill added: 'He was in quite humble circumstances and I was greatly touched.'

In each of his letters to Clementine, Churchill reported on their son's progress, writing that he was an 'admirable companion'. He also reported that Randolph had made 'a good impression' on everyone who had met them.

Randolph and his father were enjoying their travels together immensely. Riding near Calgary one morning, 'on sure-footed ponies galloping up and down the hills', Churchill wrote, his son was in his 'seventh Heaven'. Randolph described their riding expedition in his diary: 'Papa came out looking magnificent. Jodpur riding suit of khaki, his ten gallon hat, a malacca walking stick with gold knob, and riding a pure white horse. We rode up to the Lake of the Clouds and then on to the edge of the moraine where we had lunch at two o'clock.' Soon afterwards they reached a glacier and Randolph recorded how 'Papa, Johnny and I climbed all over it – Papa with especial vigour.'

During their visit to the oilfields at Calgary, Randolph recorded in his diary: 'I happened to say (after seeing the Calgary oilfields) that it was a depressing thing to see all these oil magnates pigging up a beautiful valley to make fortunes and then being quite incapable of spending their money, and went on to criticise their lack of culture. Instantly Papa flared up, "Cultured people are merely the glittering scum which floats upon the deep river of production!" Damn good.'

On the following afternoon the Churchills went fishing. 'I hooked no less than three', Randolph wrote, 'but each time although I let them have their heads the hook on the spoon broke. It was most disappointing. However as Papa remarked, "'Tis better to have hooked and lost, than never hooked at all."'

In each of his letters to Clementine, Churchill wrote of Randolph's own progress. Never before had the two of them spent so much time together, and Randolph was even making short speeches at his father's side. 'He speaks so well,' Churchill wrote, 'so dextrous, cool and finished.' As for his son's habit of sleeping for ten and even twelve hours a night, he wrote, 'I suppose it is his mind and body growing at the same time.' And Churchill added: 'I love him very much.'

Overwhelmed by the warmth of his welcome in Canada, Churchill told Clementine that 'the workmen in the streets, the girls who work the lifts, the ex-service men, the farmers, up to the highest functionaries have shewn such unaffected pleasure to see & shake hands that I am profoundly touched.'

From Vancouver the Churchills drove south into the United States. Since his youth, Churchill had believed in the strength of America, and been impressed by its buoyant democracy. 'A great, crude strong young people are the Americans,' he had written to his brother at the turn of the century, 'like a boisterous healthy boy among enervated but well bred ladies and gentlemen.' In the last year of the First World War, when it seemed that Germany might win, he had written to Archie Sinclair: 'I fear the tendencies are no longer as favourable as they used to be. Still, America, dear to your heart and mine, is please God, a final makeweight.' As Minister of Munitions he had worked in closest harmony with his American opposite number, Bernard Baruch, and he hoped that cooperation with America would continue after the war. The one great reward of the war, Churchill declared in a public speech in July 1918, would be the 'supreme reconciliation' of Britain and the United States: that, he said, was 'the lion's share'.

Churchill always kept this 'supreme reconciliation' in the forefront of his thinking', telling his constituents, during a bout of wartime British anti-Americanism in 1918: 'We must keep in step with them. They are our kinsmen from across the ocean. They are our sons returned from a long estrangement.'

After 1919, much as he was saddened by America's abrupt withdrawal from Europe, and angered by the constant American pressure for disarmament, Churchill always looked forward to a return to the comradeship of the war, and to the substantial improvement of Anglo-American relations, urging Lloyd George, at the height of the quarrel, to try to establish 'personal friendly relations' with the President as a means of reaching a common policy.

In California, Churchill himself took on the task of urging Anglo-American amity on the leading businessmen of the State, many of whom favoured America's total isolation. His efforts were not in vain, for, as the British Consul reported to London, Churchill had been very successful in influencing those who had been hostile to British interests.

One of Britain's strongest critics, the newspaper-owner William Randolph Hearst – the legendary 'Citizen Kane' of the cinema – was persuaded by Churchill to let him write for the Hearst newspaper chain, with outlets all across America: and to write on politics and international affairs with no editorial restrictions.

As guests at Hearst's castle, the Churchills enjoyed the 'extreme personal courtesy' they received. Churchill liked Hearst's 'strong, liberal and democratic outlook', but described the newspaper-owner as 'a grave simple child – with no doubt a nasty temper – playing with the most costly toys'.

From Hearst's castle, Churchill travelled to Hollywood, where he was introduced to Charlie Chaplin. Churchill was captivated by Chaplin. 'He is a marvellous comedian', he reported to Clementine, 'bolshy in politics and delightful in conversation.'

At the beginning of October the Churchills arrived in New York, as guests of Bernard Baruch. Randolph described Baruch in his diary as 'the greatest speculator there has ever been. He actually bought a seat on the New York Stock exchange costing one hundred thousand pounds solely in order to transact his own business. During the war he was Chairman of the War Industries Board, and came into considerable contact with Papa. He is a tall man about six foot five inches, of great dignity and with a magnificent carriage and personality.'

During his stay in New York Churchill arranged to write a series of twenty-two magazine articles for the Hearst syndicate, articles which were to earn him £40,000 in under a year. This was an incredible sum of money for a journalistic assignment, the equivalent of more than half a million pounds in 1981.

After visiting the battlefields of the American Civil War, Churchill returned to New York to complete the purchase of large blocks of American shares, using his past literary earnings to the full, and even sinking some of his capital into the most promising ventures on the American stock exchange. He was able to put up for his speculative purchases a total of £20,000, as a result of money earned during his American visit both as an advance payment for his Marlborough biography, and for newspaper and magazine articles written or contracted for. This vast sum, he had explained to his wife, 'must not be frittered away', but kept instead 'fluid for investment'.

Churchill was guided in his investments by an American stockbroker whom he had met in California, and who encouraged him to take up American stocks with the greatest prospects. But these prospects were illusory. Even as Churchill put his fortune into the shares, the market collapsed. The Great Crash had begun. Churchill was one of its victims.

On the night of the Crash – 'Black Thursday' – Bernard Baruch was entertaining Churchill and introducing him to some forty leading American bankers and financiers, one of whom, in proposing Churchill's health, addressed those assembled as 'Friends, and *former* millionaires'. On the following day Churchill visited the New York stock exchange, witnessing for himself the brokers 'walking to and fro like a slow-motion picture of a disturbed ant-heap, offering each other enormous blocks of securities at a third of their old prices', and for many minutes together, he later recalled, 'finding no one strong enough to pick up the sure fortunes they were compelled to offer'.

Churchill had faith in America's economic recovery, believing that the financial disaster would prove to be a 'a passing episode in the march of a valiant and serviceable people'. But many did not share his confidence. From the very apartment block in which he was staying, he later recalled, and under his own window, 'a gentleman cast himself down fifteen storeys and was dashed to pieces, causing a wild commotion and the arrival of the fire brigade'.

On 30 November 1929, back at Chartwell, Churchill celebrated his fifty-fifth birthday. But it was not a time for rejoicing. Economically his finances were in disarray. Politically he was on the verge of a breach with his Party and its leader. The Conservative defeat in June 1929 had revealed that Churchill's position as a leading Party luminary was based far more upon his abilities as a Minister, his Parliamentary skills as a defender of the Government, and his friendship with Baldwin, than on any popularity he might have acquired from the traditional, non-reforming stream of Conservatism which, as Chancellor of the Exchequer, he had tried so hard to influence and change.

Even during Churchill's three months travelling across Canada and the United States, while he was urging his audiences not to write off Great Britain as a source of power and influence, the Labour Government had decided to take a further step towards Indian self-government. And it had done so with Baldwin's support, and in the absence of many of the leading Conservatives. Even Churchill, though still one of the most senior members of the Shadow Cabinet, had been excluded.

Chapter Two

'These anxious
and dubious times'

The Government's new India policy had been embodied in a Declaration issued by the Viceroy of India, Lord Irwin, on 31 October 1929, in which the natural outcome of constitutional progress in India was defined as 'the attainment of Dominion status'. Churchill was distressed, and immediately on his return from America, he wrote in the *Daily Mail* that, in his view, Dominion status could not be attained by a community which continued to brand sixty million of its fellow human beings as 'untouchables', and whose very presence was considered 'pollution'.

Henceforth, for more than five years, Churchill was to write and speak against this transfer of power in India. Dominion status would place power in the hands of a minority who would, in his view, abuse it: Hindus, who would continue to treat the Untouchables as creatures of contempt; and a small group of extremist politicians whose real aim, he believed, was not Dominion status but full independence.

The decision to work towards Dominion status for India had been taken by the Labour Government. But it was Baldwin's support of the Government's policy that gave it impetus. Many leading Conservatives shared Churchill's dislike of the decision. But Baldwin had outwitted them. To those of his closest colleagues who protested he stated blandly 'that he had only approved of it in his personal capacity and not as leader carrying the Party with him'. His personal approval, however, influenced many Conservative backbenchers to support the Labour move. The fact that Irwin had been sent to India as Viceroy by Baldwin himself three years earlier further contributed to Conservative acceptance of the Declaration.

All this took place in Churchill's absence: his ship only docked at Southampton five days after the Irwin Declaration had been made public, and Baldwin's support of it assured. The principal decisions had been taken without Churchill having been consulted, and indeed while he was on board ship in mid-Atlantic, even though he was still one of the most senior members of the Shadow Cabinet.

Churchill had reached Britain on 5 November 1929. Three days later the Labour Government's new India policy was debated in the House of Commons. During the debate, Baldwin announced the Conservative Party's support for MacDonald's move. But his support was met by a hostile reception. It appeared indeed to one of Baldwin's closest advisers that as many as a third of all

Conservative MPs were prepared actually to vote against the Irwin Declaration, despite Baldwin's own support of it.

One of the few senior Conservatives who supported Baldwin was Sir Samuel Hoare. He was a shrewd politician who had previously been Secretary of State for Air while Churchill was Chancellor of the Exchequer. Together they had successfully worked, at a period of economy in all branches of Government, to prevent cuts in air force expenditure, and had become friends. But as the India debate began he was to find himself in a direct clash with his former colleague. After the November debate he informed Lord Irwin of his concern that scarcely anyone in the Party approved of the Irwin Declaration and that Churchill was 'almost demented with fury' during the debate, and had spoken to no one since.

Over Indian policy, however, the battle-lines were not yet clearly drawn. But in the turmoil of Baldwin's virtual pact with MacDonald, it seemed that the Conservative Party might split, and that Churchill would return to the centre of British politics, at its most stormy and unpredictable. But Baldwin had strong backing for his policy, in spite of its unpopularity in the Party. He could command the support, not only of the Party machine and the Party Whips, but of the editor of *The Times*, Geoffrey Dawson, and the Director General of the BBC, Sir John Reith.

Churchill learned just how strong this phalanx of opponents could be when he asked Reith if he could make a ten-minute broadcast against the India policy. Reith, after consulting the Labour Government's Secretary of State for India, turned down his request.

Central to Churchill's political beliefs was the conviction that the public would respond fairly to a good case, well presented. He was bitter that Reith was, as he wrote to him, 'obstructing' him. But the ban remained in force.

When Churchill was asked to give the annual Romanes lecture at Oxford University, he took the opportunity to point out that democracy depended on free expression and debate. During his speech he said that he regarded Britain's democratic parliamentary institutions 'as precious to us almost beyond compare'. They seemed to give, he said, 'by far the closest assocation yet achieved between the life of the people and the action of the State'.

Throughout 1930 Churchill also made clear his anxiety about the Labour Party's decision to accept a limitation of British naval power, as part of world disarmament. From the moment that he had become Prime Minister in the summer of 1929, Ramsay MacDonald had made disarmament a central feature of his policy. When in April 1930 the Admiralty were forced to accept a maximum British naval strength substantially below what the Naval Staff regarded as the minimum for Britain's 'full defence requirements', the Admiralty experts asserted that the reduction in strength, compared with the rest of Europe, would be dangerous should there be a rise in international tension.

Churchill shared this view, and was one of the leading speakers in the House of Commons against the new naval limitations. Suddenly he found himself, for the first time in his career, with allies on the Right. The newspaper of the Right, the *Morning Post*, which in 1917 had described Churchill, cruelly, as 'the floating kidney in the body politic', now praised his efforts to halt any further naval disarmament. 'I think this naval business is going to carry us a long way', Churchill wrote privately to the Editor. 'It may become part of a definite movement to a strong assertion of the life-strength of the British Empire.'

The Labour Government's Naval Treaty was supported, however, by Baldwin, as its India policy had been, and in the House of Commons more than half of the Conservative MPs refused to sign a protest motion rejecting part of the Treaty.

Churchill, however was supported by professional naval opinion. When the naval historian, Professor Richmond, wrote to deplore the Treaty, Churchill replied: 'of course the worst thing about these agreements is that they deprive us of all that flexibility and authority in variants of design which are our birthright'.

The Naval Treaty was passed in the House of Commons with Labour, Liberal and Conservative support. Those who shared Churchill's views were in a minority, despite their often senior status. The Treaty was judged a triumph, not only for MacDonald, but for the Secretary-General of the Conference, Sir Maurice Hankey, who was also Secretary to the Cabinet, and to whom MacDonald wrote, when the Conference was over: 'I do not know what we should have done without you. You were the master engineer.'

Churchill remained deeply worried about political and European developments. His concern was noticed by visitors to Chartwell and by his friends: 'Winston talks long and sadly', a visitor to a country house in Wiltshire wrote in July 1930, as he listened to Churchill warning the guests that Lord Beaverbrook's growing campaign for Tariffs would 'hand over South America to the Yanks, split the Empire for ever, and shatter the Conservative Party into smithereens'. Churchill also told the Wiltshire house party of the three books he was now writing: a sixth and final volume of his war memoirs, to be called *The Eastern Front*, the massive biography of Duke John, and a short book of early reminiscences, *My Early Life*. As often happened, Churchill became the centre of the guests' attention, one of them noting how, as he talked, he was in 'gentle and intelligent form'.

Visitors to Chartwell recalled how Churchill sometimes sat silently at the start of a meal, paying no attention to the chatter of the guests, until some chance remark provoked him to a sombre outburst. But he could also be a witty and kind host, encouraging the young people present to speak their mind, and drawing from his deep well of experience to entertain or to set out his view of events.

Churchill's friends delighted in his friendship and humour. As one young man wrote to him after receiving *My Early Life* as a gift: 'I shall recapture some of the magic of those long evenings at Chartwell, when you were in reminiscent mood, and I was exceptionally content to listen in fascinated and happy silence'.

My Early Life, gave pleasure to all Churchill's friends and former colleagues. 'I have read it with real delight', Baldwin told him, and Lawrence of Arabia wrote, from his RAF station: 'The ripe and merry wisdom, and the courage and flair and judgment, I take rather for granted, having seen you so much in action: but as your reputation is not all made by your friends, the book will do you good amongst your readers.'

Lawrence had a further comment on finishing the book. 'Not many people', he wrote, 'could have lived 25 years or so without malice.'

While writing his account of his early years, and in particular of his school-days, Churchill reflected on the changes which had occurred since the distant days of the 1880s and 1890s, the two decades of his early life and school days. 'I was a child of the Victorian era', he wrote, 'when the structure of our country seemed firmly set, when its position in trade and on the seas was unrivalled, and when the realization of the greatness of our Empire and of our duty to preserve it was ever growing stronger.' In those days, he reflected, 'the domin-ant forces in Great Britain were very sure of themselves and of their doctrines. They thought they could teach the world the art of government, and the science of economics. They were sure they were supreme at sea and conse-quently safe at home. They rested therefore sedately under the convictions of power and security.'

'Very different', Churchill mused, 'is the aspect of these anxious and dubi-ous times'; and in a long and thoughtful letter to Lord Beaverbrook in the autumn of 1930 he urged his friend of former years to use the influence of his newspapers, including the multi-million circulation *Daily Express*, to help to improve Britain's increasingly 'rotten state'.

Churchill wrote that, considering the enormous sacrifices of blood and money which had been made in the First World War in order to hold some small village or town on the western front, he could not understand why it was that 'we should now throw away our conquests and our inheritance with both hands, through helplessness and pusillanimity'.

Churchill then surveyed the twelve months that had passed, and the series of Government decisions which had caused him such distress. Naval dis-armament, the weakening of authority in Egypt and the rapid decline of Britain's position in India to the point where it seemed possible that she would be forced to abandon India altogether, all contributed to what Churchill described as the 'disastrous' nature of the year 1930. 'My only interest in politics', he told Beaverbrook, 'is to see this position retrieved', and it could only be retrieved, he believed, if a 'real majority' of the nation were behind the Government.

Churchill was certain that a 'real majority' of the nation was opposed to the Labour Party's India policy. It was certainly true that, in spite of Baldwin's support for MacDonald, many Conservatives shared his sense of unease. 'The tide here is running pretty strongly against your ideas', the editor of *The Times* informed Lord Irwin in a private letter in the summer of 1930, while Mac-Donald himself warned Irwin that even Baldwin's closest counsellors were 'opposed' to the Irwin Declaration, with its implication of eventual Indian self-government.

In order to advance the Indian reforms, MacDonald announced a plan to invite the leading Indian politicians to London, to meet senior Labour Ministers, as well as the Liberal and Conservative leaders, at a Round Table Conference. Churchill believed that such a conference would only encourage 'false hopes' among politically minded Indians, who would regard Dominion status as only one step away from full independence, a goal to which even the Labour Government was opposed.

It was wrong, Churchill argued in a public speech in August 1930, 'to lure and coax' the Indian political leaders to London, 'with vague phrases about Dominion status in their lifetime'. These leaders, among then Gandhi and Nehru, were in any case, he argued, 'only a handful compared to the vast Indian masses for whom we are responsible'.

The Congress Party in India, inspired by and supported by Gandhi, started a civil disobedience campaign in September. Soon there was violent rioting and attacks on British officers. Much of the British administration, including that already in Indian hands since the reforms of 1919, was brought to a halt. On Lord Irwin's orders, tens of thousands of Indians were arrested and imprisoned: but the non-cooperation spread, and by the end of 1930 sixty thousand Indians were in prison, including Gandhi himself.

In Britain, however, the Indian crisis was momentarily eclipsed by a new Conservative lurch towards Tariffs, marked by Neville Chamberlain's public demand that at the next election the Conservatives should pledge themselves to introduce a series of taxes on imported goods. For Churchill, this demand by Chamberlain marked the first step in his formal break with the Conservative leadership. First India, and now Tariffs, marked the breach. On the night of 14 October 1930 Baldwin wrote to Churchill to express his 'profound regret that there is a real parting of the ways'. Their friendship, Baldwin wrote, had grown up 'through six years of loyal and strenuous work together'. At the beginning of those six years, Baldwin added, 'we knew little of each other. We have had good times and bad times, and we have come through side by side, and the memory of them will abide.'

That same week Clementine Churchill wrote to Randolph, 'politics have taken an orientation not favourable to Papa'. Sometimes, she added, he was gloomy about this, 'but fortunately not increasingly so'. Churchill remained on only one official Conservative body, the 'business committee' of the Party: its Shadow Cabinet. But he was no longer a member of any of the Party's specific policy making bodies in the economic sphere.

A deep personal cause for sadness was the death that autumn of Lord Birkenhead – formerly F. E. Smith – and for nearly twenty years one of Churchill's most intimate friends. On the day after Birkenhead's death

Clementine Churchill wrote to his widow: 'Last night Winston wept for his friend. He said several times "I feel so lonely".'

Birkenhead, whom Churchill had known since 1906, had shared Churchill's views on many subjects, including India. That Birkenhead had died at a moment when his talents and experience would have been of decisive help in the growing debate about the future of India, added to Churchill's sadness. To a private gathering of F.E.'s friends, Churchill lamented: 'Just at the time when we feel that our public men are lacking in the power to dominate events, he has been taken. This was the occasion, and these were the very years, for the full fruition of his service to our country.'

Lord Birkenhead's death, coming so soon after the Tariff breach, and the announcement of the Round Table Conference, made Churchill feel totally isolated. When the Conference opened in London on 12 November 1930, with Sir Samuel Hoare as one of the four official Conservative delegates, Baldwin wrote to a friend that the delegation was starting well, while Churchill was 'in the depths of gloom'.

Churchill refused to give way to despondency, however. Believing the proposed India reforms to be misguided, he now determined to put forward his opposition to them whenever possible, and to rally support, especially in Parliament. The centre of Churchill's argument was that there was no single group in India capable of taking responsibility for the whole of India, or prepared to act in the interests of the many different and conflicting Indian interests. Only the British Parliament could do that. The individual provinces of India, each one many times larger than Britain, could indeed, he believed, be governed by Indians. But the control of all-India, the linking together of the wider needs, the safeguarding of minority interests, these could only be done fairly and effectively by a British controlled central government in Delhi and an ever-vigilant and beneficent Parliament at Westminster.

This had always been Churchill's view of Empire. A quarter of a century earlier he had told the House of Commons, during a discussion of the ill-treatment of negro mine-workers in South Africa, that it was important to 'establish clearly that in all the wide dominions of the King there was no man so unfortunate and so humble as to have his ill-treatment beneath the notice of that House' – the House of Commons – and that there was no province in the British Empire 'so distant as to be beyond their reach'.

The reach of Parliament, in Churchill's view, was to be used in order steadily to improve the lot of the masses, and to challenge injustice, including the injustice whereby sixty million Indians, the so-called 'Untouchables', were denied by their fellow Hindus 'even the semblance of human rights'. There was also the need for an external power to curb the fierce sectarian disturbances, as when, at Cawnpore, Hindus attacked Muslims and at least 300 people were killed. As Churchill pointed out, women and children had been butchered at Cawnpore 'in circumstances of bestial barbarity, their mutilated bodies strewing the streets for days'.

Churchill believed that Gandhi, Nehru and the Congress Party had used the grant of greater Indian participation in both local and central Government since 1919 'not for the purpose of improving the well-being of India, but merely as convenient tools and processes for political agitation and even sedition'.

His views were far from unpopular; on Christmas Eve 1930 a friend wrote to Lord Irwin that Churchill's influence was so great in the Conservative Party now that he doubted Baldwin's ability to carry the Party in any decision he might choose to make.

Churchill was totally absorbed in the Indian issue. 'It is a great comfort', he wrote to his son in January 1931, 'when one minds the questions one cares about far more than office, or party, or even friendships'.

The Round Table Conference came to an end on 19 January 1931, when Ramsay MacDonald promised that India would now be allowed to advance towards self-government. But before independence could be granted, the British Government's aim would be to devise a new constitution for India, linking Hindu, Muslim, Princely and other interests in a single All-India Federal Parliament, and with British supervised safeguards for minorities. Britain would also retain power over imperial defence, foreign affairs and the army.

Many moderate Indian politicians were much tempted by this offer, which went far beyond the local and central participation granted in 1919. But with Gandhi still in prison, the Congress Party refused to abandon its campaign of non-cooperation, even after MacDonald had offered to bring the Congress into all future negotiations. Led by Nehru, the Congress Party refused to give up their protest, which was crippling all administration. Then, in an attempt to break the deadlock, Lord Irwin allowed Gandhi to go free.

Churchill was angered by an act which he regarded as one of supreme weakness. In the House of Commons he criticized the Government's plan. He pointed to what he believed to be its central weakness, that while offering the 'excitable' Indian masses eventual self-government, the Viceroy would be retaining 'formidable' powers. If the Viceroy attempted to use his great powers under the proposed constitution, he would quickly become an object of popular hatred. This, Churchill warned the House of Commons, must soon result in a serious, even violent conflict. In reply Baldwin, and not the Government spokesman, defended the Government's plans. He went even further, pledging the Conservative Party to support the implementation of the proposed constitution.

Baldwin's answer was not entirely popular with his own Party. As a former Conservative Minister, George Lane-Fox, wrote to Irwin – his brother-in-law – many Conservatives had told him that Baldwin's pledge 'was a surprise to them, and emanated from him alone'.

Lane Fox explained to Halifax that during the debate Baldwin had been 'vigorously cheered' from the Labour benches, while there had been an 'ominous silence' from fellow Conservatives. 'I don't believe he has ever consulted his colleagues,' Lane Fox added, 'except Sam Hoare, with whom he had obviously been dining. And my impression is that he just went into the debate without having thought the matter out carefully, and just drifted on, following his own line of thought.'

Once more, Baldwin had committed the Conservative Party to a major policy development without serious consultation. Churchill now wrote to Baldwin, formally resigning from the Conservative Party's business committee. He did so, he said, because the divergence of their views on India policy had now become public, as a result of the debate.

Baldwin accepted Churchill's decision at once, and did so with 'regret'. But in his letter of acceptance he agreed that Churchill was right to go. Nevertheless, Baldwin added, 'Our friendship is now too deeply rooted to be affected by differences of opinion whether temporary or permanent.' Baldwin referred to the 'testing times' they had fought through together and how they had come to appreciate each other's good qualities and to be 'indulgent to qualities less good', if they indeed had any.

Having publicly declared his opposition to Baldwin's cooperation with MacDonald over India, Churchill at once began to attack the Prime Minister for his weakness and political ineptitude. On 28 January 1931, during a debate on the Trade Disputes Bill, he insulted MacDonald by describing the Prime Minister's remarkable ability in falling down but coming up smiling, 'a little dishevilled but still smiling'. He recalled being taken as a child to Barnum's Circus for an 'exhibition of freaks and monstrosities' but that his parents had prevented him from seeing the spectacle described as 'The Boneless Wonder', judging it to be 'too revolting' for a child. 'I have waited', he added, 'fifty years to see the boneless wonder sitting on the Treasury Bench.'

Churchill's invective offended not only MacDonald's supporters but also many Conservatives. Brendan Bracken liked it, however. The 'boneless wonder' speech, he wrote to Randolph, 'is immortal'.

The weakness of Churchill's position became clear during a further debate on 12 February 1931, when Baldwin not only supported the Government's India policy, but also warned his Conservative followers 'to keep India out of party politics'. When Churchill rose to reply, and to present his detailed criticisms of a policy that would bring what he called 'bloodshed and confusion', his arguments were met throughout by hostile cries from Conservative, Labour and Liberal MPs. On the following day one of Baldwin's friends wrote to the Conservative leader that 'yesterday's triumph' had put Baldwin on top again.

Nevertheless, as 1931 progressed, Churchill was determined to mobilize as wide support as possible against the proposed All-India Federation. To his friend Lord Rothermere, owner of the *Daily Mail*, he wrote: 'I am sure that it is not possible to frame a workable scheme which safeguards our essentials, nor to win in any circumstances an agreement with the forces which are trying to drive us out of India.' And to a young MP who had offered his support,

33

Churchill replied: 'India is a symbol as well as a cause, and it may well be the means by which a general reassertion of British will to live may come to pass.'

Churchill also believed there was 'plenty of time', as he told Rothermere, 'for a slow, steady marshalling of those who will defend our interests in India', and to Lord Carson he wrote of what he envisaged as 'a grim but *victorious* fight'. The emphasis was Churchill's own.

Churchill now began a systematic campaign of public speaking. 'Steadily working up of a great cause', he wrote to Rothermere, 'will produce a political situation of deep interest and probably an acute tension.' As long as he was fighting a cause, Churchill added, he was not afraid of anything, 'nor', he added, 'do I weary as the struggle proceeds'. The Party machine, Baldwin, public office: all these, he said, were 'mere irrelevancies'. Policy alone was what counted: 'win there, win everywhere'.

The Conservative Party machine was not idle, however, and quickly launched a campaign aimed not only at making Dominion Status seem respectable, but also at casting doubts on Churchill's sincerity. For his part, Churchill again approached the BBC, and asked to be allowed to give his views about India. But once again, the BBC refused. Nevertheless, Churchill wrote to his son, who was then in America, that he had become 'quite popular in the Party' and in great demand as a speaker. His own constituency, he had been told, was 'in a bright flame of enthusiasm'.

On 17 February 1931 Lord Irwin met Gandhi in Delhi, and then continued discussions with him week by week. It was less than a month since Gandhi had been released from prison, having first promised to seek to curb the formidable forces of disorder and non-cooperation which he had encouraged throughout India. This disorder had still not ceased. The Congress militants still saw their path, under Gandhi's guidance, as that of trying to make British rule impossible. Six days after Gandhi's first meeting with Irwin, Churchill told the Conservatives of West Essex: 'It is alarming, and nauseating to see Mr Gandhi, a seditious Middle Temple lawyer, now posing as a fakir of a type well-known in the East, striding half naked up the steps of the Viceregal palace, while he is still organising and conducting a defiant campaign of civil disobedience, to parly on equal terms with the representative of the King-Emperor.' This spectacle, Churchill warned, would encourage the forces of disorder and opposition to British authority throughout India.

Despite the stridency of his description of Gandhi, Churchill's speeches were well received in Conservative circles. Indeed, the Party's Principal Agent warned Neville Chamberlain that many Conservatives were more sympathetic to Churchill's position than to Baldwin's. And Churchill himself, in confident mood, told Clementine that all they needed was time.

But time was against Churchill. On 4 March 1931 Irwin and Gandhi, their series of talks concluded, came to an agreement whereby the Congress Party would end civil disobedience, and Britain would invite the Congress leaders to a new Round Table Conference. Although Gandhi also agreed to accept the principle of continuing British safeguards – involving Viceregal control of war and defence policy, and foreign affairs and minority interests – he also demanded India's right to secede from the British Empire.

Churchill was as opposed to the Gandhi–Irwin pact as to the Federal Parliament scheme. But although he expressed his opposition publicly on at least twenty occasions between March and December 1930, Baldwin still managed to retain, often only with difficulty, a majority of Conservative support.

Baldwin had all the advantages of being Party leader, and controlling the Party machine. He was also lucky in the general Conservative distrust of Churchill, which often overrode the specific issues. 'My late colleagues', Churchill wrote to Robert Boothby on 2 April 1931, 'are more interested in doing me in, than in any trifling questions connected with India or tariffs.' And yet, Churchill added hopefully, 'I have a strong feeling they will not succeed, but anyhow my course is clear.'

Helped by the Indian Empire Society – a growing organization of like-minded critics of the Federation scheme – Churchill followed the course he had set himself. But despite his optimism it was uphill work, with the Conservative, Liberal and Labour Parties in such close but unofficial collusion.

Churchill also found himself strongly in opposition during 1930 and 1931 to MacDonald's policy of disarmament. He had always feared Germany's ability to rearm and by June 1931 he was convinced that the danger was imminent. Since the summer of 1930 the rise of Adolf Hitler had led to a marked increase of violence in the streets. The National Socialist, or 'Nazi' movement, was committed to the complete overthrow of the parliamentary system by which Germany had been ruled since the end of the war.

By July 1930 unemployment in Germany had risen to almost three million. Nazism fed on the poverty and fear which these figures created. It also cried out for a new racial order: for the destruction of liberal democracy and western culture, and its replacement by the so-called 'pure Aryan' social order. Jews were pointed out as the special enemies of the Hitler movement, and German citizens were incited to anti-Jewish feelings and actions. Nazi thugs attacked Jews in the street and beat up without mercy those, Jew and non-Jew alike, who criticized the Nazi creed.

In September 1930 elections had been held throughout Germany. During the campaign, Nazi agitators in the streets perpetrated outrages which often led to bloodshed. But when the election result was announced, it emerged that the Nazis had polled six and a half million votes. This vast vote made them the second largest party in the Reichstag, with 107 seats. The only larger party, the Social Democrats, held 143 seats. The Communists, with two million votes less than the Nazis, won 76 seats. The former dominant Central Party, headed by the Chancellor, Dr Brüning, won only 69 seats.

Ten days after the election, Hitler announced that if the Nazis came to power they would tear up the Treaty of Versailles with its clauses forbidding Germany to have a standing army, a navy, or any air force at all, and that 'heads will roll in the dust'.

The Reichstag met for the first time since the election on 13 October 1930. Brüning remained Chancellor, but Hitler had become the focal point of attention. That same afternoon, groups of Nazi hooligans milled through the main streets of Berlin, breaking the windows of any shops which belonged to Jews. In order to free himself from dependence on Nazi votes, and to maintain his position as Chancellor, Brüning introduced an Emergency Decree, which enabled him to rule without a Reichstag majority. For the Brüning Government this suspension of German democratic rights – for the first time in over twenty years – seemed the only way to preserve Parliamentary democracy from the Nazi threat.

On 18 October 1930 Churchill had been a guest at the German Embassy in London, and had held a long talk with a senior member of the Embassy staff, Prince Otto von Bismarck, a grandson of the 'Iron Chancellor'. Bismarck had recorded their talk in a secret dispatch. He reported that Churchill had been reading newspaper accounts of developments in Germany with close attention, and that he was 'pleased' about Brüning's success in maintaining control of the Parliamentary system, and in preserving it.

Churchill had gone on, however, to describe National Socialism in what Bismarck called 'cutting terms', and had stressed the extent to which Nazi policies were causing anxiety in Europe, especially in France, and were leading to a 'considerable deterioration' in Germany's foreign position.

Churchill had also told Bismarck that Germany should not fear a strong French army, since the French had no aggressive designs on other powers. He pointed out that the construction of the Maginot line illustrated France's fear of an aggressive Germany: it was a defensive line, suitable only as a barrier against invasion, not as a means of attack.

In reply Bismarck told Churchill that Hitler had declared in a number of public statements that he did not wish to embark on any external military adventures. But Churchill was not convinced, telling Bismarck that while Hitler had indeed declared publicly that he did not mean to wage 'a war of aggression', he, Churchill, was 'convinced that Hitler or his followers would seize the first available opportunity to resort to armed force'.

This account of Churchill's views, so sharp in their perception and foresight, was sent to the German Foreign Office in Berlin.

Five months later, in April 1931, Austria and Germany announced the establishment of a Customs Union. No other nation had been informed in advance, nor had the League of Nations been consulted. Both the British and French Governments had protested about the union, and in an article syndicated through the United States, Churchill explained the reasons for these protests. 'Beneath the Customs Union,' he wrote, 'lurks the *Anschluss*, or union, between the German mass and the remains of Austria.' Once these two States were linked, two other States, France and Czechoslovakia, would both feel themselves in danger. Nor, in Churchill's view, was this danger imaginary. France, he wrote, 'with her dwindling but well-armed population sees the solid German block of seventy millions producing far more than twice her number of military males each year, towering up grim and grisly'.

It was impossible, Churchill wrote, to ask France to treat this as a 'trivial' matter, and he went on to explain that when 'you have been three times invaded in a hundred years by Germany and have only escaped destruction the last time because nearly all the other nations of the world came to your aid, which they certainly do not mean to do again, you cannot help feeling anxious about this ponderous mass of Teutonic humanity piling up beyond the frontier'.

Churchill was also concerned about the future of Czechoslovakia. His sympathies were strongly for her leaders, Thomas Masaryk and Eduard Beneš, who had 'refounded an ancient nation on democratic and anti-communist principles'. But inside Czechoslovakia's border, in the Sudeten region, were three and a half million German-speaking people. These 'Sudeten Germans', as they were called, had never been a part of Germany, but of the Austro-Hungarian Empire, which had disintegrated in 1918. Now they were a dissatisfied minority, themselves divided between democratic and socialist groups on the one hand, and right-wing groupings on the other. Hitler's German Nazis had made the 'liberation' of the Sudeten Germans one of its slogans. But both the Czechs and Sudetens were working to resolve their differences within the existing borders of Czechoslovakia, on the basis of greater Sudeten autonomy.

Churchill warned that if Germany were to annex Austria, the geographic result would be dangerous, for 'Czechoslovakia will not only have the indigestible morsel in its interior, but will be surrounded on three sides by other Germans'. Churchill did feel, however, that there might be one advantage in the Austro-German Customs Union if it were clearly restricted to creating economic, and not political links. Such an economic union might provide the Brüning Government with a popular success and bolster it against the Nazi movement. The 'mastery of Hitlerism by constitutional forces in Germany' would, he wrote, greatly contribute to peace in Europe in the immediate future.

For Churchill, the conflict in Germany was now clearly defined, between the 'dangerous Hitler movement' on the one hand, and the struggling 'constitutional forces' on the other. But until the outcome of the struggle became clear, he believed disarmament to be a policy fraught with danger.

The British Government's hopes for peace in Europe, however, continued to lie, as Ramsay MacDonald told the House of Commons on 29 June 1931, in European disarmament. The threat of war came, in MacDonald's view, not from a disarmed Germany but from the other European nations and their armed forces. The French army in particular, which Churchill regarded as a guarantee of European peace, was seen by MacDonald and the supporters of disarmament as a provocation and a danger.

MacDonald told the House of Commons that Britain's aim at the forthcoming disarmament conference was a general reduction in armaments, and then, when the conference was over, the planning of yet further reductions.

It was Churchill who rose to challenge MacDonald's proposals. He declared that since the Washington Naval Conference of 1921, British disarmament had reached a dangerous level, cutting the army 'to the bone' and leaving the air force with only an eighth the strength of France, the largest European air force at that time.

Churchill had always been an advocate of the importance of air power, not only as a factor, but as a decisive factor, in war. As early as 1909 he had urged Asquith's Cabinet to put themselves in direct contact with the Wright brothers, in order to study the most recent air developments. On the outbreak of war in 1914 he had become responsible, at Lord Kitchener's request, for the air defence of Britain. During the first nine months of the war he had been a pioneer in the use of reconnaissance aircraft, both in Flanders and at Gallipoli. In 1917, as Minister of Munitions, he had been insistent upon aircraft production being given priority for the use of steel and other scarce raw materials. In 1918 he had urged Lloyd George not to embark on any further offensives on the western front, until British and American air superiority was certain. From 1919 to 1921, as Secretary of State for Air, he had preserved the Royal Air Force as an independent entity, and created its distinctive ranks and badges. He himself was a former trained pilot with many hours, and one nearly fatal accident, behind him. He had many friends in the air force: those who had first taught him to fly in 1913, and those with whom he had worked between 1917 and 1922. By 1931 he had become convinced in his own mind of the need for a strong air force, both for national defence, and as a deterrent to aggressive action by others. Yet since the summer of 1929, under the second Labour Government, even the modest Air Programme laid down in 1923 had fallen into arrears, and the forty-two squadrons planned to be operational by 1933 would not in fact be ready.

Hence Churchill's sense of alarm, and anger, in opposing the ever more real and effective efforts at disarmament upon which MacDonald was embarked, not only cutting back Britain's military and air preparedness, but putting international pressure on France to cut back likewise. French disarmament, under duress from Britain or America would, Churchill warned the House of Commons during the debate of 29 June 1931, lead to terrible repercussions everywhere in Eastern Europe, the States of which, from the Baltic to the Black Sea, looked to France for leadership. Such French disarmament, when combined with British military weakness could 'open the floodgates of measureless consequence' in Europe.

A weak Britain, as Churchill saw it, would be forced to watch other States make concessions to an aggressor, and might herself be forced to make concessions, not on the basis of the rights or wrongs of the issue, but through weakness alone.

A strongly armed Britain, on the other hand, would deter military action and bullying by other powers. It was clear to Churchill that the greatest threat to peace was from a Germany determined to remove the restrictions put on her by the Treaty of Versailles. Such restrictions would never be accepted, he warned, by the youth of Germany, now 'mounting in its broad swelling flood'.

In the summer of 1931 Churchill went on a motoring holiday to France with his wife and son. While they were away, the Labour Government was confronted with the worst British economic crisis of the decade: the effects of the American Crash having finally struck at European financial stability. Churchill broke off his holiday to hurry back to London, hoping to prevent the Conservatives from joining a coalition with Labour to deal with the crisis on a 'national' basis. But his presence in London in no way altered the political situation.

After brief talks with various Conservative politicians, Churchill returned to France, to Juan-les-Pins on the Riviera. In London, the Labour Government struggled with plans to rescue the economy. One plan was a cut in unemployment benefit. But the Trade Unions made it clear that this would be unacceptable to them. Several senior Ministers supported the Trade Union view. MacDonald was emphatic, however, as was Philip Snowden, his Chancellor of the Exchequer, on the need for the cuts. There were mass resignations from the Cabinet. Then, on 24 August 1931, at a conference at Buckingham Palace, the King asked Ramsay MacDonald to remain Prime Minister, at the head of an all-Party Government.

The Coalition which had existed in spirit over India now came into effect officially in Parliament. Baldwin, Chamberlain and Sir Samuel Hoare entered the Cabinet. Lloyd George being too sick to participate in the crisis, two other leading Liberals, Sir John Simon and Sir Herbert Samuel, likewise joined the new administration. Churchill's absence, as Sir Samuel Hoare told a friend, was regarded as 'good luck'. Churchill was not, as he had believed he might be, offered a position in the new Cabinet.

The National Government had come into being. Although intended as an emergency measure, it was to last for nearly nine years. One of its first acts was to endorse the previous Labour Government's India policy. Gandhi himself came to London a few weeks later to participate in a second Round Table Conference. At the opening of the Conference, Ramsay MacDonald made it clear that the change of Government did not alter the Government's determination to grant India full Dominion status.

In October MacDonald called a General Election. The Labour Party, rejecting MacDonald's appeal to maintain the National Government, was reduced from 288 to 52 seats, a staggering collapse. The Conservatives won a massive majority: 473 seats out of 615. MacDonald remained Prime Minister, but the majority of his Ministers were Conservatives, headed by Baldwin as Lord President of the Council, Neville Chamberlain as Chancellor of the Exchequer, and Sir Samuel Hoare as Secretary of State for India. In all the Conservatives held eleven Cabinet posts, National Labour three and National Liberal two. The Conservatives' dominance was complete.

Once again, Churchill was not asked to join the new administration. Of a total of 615 MPs, only 20 were members of the Indian Empire Society.

Although Churchill nearly doubled his own majority at Epping, he was more isolated politically than he had ever been. But at Chartwell there were distractions at hand: bricks to lay, canvasses to paint, a swimming pool to be built, lakes to extend and many articles to be written. The theme of these articles was varied: politics, painting, reminiscences, economics and philosophical reflections.

By his writing during 1930 and 1931 Churchill was able to make up, and more than make up, his losses in the Great Crash. In all, his earnings during that single tax year were more than £35,000, of which only £500 was his Parliamentary salary, and £1,000 from new investments. The bulk of his earnings was from books and articles.

Churchill now prepared to go on a substantial lecture tour of the United States, hoping to earn enough money to build a substantial reserve of capital. But he postponed his departure in order to speak in the House of Commons in the debate on the second Round Table Conference. During the debate, Samuel Hoare stated that the National Government would maintain both the promised safeguards, and Westminister's ultimate responsibility for all decisions on India.

Churchill was sceptical of these assurances, so much so that he insisted on forcing the House to vote. He repeated his view that British authority and mediation would be required for many years to prevent Hindu–Muslim strife and the persecution of minorities in India.

Baldwin defended the Government's India policy. When the vote was taken only 43 MPs supported Churchill, as against 369 who voted for the Government. MacDonald, now supported by Parliament, set up three special Commissions of Inquiry to go out to India, and to make detailed proposals for a working reform.

Churchill set sail for America, together with his wife, and their daughter Diana. Travelling with him was his former detective from his Ministerial days, W. H. Thompson, sent with him by Scotland Yard, as a result of threats to Churchill's life by Indian extremists. Reaching New York on 11 December 1931, Churchill gave his first lecture on the following day at Worcester, Massachusetts. His topic: 'Pathway of the English-speaking People'. His theme: the essential unity of purpose of Britain and the United States: 'the only hope to bring the world back to the pathway of peace and prosperity'. Wherever that pathway might lead, Churchill declared, 'we shall travel more securely if we do it like good companions'.

On December 12 Churchill returned to New York. He had thirty-nine more lectures to prepare, for a guaranteed minimum income of £10,000, and a series of articles to write for the *Daily Mail*, on his American experiences, for a further £8,000. That night he went by taxi to dine with his friend, Bernard Baruch, but late, and unable to find the house, he asked the taxi-driver to set him down opposite where he remembered the house to be from his visit two years before. Then he set off to cross the road. He forgot to look left as well as right. As he stepped into the road he was knocked down by a car.

Churchill was crushed by the impact, dragged along by the car for some yards, and then thrown into the road, badly injured both in the head and the thighs. In great pain, he lay in the road. A crowd gathered, and flagged down a passing ambulance, but it already had a badly injured person on board, and drove on. Finally a taxi-driver took him to hospital. Blood was streaming down his face. 'What is your name and profession?' he was asked. 'I am Winston Churchill, a British Statesman,' he replied.

Churchill was carried into the hospital on a wheelchair, feeling as he recalled, 'battered but perfectly confident'. His scalp was cut to the bone. 'I do not wish to be hurt any more,' he said, 'Give me chloroform or something.' The anaesthetist was already on the way. 'A few deep breaths', Churchill wrote 'and one has no longer the power to speak to the world.'

Churchill was seriously ill for several days. As his detective hurried to his bedside, he said: 'They almost got me that time, Thompson.'

Churchill quickly developed pleurisy in addition to his cuts and bruises. Forty-eight hours after the accident he was well enough to telegraph to his son that his progress was satisfactory.

It was a week before Churchill was able to leave hospital. Then, much better in spirit, buoyant even, and despite the continuing pains, he at once arranged with the *Daily Mail*, by an exchange of telegrams, that he would write a special article on his accident. He wrote the article on board ship, on the way to the Bahamas to recuperate, and before taking up the lecture tour again. The *Daily Mail* paid him £600 for the single article, more than a year's Parliamentary salary.

While preparing his article, Churchill decided to include a note about the logistics of the accident. To obtain the technical details which he needed, he therefore telegraphed to Professor Lindemann: 'Please calculate for me following. What is impact or shock to stationary body two hundred pounds, of motor car weighing two thousand four hundred pounds travelling thirty or thirty-five miles per hour?' This shock, Churchill added, 'I took in my body, being carried forward on the cow-catcher until brakes eventually stopped car, when I dropped off.' Churchill went on to explain to Lindemann that 'brakes did not operate till car hit me', and he then told the Professor that he needed the figure for his article. 'Think it must be impressive', Churchill ended. 'Kindly cable weekend letter at my expense.'

Lindemann, true to form, replied with the necessary details as follows: 'Just received wire. Delighted good news. Collision equivalent falling thirty feet on to pavement. Equal six thousand foot pounds energy. Equivalent stopping ten pound brick dropped six hundred feet or two charges buckshot pointblank range. Rate inversely proportional thickness cushion surrounding skeleton and give of frame. If assume average one inch your body transferred during impact at rate eight thousand horsepower. Congratulations on preparing suitable cushion and skill in bump.'

In the article itself, Churchill not only described his accident, but reflected on its personal and philosophical implications. 'I certainly suffered', he wrote, 'every pang, mental and physical, that a street accident or, I suppose, a shell wound can produce. None is unendurable.'

'Nature is merciful', Churchill reflected, 'and does not try her children, man or beast, beyond their compass. It is only where the cruelty of man intervenes that hellish torments appear.' Otherwise, he wrote, 'live dangerously' and 'take things as they come; dread naught, all will be well.'

The accident article made a considerable impact; making one feel 'that one had been through every stage of the accident with you', his former Parliamentary Private Secretary, Bob Boothby, wrote to him from London, 'and caused a tremendous stir over here. What a time you have had.' The danger, Boothby warned, was the possibility of 'delayed shock', and with it, severe depression. In a recent accident of his own, Boothby added, 'I found it comforting, in moments of the most savage depression, to reflect that there was a definite physical cause for my psychological condition, and – although this was more difficult to believe – that it was only a passing phase.'

Boothby's warning was all too accurate. As Churchill recuperated in the Bahamas, he found recovery slower than he had expected. 'Vitality only returning slowly', he telegraphed to his American lecture tour manager on 3 January 1932, and he added: 'Premature efforts would court disaster.' He had hoped to return to his lecture tour before the end of January. But the doctor who had attended him in New York, Otto C. Pickhardt, warned him not to do so. 'First remember', the doctor telegraphed on January 5, 'forceful impact, with shock and shaking of brain cells. Real rest, mental as well as physical, imperative in building for your future and present usefulness.'

The lecture agent pressed Churchill to return to America by January 15. With each week's delay, another dozen engagements were being lost, and several thousand dollars. But Clementine was emphatic that Churchill should not risk a relapse. 'If my husband were to resume lecturing prematurely', she telegraphed on January 7, 'his health might be permanently impaired.'

Churchill was relieved to be allowed the whole of January to recover. He had begun to walk and swim a little more each day, but had lost the mental energy which had been so strong while he was writing his article on the accident earlier in the month. Since then, as he wrote to Dr Pickhardt on January 8, he had found 'a great and sudden lack of power for concentration, and a strong sense of being unequal to the task which lay so soon ahead of me'. In addition, both his arms, and his right side, were 'plagued', as he put it, with sharp pains which made them at times about as sore as two or three days after the accident. 'I have to take a quarter dose of the sleeping medicine at every night,' he wrote, 'and from time to time have some depression of spirit.' He was not, he added, trying to combat 'this unusual mood', of seeking to avoid both mental and physical exertion. He was sorry, also, for the lecture organizers, who, as he told his doctor, 'have been almost as much knocked about by the changes of programme as I was by the motor car'.

Despite the continuing pains, Churchill fought to overcome the nervous reaction. He was slowly throwing off both the insomnia and the neuritis, as he explained to a friend in England on January 8, 'by sea and sunbathing, massage and other aids', and three days later he told his New York lecture agent: 'I have made great progress here, but the shock was grave and deep.'

Suddenly, on January 12, Churchill became morose at his continuing pains and slow recovery, telling his wife that he had suffered three heavy blows in the past two years: the loss of money in the Crash, the loss of his political position in the Conservative Party, and now terrible physical injury. He told Clementine that he did not think he would 'ever recover completely from the three blows'.

Because of the pain which often made sleep impossible, Churchill now had to employ a night nurse. He told his lecture agent that he was still 'astonishingly feeble; even the act of dressing or shaving tires me. I spend eighteen of the twenty-four hours in bed.' Yet, despite feeling 'very weak and debilitated', his mind was 'becoming active again', and by January 17 he was able to sketch out the plan of his two principle lectures, one on Anglo–American unity, the other on the economic crisis. His spirit was on the mend.

The physical blow which Churchill had suffered was considerable, and he was to feel its effects for many months and even years. No man of fifty-seven can take so fierce a shock without substantial and unpleasant after-effects. Even as he prepared to return to his lecture tour, he realized that he was not in any way as fit as he had been a month before. 'You will find me, I am afraid, a much weaker man than the one you welcomed on December 11th,' he wrote to his lecture agent in his letter of January 17. 'I walk about five hundred yards every day and swim perhaps one hundred and fifty. But I tire so quickly and have very little reserve.'

Churchill now set about planning fourteen lectures. The itinerary planned for him was a punishing one: a different city almost every day between January 28 and February 15, including Rochester, his mother's birthplace outside New York. 'I am steadily improving and gaining strength', he wrote, while still in the Bahamas, to his agent, ten days before the first of the lectures, 'and also, though more slowly, punch.'

In preparation for his return to the United States, and to the land of Prohibition, Churchill acquired a note from Dr Pickhardt which was to save him adopting his earlier stratagem of 1929, of smuggling brandy into America in stone hot water bottles. 'This is to certify', wrote the good doctor, 'that the post-accident convalescence of the Hon. Winston S. Churchill necessitates the

43

use of alcoholic spirits especially at meal times. The quantity is naturally indefinite but the minimum requirements would be 250 cubic centimeters.'

Churchill now embarked on his lecture tour. On 28 January 1932, in the first lecture since his accident, Churchill spoke to an audience of 2,000 people at the Brooklyn Academy of Music. He argued in favour of closer Anglo–American cooperation, as a counterweight to both Europe and the Soviet Union, telling his audience: 'England and America are going in the same direction. They have the same outlook and no common discords. Why, then, do we not act together more effectively? Why do we stand gaping at each other in this helpless way, ashamed that it be said that America and England are working together, as if that were a crime? We must be the strong central nucleus at the council board of the nations.'

To an American magazine publisher, who wanted him to write some witty, and perhaps critical articles about the United States, Churchill wrote: 'I must tell you that I have become a great admirer of your people, and have developed many extremely cordial sentiments towards them during my travels.'

In Washington, Churchill met several leading Senators, and had a short talk with President Hoover. The effects of the economic crisis were still everywhere in evidence. 'Everyone has been most kind over here', Churchill wrote to his cousin, Sunny, the Ninth Duke of Marlborough, 'and I cannot help being very much drawn to these people in their great distress.'

Churchill completed his lecture tour without the collapse which both he and his wife feared. For three days he had been in acute pain from a sore tonsil, but managed, as he told his doctor, 'to shake it off'. Despite the strain of travel and the fatigue of seeing so many people, he added, 'I have strengthened steadily every day.'

The tour had further confirmed Churchill's admiration for the American people. He was never to lose this sympathy, nor to lose his faith in America's powers of economic recovery. In a letter to his British stockbroker he confided, in the summer of 1932: 'I do not think America is going to smash. On the contrary I believe that they will quite soon begin to recover. If the whole world except the United States sank under the ocean that community could get its living. They carved it out of the prairie and the forests. They are going to have a strong national resurgence in the near future.'

Following the election of President Roosevelt, Churchill felt drawn, from afar, to this man of courage and vision, grappling with economic chaos. One weekend at Chartwell in October 1933, Roosevelt's son James was among the guests. After dinner Churchill began a guessing game, asking each guest in turn to tell the assembled company his or her 'fondest wish'. Finally, when the question was put to him, he answered without a moment's hesitation: 'I wish to be Prime Minister and in close and daily communication by telephone with the President of the United States. There is nothing we could not do if we were together.' Then, turning to a secretary, he called for a piece of paper on which he inscribed the insignias of a pound and a dollar sign intertwined. 'Pray, bear this to your father from me', he said to James Roosevelt. 'Tell him this must be the currency of the future.'

Churchill's support for Roosevelt was frequently repeated in his articles in both Britain and America. 'I am,' he wrote in *Colliers* magazine in the first year of Roosevelt's presidency, 'though a foreigner, an ardent admirer of the main drift and impulse which President Roosevelt has given to the economic and financial policy of the United States.' And when, at Oxford, an undergraduate echoed the prevailing anti-American feeling by asking Churchill if he approved Roosevelt's policy 'of neglecting the affairs of the rest of the world for the especial benefit of the United States', Churchill replied with feeling: 'The President is a bold fellow. I like his spirit.'

His lecture tour completed, Churchill prepared to leave New York for England. Before he left he was interviewed on the local radio. The interview was broadcast that same day, 10 March 1932. That Churchill would eventually become Prime Minister, the interviewer declared, 'is the exultant hope of his friends, who are legion, and the apprehension of his political foes, who are by no means few'. Next to the King, the interviewer added, Churchill was 'probably the best-liked man under the Union Jack'.

After being questioned about his accident, Churchill was asked whether he believed that there might be 'another World War'. Do you think, the interviewer pressed, 'a war between two or more powers is about to take fire?'

'I do not believe that we shall see another great war in our time', Churchill replied, and he went on to explain why. 'War, today' he said, 'is bare – bare of profit and stripped of all its glamour. The old pomp and circumstance are gone. War now is nothing but toil, blood, death, squalor, and lying propaganda.'

Churchill stressed in this interview that for as long as France had a strong army, and Britain and the United States had good navies, 'no great war is likely to occur'.

'I take it,' replied the interviewer, 'that you haven't a high opinion of these Disarmament Conferences?' Churchill replied emphatically: 'No, I have not! I think that since the Great War they have done more harm than good.'

On 11 March 1932 Churchill sailed from New York for England. Awaiting him at Southampton was a 'surprise' gift of a Daimler, organized by his friend, the young Conservative MP Brendan Bracken. Bracken was a thrusting, exuberant Irishman. Churchill had first met him in 1923 when Bracken arrived spontaneously to help his childhood 'hero' in the election. Although Churchill had lost the election, he had been impressed by Bracken's energy, enthusiasm and organizing powers as a canvasser and mobilizer of votes. One observer of the 1923 campaign described Bracken as 'a tall youth, who looked like a golliwog. His head was covered with a thick thatch of reddish curls. In manner he was very self assured. He was a strong and downright personality.'

Clementine had not like Bracken at first, but his devotion to Churchill was total and she was gradually won over by his loyalty. He also had a considerable capacity for ferreting out political gossip and for transmitting it. Some said that

Bracken was Churchill's illegitimate son, a fiction to which Churchill reacted with amused indifference, but which Randolph found somewhat vexatious.

In the late 1920s Bracken had become a financial journalist, and owner of the *Financial News*. His business acumen was acute, particularly when it came to raising money. To buy Churchill's Daimler, £5,000 had been needed. Bracken had drawn up a list of more than a hundred of Churchill's personal friends, then cajoled £50 from each. With so much sympathy for Churchill after his accident, the task was not too difficult: and with a sense of pride, Bracken sent Churchill himself a copy of the list, so that Churchill could send a hundred thank you telegrams.

The Prince of Wales himself, Bracken reported to Churchill while he was still in America, 'has associated with this gift, but wishes that his part be kept completely secret'. Churchill had known Edward since his investiture as Prince of Wales at Carnaervon Castle in 1910, when Churchill, as Home Secretary, had been in charge of the event. Other donors included two former Foreign Secretaries, Sir Austen Chamberlain and Lord Grey of Fallodon, the Secretary of State for India, Sir Samuel Hoare, two Professors, J. M. Keynes and Lindemann, the former High Commissioner in Cairo, Lord Lloyd, the young Tory MP Harold Macmillan, the financier Sir Henry Strakosch, and three press Lords – Beaverbrook, Rothermere and Riddell. Also in the list were the architect Sir Edwin Lutyens, the painter Sir John Lavery, and Charlie Chaplain – whom Churchill had first met in the United States in 1929.

Even the small selection above, a cross-section of Churchill's friends, gives an indication both of the wide range of his friendships, and of the broad spectrum of the society, or indeed societies, in which he moved. 'I cannot tell you what pleasure the gift of this lovely motor car has been to me', Churchill telegraphed to each of the hundred donors. 'Most of all for the friendship which inspired it.'

Another donor had been Randolph himself. Although he had only completed his first year at Oxford, Randolph decided not to return to university, but to lecture instead in the United States. Before his son set off, Churchill gave him a birthday dinner at Claridges, having, as he told one of the guests, 'high hopes' of Randolph and his extraordinary gifts of expression. He also hoped that Randolph would use diligence and hard work to develop his youthful potential.

Despite many fierce quarrels and angry disagreements, father and son were to fight many battles side by side, against the outside world, and were to feel a common purpose rare in father-son relationships. Randolph's admiration for his father, and Churchill's hopes for his son, often ran into stormy waters. But the strength of their relationship was real, and the affection abiding. This became particularly clear when Randolph decided to go on a lecture tour, to help pay off the mounting debts which he had incurred at Oxford. 'Everybody except my father thought I was crazy', Randolph later recalled.

Churchill encouraged his son to go to America, and shortly before Randolph left, asked him if he had yet prepared his lectures. 'I said no', Randolph wrote, 'I would do that during the three weeks which I was planning to spend in Venice. He chuckled.'

Randolph did not in fact prepare his lectures even in Venice, and, when he came to say his final farewell to his father, he now said he would prepare the lectures on the journey. Churchill commented whimsically: 'Ah, the first day you are on the ship you won't be feeling very well. The second day you will be feeling better. The third day you will meet a pretty girl and then you will be nearly there.' Randolph later recalled that his father had been absolutely right.

Although the years 1930 and 1931 marked the lowest point of Churchill's personal and political fortunes, they also produced two compelling reasons for him to remain in politics to fight for the causes in which he believed. Not only the problems of India but also the 'European Quarrel' had re-emerged to prevent him, as he expressed it, from 'forsaking the dreary field for pastures new'.

Chapter Three

'If we lose faith
in ourselves . . .'

Throughout 1932 Churchill watched with growing concern as the forces for
totalitarianism struggled for mastery over the German people. By February
1932 membership of Hitler's semi-military Stormtroopers had reached 400,000,
and Nazi Party membership climbed steadily above two million. Two months
later, in the second ballot for the Presidential Election, the incumbent President
since 1925, Marshal Hindenburg, was re-elected with nineteen million votes.
But Hitler, his most serious challenger, received thirteen and a half million
votes.

The demands of Hitler and the Nazi Party remained strident, clear and
simple: an end to the Treaty of Versailles, the removal of German Jews from all
walks of German life, and rearmament. With this platform Hitler had obtained
almost 40 per cent of all votes cast on 10 April 1932. Eleven days later Ramsay
MacDonald had travelled to Geneva, to urge the World Disarmament Conference that now was the time for the well-armed nations, and particularly
France, to disarm.

On 13 May 1932 Sir John Simon, the Foreign Secretary, and one of the few
Liberal Cabinet Ministers in the National Government, asked the House of
Commons to support the Government's plans for disarmament. Peace could
only be maintained, he argued, through a reduction in the level of armaments
throughout Europe, and he asked for sympathy for a disarmed Germany
looking fearfully across her border at a powerful well-armed France.

Simon's speech was well received. But Churchill was deeply worried. 'I
should very much regret,' he said, 'to see any approximation in military
strength between Germany and France. Those who speak of that as though it
were right, or even a question of fair dealing, altogether underrate the gravity
of the European situation.' As the House listened coolly, Churchill declared: 'I
would say to those who would like to see Germany and France on an equal
footing in armaments: "Do you wish for war?",' and he added: 'For my part, I
earnestly hope that no such approximation will take place during my lifetime or
that of my children.'

Churchill sought in his regular newspaper articles to point out the dangers of
disarmament to the general public; a public which was attracted by what
Churchill believed to be the misguided and over simple appeal of the Disarmament Conferences at Geneva. In one such article he warned that the horror
of war meant that people were now inclined to grasp at unrealistic platitudes,

48

and to accuse those who warned of the true situation of 'warmongering'. As Churchill saw it, the 'truth' was that each country went to the conferences to obtain the reduction of other countries' armies, while maintaining its own. Disarmament was a dangerous sham.

In an article in the *Daily Mail* on 26 May 1932, Churchill wrote bluntly that the cause of disarmament 'will not be attained by mush, slush and gush. It will be advanced steadily by the harassing expense of fleets and armies, and by the growth of confidence in a long peace. It will be achieved only when in a favourable atmosphere half a dozen great men, with as many first class powers at their back, are able to lift world affairs out of their present increasing confusion.'

Four days after this article appeared in London, Count Franz von Papen succeeded Brüning as Chancellor. Von Papen saw the possibility that his Government could last for a number of years with Hitler's tacit support, even though no Nazis were asked to join his Cabinet. The Nazis, however, went from strength to strength, increasing their percentage of the votes from 37 to 44 per cent in the Hesse provincial election in June.

The Nazis celebrated this victory, which made them the largest party in Hesse, by attacking and killing political opponents on the left, as well as their families.

On 16 June 1932 the British Prime Minister, Ramsay MacDonald, and the German Chancellor, Franz von Papen represented their countries at another international conference. The aim of this new conference, held at Lausanne, was to reduce Germany's remaining Reparation liability. When the conference agreed to Germany's demand that only a token payment of 3,000 marks be made, Churchill was angered by Hitler's comment that this money 'would be worth only three marks in a few months'. Churchill also pointed out that Germany had not suffered as much from reparations as was generally believed, as she had received massive loans from the United States with which she had completely modernized her industry.

The British Government, nervous of upsetting those who still wanted to 'make Germany pay', hesitated to publish full details of what had been agreed. But there was no way in which the historic 'ending of reparations' could effectively be hidden, and rumours abounded. 'In the present unfortunate circumstances', Churchill wrote privately to the Foreign Secretary, Sir John Simon, 'it seems to me better to make a frank publication of all the agreements, instead of letting things be dragged out piecemeal by foreign disclosures, or by the need of answering American rumours and exaggerations.'

This was always Churchill's view, echoing his friend Lord Birkenhead's slogan, 'Tell the truth to the British people.' And it rested equally on the arguments of morality and expediency. 'I am sure', Churchill told Simon, 'you will have to publish in the end.'

Publication took place a week later, with the aim, as Simon wrote to Churchill, of allaying 'a good deal of apprehension'. But the ending of reparations did not help the moderate or liberal elements in Germany. In every city, Nazis marched through the streets, demanding an end to the Treaty of Versailles.

A German General Election took place in July 1932. The reporter for the *Sunday Graphic* was Randolph Churchill, and he flew in Hitler's aeroplane with several other journalists as the Nazi leader addressed meeting after meeting. Randolph was amazed by the adulation which Hitler received from the crowds, and in his first report to his newspaper he made it clear that a Nazi success 'sooner or later means war', a prescient remark which echoed his father's warnings to Prince Bismarck nearly two years earlier.

In this new election the Nazis won 230 seats, well ahead of the Social Democrats who won 133 seats and the Communists with 78 seats. The Nazis were now Germany's largest single political party, with 13½ million votes. They did not achieve an absolute majority, however, and von Papen was able to form a Government without a single Nazi in his Cabinet.

Hitler's response to this snub was swift and violent: political opponents on the left were murdered in their homes and on the streets, while Jewish-owned shops were once more smashed and looted. On 29 August 1932 a shaken von Papen offered Hitler the Vice-Chancellorship, but Hitler would accept nothing less than the Chancellorship itself, and remained in defiant opposition, supported by a growing private army.

At this very time, as part of the research for his Marlborough biography, Churchill left England for Germany, and for a visit to the battlefields of Blenheim. With him on this expedition went Clementine, Sarah, Randolph, Prof, and a leading military historian, Lieutenant-Colonel Pakenham-Walsh.

After visiting the scenes of Marlborough's battle triumphs at Ramilles and Oudenarde – in Belgium – the party drove on to Munich, before proceeding to Blenheim. While they were in Munich, Randolph was keen to set up a meeting between his father and Hitler.

While reporting the election in July, Randolph had met, and enjoyed the company of one of Hitler's friends, Ernst Hanfstaengel, a Harvard graduate, and a friend also of the then Governor of New York State, Franklin Roosevelt. Randolph now asked 'Putzi', as Hanfstaengel was known, to use his influence to bring Churchill and Hitler together. Churchill dined with Hanfstaengel who spoke in a bewitched manner about Hitler and his policies. It soon emerged that almost every day Hitler visited the very hotel in which Churchill was staying. Hanfstaengel was therefore certain that a meeting could easily be arranged.

Although Churchill gave Hanfstaengel his permission to arrange the meeting, Hitler was not keen. He was indeed quite nervous of the prospect, dismissing Churchill, according to Hanfstaengel's own account, as a 'rabid Francophile'.

Despite Hitler's unease, Hanfstaengel still hoped that the Nazi leader might decide to join Churchill's party for coffee. At dinner, while Hanfstaengel chatted with Churchill and Clementine, Churchill pressed him about Hitler's anti-Semitism. 'I tried to give as mild account of the subject as I could,' Hanfstaengel recalled, 'saying that the real problem was the influx of eastern European Jews and the excessive representation of their co-religionaries in the professions.' To this Churchill listened carefully. Then he told Hanfstaengel: 'Tell your boss from me that anti-Semitism may be a good starter, but it is a bad sticker.'

Hitler never appeared for coffee. Hanfstaengel made one more effort the next day to persuade him to meet Churchill. Refusing yet again, Hitler asked what could be achieved by meeting a man who was not a member of the Government and to whom no one listened. 'People say the same thing of you', Hanfstaengel replied. Altering his routine, Hitler avoided the hotel during the remaining two days of the Churchills' visit.

Churchill and his party then drove to Blenheim, where Pakenham-Walsh showed him the scene of his ancestor's triumph. To Churchill's joy, the topography of each of the battlefields was unchanged, and in his mind he was able to 'repeople them with ghostly but glittering armies'.

Churchill was deeply moved by these scenes and looked forward to bringing them to life in his biography. He now planned to leave Germany, to drive southwards through the Austrian Alps to Venice, there to combine a family holiday with writing up his first draft of the Marlborough battles. But as he set out on this last lap of his journey, he was suddenly taken ill with paratyphoid, and taken to a sanatorium in Salzburg.

The doctors at Salzburg insisted on Churchill remaining in bed for several weeks. His illness, combined with the lingering effects of his New York accident, had weakened him considerably. At home the news of Churchill's illness was widely and sympathetically reported.

Churchill was impatient to return to Chartwell, and to continue both his work and convalescence amid familiar surroundings. He therefore discharged himself from the sanatorium, and took the train for Calais. A British doctor, who was also on his way home, later recalled finding Churchill and his wife in the restaurant car. After a while Clementine went up to the doctor, whom she had known in England, and said to him: 'Can you help me with Winston. He has just discharged himself, against the doctors' advice, from the nursing home in Salzburg where he has had bad bleeding and insists on eating a full lunch with salad, wine etc. Will you kindly give him your advice as a doctor?'

'I will,' the doctor replied, 'but I doubt if he will take my advice.' Whereupon he went over to Churchill and talked to him 'like a Dutch uncle', and, as he later recalled, 'he took it quite well.'

Safely back at Chartwell, Churchill began a punishing schedule of writing. Within only a month he had written as many words as fill this book.

A young historian, Maurice Ashley, a recent Oxford graduate, provided Churchill with copies of documents from the archive at Blenheim, and from previously unexamined archives in several country houses. Churchill and Ashley then discussed the meaning of these documents, and prepared outlines and then drafts of the unfolding story. Then Churchill dictated to his new secretary, Violet Pearman, the thoughts which these documents and discussions provoked. Once his dictation was typed out, he then read it aloud to Ashley, listened to Ashley's comments, corrected, re-wrote and even re-dictated.

It was a long, difficult, and constructive process: every sentence beaten into shape by a master of words and argument. He also continued to work on his series of 'great stories retold', following *The Tale of Two Cities* with *Anna Karenina*.

All this work had to be done in bed, as Churchill had not fully recovered from his second serious physical setback within a year. As Ashley sat on one side with the documents, Mrs Pearman sat on the other side with her note pad, taking dictation. Impatient to make progress, Churchill insisted, however, on walking with Ashley up and down the great lawns at Chartwell, to discuss the meaning of the latest discovery of Marlborough's early and tortuous career.

Ashley later recalled how, as the two men walked and argued, Churchill suddenly 'got whiter and whiter'. Then he collapsed with a severe haemorrhage, the result of a paratyphoid ulcer. An ambulance was summoned, and Churchill was driven off to a nursing home in London. 'We hope he will recover shortly,' Mrs Pearman wrote to a friend, 'in his usual marvellous way.'

Churchill's friends rallied round, and did what they could to be of good cheer. 'You have my sympathies and my prayers for a genuine recovery,' Desmond Morton wrote to Clementine, and Stanley Baldwin wrote from 11 Downing Street, now his official residence as number two to Ramsay MacDonald: 'My dear Winston, so far I have refrained even from good words, but I do want you to realize with what profound sympathy I see you laid up and rendered immobile for the time being. No greater trial could there be to your ardent spirit.'

Baldwin's handwritten note went on: 'For all our sakes you must devote yourself to regaining your strength, and no one will be more glad to hear you from your corner, invoking once more blessings or curses on our heads as may seem good to you on occasion.'

In his reply to Baldwin, dictated to Mrs Pearman from his sick bed, Churchill reported that as a result of his haemorrhage he had lost 'about two-fifths of my blood', and that it would be at least six weeks 'before I have my ordinary vigour back'.

'I am recovering, and recruiting red corpuscles at about 100,000 a day,' Churchill wrote to a friend. And he added: 'At present, though increasing in numbers rapidly, they are still rather a raw militia and I do not feel that I could wisely commit my army to any first class operations.'

As always, Churchill's mail bag reflected the enormous affection in which he was held, even by political opponents, and strangers. It was now more than thirty years since he had become 'Winston' to the newspapers, the cartoonists and to millions of people whom he would never know. Baldwin remained 'Baldwin' to the public, and was 'Stanley' only to his friends. The same was true of Neville Chamberlain and 'Sam' Hoare. But 'Winston' was Winston to the masses. 'The world is a dull place without your pungent wit', wrote one of his myriad correspondents, 'so come back to public life as soon as you can do so without danger to health.'

Among those who were concerned about Churchill's well-being was his brother's wife, Gwendeline, known in the family as 'Goonie'. Churchill had first met her twenty-five years before, at the time of his own marriage to Clementine, and had been instantly attracted by her vivacious character and warm personality. The two had become devoted friends, and greatly enjoyed each others company. In the summer of 1915 it was Goonie who encouraged Churchill, then in the depths of depression over events at the Dardanelles and his own political demotion, to try painting as a solace. The suggestion had worked, opening up for Churchill a wonderful world of paints and canvasses, colours and relaxation. Henceforth Jack and Goonie were frequent visitors at Chartwell, often spending Christmas and New Year there. Goonie's presence in the family circle was a source of pleasure to them all, and her three children, Johnny, Peregrine and Clarissa, were likewise drawn into the Chartwell scene.

As soon as he was well enough to return to Chartwell, Churchill began to put together yet another book, *Thoughts and Adventures,* a collection of newspaper articles which he had written over the past twenty years, on his flying adventures, his air crash, painting as a pastime, a near escape from death on the western front, cartoons and cartoonists, elections, and economics. 'You have been very generous', wrote Neville Chamberlain on receiving a copy, 'in sending me your books, which I have enjoyed for themselves, and much more because they came from you to me. But I did not expect you would continue such generosity when we were no longer constantly meeting as colleagues, and I was equally touched and gratified on receiving *Thoughts and Adventures.'*

While Churchill was recovering and writing, ominous events were taking place in Germany, where von Papen's new Minister of Defence, Kurt von Schleicher, demanded for Germany 'equality of status' in armaments. The British official view, in the form of a note issued on 18 September 1932 by Sir John Simon, was that Germany should not be allowed to rearm and that all the clauses of the Treaty of Versailles to this effect were still binding. Germany's response was to withdraw from the Disarmament Conference. Thus von Papen found himself endorsing Hitler's denunciations of Versailles.

Churchill supported the Simon Note, although many in Britain felt that an unarmed Germany was at a disadvantage against France, and looked with some sympathy at the German demands. Churchill was convinced, however, that a firm stand against German rearmament was essential. Every right-wing party in Germany, he noted, was trying to win votes by standing up against foreign governments opposed to the resurgence of Germany as a military power. Churchill saw von Papen being pushed further and further towards extreme policies by Hitler's popularity, only to have Hitler outdo him by taking an even more extreme position. In an article published in the *Daily Mail* on 17 October 1932 Churchill, after describing General Schleicher as 'the main repository of force in the new German autocracy', reminded his readers that Schleicher had already declared that Germany would disregard the opinion of foreign powers with regard to rearmament. With such a development, he warned that the British might be plunged into 'a situation of violent peril' within an incredibly short time.

Churchill feared that any British encouragement for German rearmament might provoke the French into reoccupying the Rhine Bridgeheads, a move which Germany would rapidly use to bring her army to a wartime level.

On 6 November 1932, for the second time in five months, the Germans held a General Election. The Nazis suffered a drop in their percentage of the vote from 37 to 33 per cent but maintained their position as the largest single party. Von Papen had no clear majority in the Reichstag, however, and when Hitler refused, yet again, to accept the position of Vice-Chancellor, von Papen's Government was in great danger of collapse.

On 10 November 1932, only four days after the German Election, the House of Commons again debated disarmament. Sir John Simon, retreating from his position of only two months before, stated that the Government was now ready to listen to Germany's claims for equality in arms. The Germans, in common with the other European States would, in return, have to promise not to resort to force in settling disagreements. As this debate came to an end, Baldwin told the Commons that the Government had been able to find no way of defending the 'man in the street' from air attack and warned that 'no power on earth' could prevent bombers getting through.

Churchill, who had missed the debate because of his illness, responded on 17 November 1932 in an article in the *Daily Mail* in which he urged the Government to devise a policy which was capable of protecting Britain from involvement in another European war against its will. Such a policy, he stressed, would require the development of an air force 'in such a position of power and efficiency that it will not be worth anyone's while to come here and kill our women and children in the hope that they may blackmail us into surrender'.

In Germany, on the same day that Churchill published his article, von Papen gave up his attempt to form a Government, and resigned the Chancellorship. President Hindenburg, attempting to form a coalition Government, asked Hitler if he would join the Government under a new Chancellor. Hitler's response was that the Nazi Party would take no part in any Government unless he himself were made Chancellor.

A few days later, on 23 November 1932, Churchill spoke of the danger posed by the new Germany. 'Do not delude yourselves,' he told the House of Commons. 'Do not let His Majesty's Government believe – I am sure they do not believe – that all that Germany is asking for is equal status. I believe the refined term now is equal qualitative status by indefinitely deferred stages.' That, he said was not what Germany was seeking: 'All these bands of sturdy Teutonic youths, marching through the streets and roads of Germany, with the light of desire in their eyes to suffer for their Fatherland, are not looking for status. They are looking for weapons and, when they have the weapons, believe me they will then ask for the return of lost territories and lost colonies, and when that demand is made, it cannot fail to shake and possibly shatter to their foundations every one of the countries I have mentioned' – France, Belgium, Poland, Rumania, Czechoslovakia and Yugoslavia – 'and some other countries I have not mentioned.'

Churchill urged the Government to 'tell the truth to the British people, they are a tough people and a robust people'. He also emphasized that he could not recall any time 'when the gap between the kind of words which statesmen used and what was actually happening in many countries was so great as it is now. The habit of saying smooth things and uttering pious platitudes and sentiments to gain applause, without relation to the underlying facts, is more pronounced now than it has ever been in my experience.'

Churchill wanted the Government to pursue a policy aimed at a 'lasting reconciliation' in Europe, and he set out what he believed was the essential, guiding principle: 'The removal of the just grievances of the vanquished ought to precede the disarmament of the victors.' To bring about anything like equality of armaments while those grievances remain unredressed, would, he warned, 'be almost to appoint the day for another European war – to fix it as if it were a prize-fight'. It would be far safer, he believed, to re-open territorial disputes like the German claim to the Danzig Corridor and the Hungarian claim to Transylvania, 'with all their delicacy and difficulty, in cold blood and in a calm atmosphere and while the victor nations still have ample superiority, than to wait and drift on, inch by inch and stage by stage, until once again vast combinations, equally matched confront each other face to face'.

Churchill's speech of 23 November 1932 held the House spellbound. Yet the warnings with which it was laced seemed to many MPs to be far-fetched and alarmist. At one point he declared, in urging the need for France to remain well-armed: 'I say quite frankly, though I may shock the House, that I would rather see another ten or twenty years of one-sided peace, than see a war between equally well-matched powers.' He did not believe in the imminence of a European war, but war could only be avoided if statesmen showed 'wisdom and skill'. Baldwin's speech about the inability to resist air bombardment had been too negative. 'It created anxiety', Churchill warned, 'and it created also perplexity'. There had been in it a sense of 'fatalism, and even perhaps of helplessness'.

Churchill then set out his own belief about the part which Government must play in the defence debate in Britain, telling the House of Commons that the responsibility of Cabinet Members 'to guarantee the safety of the country from day to day and from hour to hour' was 'direct and inalienable'.

On 30 January 1933 Adolf Hitler became Chancellor of Germany. The 'thousand-year Reich' was born, and its aims were now to be put into effect; the Treaty of Versailles was to be torn up. Germany was to rearm, revenge her defeat, and become the master-power of Europe. Jews were to be driven from society. Socialists, Communists, religious leaders, and all liberal-minded opponents of the regime were to be chased out of public life, and taken, if still uncowed, to special 'concentration camps', where hard labour, humiliation, and savage brutality were to be the order of the day.

Meanwhile, as a result of events in Europe, the British Government began to examine its defence deficiencies. At a meeting of the British Cabinet on 15 February 1933, both Lord Hailsham, the Secretary of State for War, and Lord Londonderry, the Secretary of State for Air, 'called attention', as the official and secret notes of the meeting recorded, 'to corresponding deficiencies in their respective departments'. But Neville Chamberlain, the Chancellor of the Exchequer, reminded his colleagues of the Treasury's opposition to any increased spending on defence. 'Today,' the Treasury had insisted, 'financial and economic risks' were by far the most serious dangers facing the country, so much so that other risks, such as that of lack of military or air preparedness, would have to be run 'until the country has had time and opportunity to recuperate, and our financial situation to improve'.

Summing up the discussion, the Prime Minister, Ramsay MacDonald, stressed the nation's financial weakness, as already described by Chamberlain, and told the Cabinet that as a result of this weakness they would have to 'take responsibility' for the deficiencies of the Defence departments. In addition, because of Japan's recent attack on China, first priority in any defence spending would have to be given to requirements in the Far East.

Churchill's fears, however, continued to focus on Germany. When the undergraduates at the Oxford Union rejected a motion to fight for King and Country, Churchill described it as an 'abject, squalid, shameless avowel', and told an audience in London, on 17 February 1933: 'My mind turns across the narrow waters of the Channel and the North Sea, where great nations stand determined to defend their national glories or national existence with their lives. I think of Germany, with its splendid clear-eyed youth marching forward on all the roads of the Reich singing their ancient songs, demanding to be conscripted into an army; eagerly seeking the most terrible weapons of war; burning to suffer and die for their fatherland.' He thought also, he added, of France, 'anxious, peace-loving, pacifist to the core, but armed to the teeth, and determined to survive as a great nation in the world'.

Three weeks later, Randolph went to Oxford to challenge the Union verdict. He was unsuccessful. But, as Churchill wrote to a friend, Randolph had stood 'a hard test'. Nothing, Churchill added, was 'so piercing as the hostility of a thousand of your own contemporaries, and he was by no means crushed under it'.

During a debate on the Air Estimates in the House of Commons on 14 March

1933 Sir Philip Sassoon, the Under-Secretary of State for Air, opened by announcing a substantial reduction in air expenditure because of 'the need for economy'. To save money, one of the four flying training schools was to be closed down. No new fighting units were to be formed either at home or abroad. 'Risks have to be taken,' Sassoon explained.

Not only Britain's financial straights, but the course of world disarmament, dictated the policy of cut-back and economy. The 1923 Air Programme, due for completion that year, was to be held 'in suspense' for another year. This was 'practical proof', as Sassoon described it, 'of the whole-hearted desire of His Majesty's Government to promote a successful issue of the deliberations of the Disarmament Conference'.

Even after the rise of Hitler, even after his strident demands for arms and for territory, the Disarmament Conference had remained in session with Nazi German delegates sitting as bemused observers. While this effort at disarmament continued, Sassoon told the House of Commons, the Government 'are once again prepared to accept the continuance of the serious existing disparity between the strengths of the Royal Air Force and that of the air services of the other great nations'.

In reply to Sassoon, Churchill told the House of Commons: 'If our discussion this afternoon were confined solely to the topics upon which the Under-Secretary of State thought it prudent to dwell, if, for instance, we were to go away, as we might easily go, with the idea that the Air Force exists to fight locusts and that it never drops anything but blankets, we should undoubtedly entertain incomplete impressions of some of the issues which are brought before the House when the Air Estimates for the year are introduced.'

Churchill then criticized at length Baldwin's recent speech. Baldwin had, Churchill said, 'aroused alarm without giving guidance'. He went on to say that the Prime Minister 'thought wars would come again some day, but he hoped, as we all hope, they would not come in our time'. Baldwin 'had apparently no real faith in the sanctity of agreements', nor did he have any faith 'in the means of defence which are open to civilized communities when confronted with dangers which they cannot avoid. He led us up to a conclusion which was no conclusion. We were greatly concerned, and yet we were afforded no solace, no solution.'

Churchill continued by saying that Baldwin had 'vividly portrayed' the evils but that in the sphere of a 'practical course of action' there was 'a gap, a hiatus, a sense that there is no message from the lips of the prophet'. Churchill then criticized the Government's latest disarmament proposals at Geneva. 'The air forces of the world', he said, 'are all to be reduced to our level, and then we are all to take together another step down to the extent of $33\frac{1}{3}$ per cent.'

Did such a proposal have any reality, Churchill asked the House of Commons, and he went on to answer his own question: 'We must not allow our insular pride to blind us to the fact that some of these foreigners are quite intelligent, that they have an extraordinary knack on occasion of rising fully up to the level of British comprehension.' He explained, 'if all the air forces of the world were to be reduced to our level, as we are only fifth in the list, that would be a great enhancement of our ratio of military strength; and the foreigners are bound to notice that'.

Although the current disarmament proposals gave 'gratification' to the pacifists and the League of Nations Union, Churchill continued, there had never been any chance of them being accepted, and the Government knew that to be the case. 'We ought not to deal in humbug,' Churchill warned. 'It is no kindness to this country, to stir up and pay all this lip-service in the region of unrealities, and get a cheap cheer because you have said something which has not ruffled anyone, and then meanwhile do the opposite, meanwhile proceed on entirely pre-War lines, as all the nations of Europe are proceeding to-day in all the practical arrangements which they are making.'

In the 'present temper of Europe', Churchill argued, France would never accept the proposition that she should 'halve her air force and then reduce the residue by one third'. The present diplomacy of 'soothing-syrup' was dangerous 'because, unless the people know the truth, one day they are going to have a very surprising awakening'.

Churchill added: 'I would far rather have larger Estimates and be absolutely free and independent to choose our own course than become involved in this Continental scene by a well-meant desire to persuade them all to give up arms. There is terrible danger there.'

There was, however, 'a means of safety open', Churchill asserted and that was 'the possession of an adequate air force'. He could not understand, he said, 'why His Majesty's Government and the representatives of the Air Ministry do not inculcate these truths, for truths they are, as widely as they possibly can'.

Churchill then set out the crux of his fears, and of the argument which underlay, in his view, the whole debate. 'Not to have an adequate air force in the present state of the world,' he declared, 'is to compromise the foundations of national freedom and independence. It is all very well to suppose that we are masters of our own actions in this country and that this House can assemble and vote as to whether it wishes to go to war or not. If you desire to keep that privilege, which I trust we shall never lose, it is indispensable that you should have armaments in this island which will enable you to carry on your life without regard to external pressure.'

Churchill had greatly regretted, and made it clear that he had regretted, Sassoon's statement that Britain was only the fifth air power, that the ten-year programme had been suspended for another year, and that no new units had been laid down. 'Why should we fear the air?' he asked. 'We have as good technical knowledge as any country. There is no reason to suppose that we cannot make machines as good as any country. We have – though it may be thought conceited to say so – a particular vein of talent in air piloting which is in advance of that possessed by other countries.' That being so, he ended, 'I ask the Government to consider profoundly and urgently the whole position of our air defence'.

After the air debate Churchill received unexpected support from within the Air Ministry itself: a letter from Sir Christopher Bullock, the Permanent Secretary at the Air Ministry, and its senior civil servant. In 1919 Bullock had been Principal Private Secretary to Churchill, when Churchill was Secretary of State for Air. In 1933 he was only forty-two years old, but at the top of his career. On the day after the air debate he sent Churchill what he called 'a strictly private line to say how much I appreciated your intervention'.

Churchill's speech had been 'very effective', wrote Bullock, 'in inducing a beginning of clearer thinking on a subject on which there has been the utmost confusion of thought, despite all our efforts to the contrary'.

Bullock was 'not quite sure', he wrote, whether he ought to write to Churchill at all. But he did want to say how glad he was 'to think you are still keeping up your interest in air strategy and factors'. And he added: 'I only wish the Prime Minister and Simon had been in the House when you spoke!'

At the Disarmament Conference at Geneva, on 16 March 1933, Ramsay MacDonald put forward Britain's proposals. These proposals were comprehensive. Military service was to be limited throughout Europe to eight months maximum. All guns and tanks were to have an upper size limit. All land forces were to be restricted numerically. Aerial bombardment was to be forbidden. Each country's number of military aircraft was set at an upper limit; 500 aeroplanes each for Britain, France, Italy, Japan, Russia and the United States. All aircraft in excess of this number were to be disposed of. The number up to which Germany could build was to be kept open.

Under this new British proposal, all armaments surplus to MacDonald's scheme were to be destroyed, while Germany, France, Italy and Poland were each to restrict their armies to 200,000 men.

Only a week after MacDonald set out this disarmament plan in Geneva, the German Reichstag in Berlin passed an Enabling Bill giving Hitler full dictatorial powers. Hitler's ability to silence criticism, to imprison opponents, and to direct Germany's rearmament as he chose, was now complete. That same day, in the House of Commons, MacDonald, just back from Geneva, defended his disarmament proposals, while at the same time telling MPs: 'I cannot pretend that I went through the figures myself.'

The British Government's intention, MacDonald told Parliament, was to give Germany 'equality of status' in all matters of arms. That is to say, Germany would be allowed to rearm up to the levels set out at Geneva. But Churchill, now recovered from his second attack of paratyphoid, and speaking as MacDonald's principal critic, derided the return of 'our modern Don Quixote', bringing with him the 'somewhat dubious trophies' collected amid the 'nervous tittering of Europe', and warned that the 'supreme object' of avoiding war would not be possible if France were pressed to disarm to the levels which MacDonald had proposed. Such a disarmament, Churchill was convinced, could only encourage Germany. And the news from Germany, he warned, was increasingly ominous. 'When we read about Germany', he told the House, 'when we watch with surprise and distress the tumultuous insurgence of ferocity and war spirit, the pitiless ill-treatment of minorities, the denial of the normal protections of civilized society to large numbers of individuals solely on the ground of race – when we see that occurring in one of the most gifted, learned, scientific and formidable nations in the world, one cannot help feeling glad that the fierce passions that are raging in Germany have not found, as yet, any other outlet but upon Germans.'

Churchill spoke with the authority of a former Secretary of State for War and Air who, for two years, throughout 1919 and 1920, had supervised the details both of post-war demobilization and military re-organization, and of the formation of the Royal Air Force. A serious student of military affairs for more than twenty years, he now pointed out to the House of Commons that if MacDonald's proposals were carried out, it would entail an automatic halving of France's army, and a statutory doubling of Germany's. Such a course, he warned, was the path to war: 'As long as France is strong and Germany is but inadequately armed', he declared, 'there is no chance of France being attacked with success', and thus no chance of Britain being drawn in to fight Germany in defence of France, under the Locarno Agreement of 1925.

Not only would MacDonald's proposals make it easier for Germany to attack France, Churchill urged, but they also ensured, and had done so already, that Britain would be 'weaker, poorer and more defenceless' should war come. The London Naval Treaty of 1930 had helped to ensure that. So too had the continuing air disarmament. Yet Britain's weakness, Churchill pointed out, could only serve as an encouragement to Germany to make war on France, knowing that Britain would be unable to come to France's aid.

Churchill's arguments were answered by the Under-Secretary of State for Foreign Affairs, Anthony Eden. At thirty-six, Eden was one of the rising stars of the Conservative Party. Without French disarmament, he said, Britain could not secure for Europe 'that period of appeasement which is needed'. Nor was Churchill right to say that Britain wished France to halve her army. 'The reduction was nothing like that,' Eden retorted. 'It was 694,000 to 400,000.'

In the House of Commons, Eden's rebuke of Churchill met with widespread cheers, while that same evening Neville Chamberlain attacked Churchill's arguments in a public speech at Birmingham, rebuking Churchill for trying 'to sow suspicions and doubts' in the minds of Governments which had expressed no such doubts themselves.

And yet these doubts existed, and when Churchill spoke again in the House of Commons on 13 April 1933, he quoted a Swiss newspaper to the effect that by his disarmament policies MacDonald was pursuing 'those pro-German sympathies which he had had for so many years', in order to bring about 'the defeat or paralysis of France'. Of course, Churchill said, this was not so. But it was nevertheless widely believed.

During the course of his speech, Churchill made a strong defence of the Treaty of Versailles, in particular with regard to the new States which it had endorsed, and whose frontiers it had drawn, in central Europe. Hitler was now demanding changes in these post-war frontiers, and using the fact that there were German-speaking minorities in some of them – especially in Poland and Czechoslovakia – to denounce those countries and their borders.

Churchill was in favour, as he told the House of Commons, of measures to 'mitigate these anomalies'; such mitigation would indeed, in his view, be a 'blessed thing'. But he was opposed to using the minorities question to tear up the Treaty itself. It was becoming a matter of fashion in England to belittle the States created at Versailles. Ramsay MacDonald had gone so far in reflecting this fashion as to call Europe a house 'inhabited by ghosts'. This, Churchill said, 'is to misinterpret the situation', and he went on to tell the House of Commons: 'Europe is a house inhabited by fierce, strong, living entities. Poland is not a ghost: Poland is a reincarnation.' Churchill continued: 'I rejoice that Poland has been reconstituted. I cannot think of any event arising out of the Great War which can be considered to be a more thoroughly righteous result of the struggle than the re-union of this people, who have preserved their national soul through all the years of oppression and division and whose reconstitution of their nationhood is one of the most striking facts in European history.' If there were aspects of Polish policy with which Britain did not agree, he argued, that did not alter the fact that 'a very great work has been achieved, a work of liberation and of justice, in the reconstitution of Poland. I trust she will live long to enjoy the freedom of the lands which belong to her, a freedom which was gained by the swords of the victorious Allies.'

Churchill went on to speak of Czechoslovakia, 'the land of Good King Wenceslas', another State whose borders had been drawn at Versailles, and whose legitimacy Hitler had begun to attack. Czechoslovakia had 'emerged', Churchill told the House, 'with its own identity established'. As for Germany, Churchill said, 'new discord' had now arisen in Europe because she was not satisfied 'with the result of the late War'. Commenting on this, he declared: 'I have indicated several times that Germany got off lightly after the Great War. I know that that is not always a fashionable opinion, but the facts repudiate the idea that a Carthaginian peace was in fact imposed upon Germany.' Churchill went on to explain: 'No division was made of the great masses of the German people. No portion of Germany inhabited by Germans was detached, except where there was the difficulty of disentangling the population of the Silesian border. No attempt was made to divide Germany as between the northern and southern portions, which might well have tempted the conquerors at that time. No State was carved out of Germany. She underwent no serious territorial loss, except the loss of Alsace and Lorraine, which she herself had seized only fifty years before. The great mass of the Germans remained united after all that Europe had passed through, and they are more vehemently united to-day than ever before.'

Churchill then discussed the whole question of German rearmament and the revision of the Treaty of Versailles. It was 'extremely dangerous', he said, 'for people to talk lightly about German rearmament and say that, if the Germans choose to do it, no one can stop them. I am very doubtful if Germany would rearm in defiance of the Treaty if there were a solidarity of European and world opinion that the Treaty could only be altered by discussion, and could not be altered by a violent one-sided breach. I, therefore, do not subscribe to the doctrine that we should throw up our hands and recognize the fact that Germany is going to be armed up to an equality with the neighbouring States in any period which we can immediately foresee.'

Churchill now set out his basic disagreement with the Government. 'The rise of Germany', he declared, 'to anything like military equality with France, Poland or the small States, means a renewal of a general European war.'

These fears concerned civil as well as military factors. For Churchill had followed closely the recent news from Germany: the removal two weeks earlier of all Jews from public office, the official Nazi order that all local organizations must begin a nationwide campaign of anti-Jewish propaganda, and the opening near Munich, at the village of Dachau, of a concentration camp large enough to hold 5,000 political prisoners and other 'enemies' of the regime. There was also the danger, Churchill told the House of Commons, of these 'odious conditions now ruling in Germany' being extended by conquest to Poland. One result of this would be, in his view, 'another persecution and pogrom of Jews begun in this new area'.

Churchill loathed Nazism because he hated persecution and prejudice. His hatred of tyranny, whether Tsarist, Bolshevik or Nazi, had always been intense. His belief that the disarmament of France would encourage German aggression was equally firmly held. Twice within sixty years Germany had invaded France, first in 1870 and again in 1914. Churchill was convinced that under Hitler's leadership, a third such attack was inevitable, unless France remained well-armed, and France's potential allies united.

Churchill was thus greatly perturbed by the lack of such unity, and when he spoke on 23 April 1933 as the guest at the annual meeting of the Royal Society of St George, he expressed these worries forcefully. In his speech, which was broadcast over the BBC, he re-iterated his faith in Parliamentary democracy.

Churchill told his listeners that Britain's difficulties arose, not from any defect in the Parliamentary system, but from 'a mood of unwarrantable self-abasement'. Nothing could do more to demoralize a people in times of difficulty than the current Government philosophy, made up of 'a vague internationalism, a squalid materialism, and the promise of impossible Utopias'.

Nothing could save England, Churchill warned, if she would not save herself: 'If we lose faith in ourselves, in our capacity to guide and govern, if we lose our will to live, then indeed our story is told.' And he added: 'If, while on all sides foreign nations are every day asserting a more aggressive and militant nationalism by arms and trade, we remain paralysed by our own theoretical doctrines or plunged into the stupor of after-war exhaustion, then indeed all that the croakers predict will come true, and our ruin will be swift and final.'

Churchill's course was now set. He was opposed to tyranny, opposed to the precipitate diarmament of the victors, opposed to a rearmed Germany seeking to impose its will on Europe, an advocate of the threatened States working together within the framework of the League of Nations, a supporter of liberal democracy and the Parliamentary system, and the advocate of increased defence expenditure, especially in the air, in order to defend that system and to deter any assault upon it.

These were to remain Churchill's themes for the next nine years. He was to urge them again and again, first when there was still time, in his view, to put them into effect; then when time began to run out; and finally when the dangers which he had forecast had come fully into view.

During 1932 Churchill continued to reassert Britain's faith in her 'capacity to govern' in India. Early in 1932 the National Government suspended its plans for Indian self-government and moved against the mounting unrest inside India itself, imprisoning Gandhi once more, for inciting civil disobedience. Churchill was relieved that firm Government had been restored. There was no doubt, he had written to Brendan Bracken immediately after Gandhi's arrest, 'that our policy is being substantially adopted'. A few days later Robert Boothby had written to him: 'India has faded into the background with the triumph of your policy. What a vindication. And so soon.'

Boothby's congratulations were premature. With law and order restored, the Government had again embarked on the course which Churchill believed to be ill-judged and dangerous. But he himself continued to be barred from broadcasting his point of view over the BBC. One idea, which his friend the Duke of Westminster suggested, was that he should broadcast from on board a yacht, just outside the three-mile limit.

During Hindu–Muslim riots in May 1932 more than 200 Indians were killed, 3,000 were injured, and 30,000 convicted of spreading unrest. But MacDonald and Baldwin had moved steadily towards their original goal. Their first act was to adopt a proposal for increasing the Indian electorate from its existing 7 millions to more than 36 millions. This proposal was intended as a necessary preliminary to a full-scale India Bill establishing Dominion Status. Churchill doubted whether democracy was suitable to India where, worse than 'conflicting opinions', he believed, there were still in existence 'bitter theological hatreds'.

Churchill's opposition to the extended franchise was widely shared. On 27 May 1932 the Secretary of State for India, Sir Samuel Hoare, expressed his concern about the fate of the proposed India Bill in a letter to the new Viceroy, Lord Willingdon. Hoare feared that the recent riots had 'hardened opinion' against the proposed constitutional changes. Sensing this change in opinion, Churchill continued to speak and write against the proposed Bill.

Despite what he had called in June the BBC's 'gagging veto', he now managed to broadcast from the Eiffel Tower. A month later, a telegram from Paramount Films offered Churchill a series of radio broadcasts from the radio station at Toulouse. Churchill accepted the offer. He warned his listeners, in the first of a series of broadcasts, that it was the Government's aim to determine the future of India without the full approval of Parliament, and without concern for the true opinion of the nation.

The Government now took a decisive step: announcing its intention to set up a Joint Select Committee, made up of MPs and Peers of all political parties. The Committee's task, set out in Parliament on 1 July 1932, would be to examine the Government's India proposals, listen to the arguments on both sides, and then report to Parliament.

Sir Samuel Hoare was delighted that the mere announcement of the intention to set up the Joint Select Committee would give what he called 'moderate' Conservatives an answer to Churchill's most damaging accusation, that the final settlement would be negotiated without consulting Parliament. But Churchill remained concerned that the Committee would prove to be nothing but a mouthpiece for Government policy. He continued to persevere with his warnings and even while laid low with paratyphoid at the sanatorium in Salzburg, he had used Professor Lindemann as his scribe to write to a number of MPs who shared his views on India, intending to lead them in a concerted protest at the next Conservative Party conference, to be held at Blackpool in October 1932. 'I propose to send out a whip to 20 or 30 of our friends to come along', he wrote to one MP, 'and make sure we are not treated with indifference.' He himself was prepared to speak, if possible in answer to a Ministerial speaker. 'It will be stern work,' he added, 'but what can we do? We must testify what we believe.'

Churchill's Blackpool plans came to nothing, the re-occurrence of his paratyphoid knocking him out just when he was ready to lead the campaign. Even while he was still in the nursing home, his constituency Vice Chairman had reported that he had found Churchill keen to go to Blackpool, even in an ambulance. But Churchill returned to Chartwell to convalesce.

A motion by Churchill challenging the National Government's India policy was put to the Blackpool Conference by Lord Lloyd, the former High Commissioner in Cairo who had been dismissed by the Labour Government three years before. Even in Churchill's absence his resolution made a considerable impact. As the debate began the Government Ministers were uncertain as to the result, and had to make a strong effort to secure it. As Sir Samuel Hoare wrote to MacDonald when the day was eventually won, Lord Lloyd had received a 'surprisingly good reception'. At the beginning of the meeting Hoare had feared that Churchill's resolution would be carried with a 'large majority'. Although, in the end, it was the Government that gained the substantial majority, Hoare warned MacDonald nevertheless that the 'sentiment' of the assembled Conservatives had been on Churchill's side.

Supporters of the Government's policy at Blackpool had laid great stress on the safeguards which would form an integral part of the India Bill, retaining in the Viceroy's hands the ultimate responsibility for foreign affairs, defence, the Indian Army, and the protection of India's many and vast minorities. But many Conservatives were uneasy as to just how firm these safeguards would be, or how firmly they would be retained, once Indian pressure mounted against them, as it surely would.

Churchill saw the Government's dilemma clearly. 'If the safeguards they have mentioned are enforced,' he wrote to Lord Carson when the Conference was over, 'responsible government is a lie.' The result would thus be 'a tissue of shams, elaborately woven, which will be rejected in scorn by every section of Indian opinion'.

An important area where the creation of safeguards was under discussion concerned the commercial interests of the Lancashire cotton mills. Hitherto, India had been their main market. But among Gandhi's leading financial backers were some of the wealthiest men of India, the mill owners of Ahmedabad, who were insisting upon the right of any Indian administration to create tariff barriers to protect, and thus subsidize, Indian cotton, and their own mills. The needs of Lancashire could not easily be brushed aside, especially with unemployment in Britain still well in excess of a million. But the India Bill intended to do just this, giving Ahmedabad a financial lever over Manchester. Hoare wrote to the Viceroy in February to tell him that one of the most difficult tasks would be to keep the Lancashire cotton people quiet, though this exercise would be much easier when they had 'got the whole question safely into the hands of the Joint Select Committee'.

On 22 February 1933 Dominion Status was upheld in the House of Commons by 297 votes to 42. But the vote revealed that less than half of all MPs were actually present. 'Nobody here or in India', Hoare warned the Viceroy, 'must imagine that things are going to run smoothly.' Most Conservatives, he told Willingdon were waiting to see whether the White Paper 'really does make the safeguards as effective as possible'.

Advocates of Dominion Status were increasingly worried about Churchill's influence as the leader of the India opposition, and feared that his campaign against the Bill might be successful. In an effort to undermine Churchill's influence, one leading Conservative politician, J. C. C. Davidson, cast doubt on Churchill's motives, declaring in a public speech that Churchill's 'ill-disguised intention' was not the safety and welfare of India, but rather 'the break-up of the National Government'.

Hoare, like Davidson, wanted to cast doubt on the motives of Churchill's campaign, telling Willingdon that Churchill's motives were to be regarded as 'completely unscrupulous', purely designed 'to smash the National Government'. Hoare added that Churchill would 'stick at nothing to achieve his end'. But Churchill's supporters were convinced of his sincerity. 'It was said that Winston was trying to break the Government over India,' one young

Conservative MP later recalled. 'I have no doubt that this was inspired by the Whips. It was deliberately put about.'

The power of the Whips did not extend to Conservative opinion outside Parliament however. At a meeting of the Conservative Central Council on 28 February 1933, a motion to repudiate the Party's India policy was defeated, but by only 189 votes to 165. The evidence of such strong support for Churchill was most worrying to Hoare, who wrote privately to Willingdon that there was a danger of 'a breakaway of three-quarters of the Conservative Party'.

The Government now began to work out the composition of the Joint Select Committee. Seeking full representation for those who shared his opinions, Churchill wrote to the Chief Whip to say that opponents of the Bill represented 'three-quarters of the Tory party in the constituencies' – an echo of Hoare's own figure. 'Anyhow', Churchill added, 'we can prove half' – a reference to the Council vote two days earlier.

To guide the Joint Select Committee in its discussions, the Cabinet now decided to issue a White Paper, setting out the proposals which it wished to see embodied in the India Bill. The secret minutes of a special Cabinet held on 10 March 1933 revealed the extent to which senior Ministers were uneasy about the policies they were proposing and pushing.

Opening the Cabinet meeting, Hoare noted that Indian critics of the proposed constitution would say at once that it was 'tied up too much' by safeguards, while critics in Britain would maintain that the safeguards were 'inadequate'. Hoare himself then explained that under the proposed safeguards the Viceroy would retain such powers that he would possess 'complete control' over both Foreign Affairs and Defence.

As Churchill had warned, and as Hoare feared, the Government's plans did indeed cause more unrest than satisfaction to the Congress Party, which saw them as a barrier to its would-be authority. Under the All-India Federation, as Hoare explained to his Cabinet colleagues, the Princes would have 30 per cent of the seats and the Muslims 30 per cent, leaving all other interests, including the Congress Party, in a permanent overall minority.

Yet even this interpretation of Dominion Status was too much for the Secretary of State for War, Lord Hailsham, who feared that under the scheme 'justice would be sold, the poor oppressed, and there would be a breakdown in the services'. Hoare agreed that he 'shared many of the doubts' expressed by Hailsham. But he went on to stress that the Muslims in particular liked the scheme, and were 'determined to have provincial autonomy', and that it was one of the 'basic principles' of Imperial policy to seek agreement with 'the Moslem world'.

Following the Cabinet's decision to go ahead with Dominion Status, Hoare authorized the setting up of what he described to the Viceroy as 'an effective organization to meet the Winston propaganda in the country'. The task was proving difficult. But Hoare had lighted upon the idea of giving a prominent part in the organization to the former President of the European Association of

India, Francis Villiers, who had earlier been a member of the Bengal Legislative Council.

Villier's proposed part in the anti-Churchill campaign was, Hoare explained to the Viceroy, 'one of the reasons why I telegraphed to you about getting him a knighthood'. Such an honour, Hoare added, 'would have helped us a great deal in getting the most out of him'. To this the Viceroy replied that, 'If you make good use of Villiers, of course I will be very glad to consider him for an honour in the future.' Villiers became Vice-Chairman of Hoare's new organization, which was known as the Union of Britain and India. He held the post until 1935, and was knighted in 1936.

On 30 March 1933 the House of Commons debated the Government's White Paper on India. The Government spokesman made it clear that the future of the White Paper would depend upon the conclusions of the Joint Select Committee, which had still not been set up. Churchill's fear, as he told the House, was that the Government would use the secret discussions of the Committee to shield the India proposals from proper Parliamentary scrutiny.

Churchill's points were greeted as much by abuse as by argument. One leading Conservative, Lord Winterton, told fellow MPs that despite Churchill's 'experience' of manual labour – a reference to his bricklaying activities at Chartwell – 'he cannot shovel enough earth over his past to obliterate it from human view'.

This outburst had been made possible by Hoare himself. As Churchill's speech proceeded, Hoare explained to the Viceroy that Churchill had 'lost the ear of the House', as a result of Hoare's own interruptions, and 'the only thing remaining was for Eddie Winterton to get up and drown him in ridicule to the delight of the House'.

At the end of the debate the Government's policy was upheld by 475 votes to 42, a massive majority. It was then decided that the Joint Select Committee would have power to frame proposals for Indian constitutional reform, on the basis of the White Paper, and as the basis for the India Bill.

The future of India seemed now to depend upon the composition of the Committee. Churchill himself was invited to join it. But when the full list of names became known, it was clear that Government supporters made up twenty-five of the thirty-four members, and he could not decide whether to accept.

For five days Churchill debated with himself and his friends. Then he decided not to serve, writing to Hoare to comment on the one-sided composition of the Committee. Three-quarters of the members, he wrote, had 'already declared themselves in favour of the principle of the abdication, at this juncture, of British responsibility in the Central Government of India. To this I am decidedly opposed.' He could see no advantage, he told Hoare, in joining the Committee 'merely to be voted down by an overwhelming majority of the eminent persons you have selected'.

Again Hoare chose to misrepresent Churchill, telling Willingdon that

Churchill had refused to join the Committee because his participation would prevent him carrying on his campaign to 'smash the Government'. Hoare even went so far as to say that Churchill was secretly dreaming that England would go Fascist, enabling him 'to rule India as Mussolini governs north Africa'.

Churchill's concern was, however, that all views should be given a fair hearing. As he wrote to a friend, 'The way in which the Committee has been picked is a scandal.' On 7 April 1933, when the composition of the Committee was debated in the House of Commons and a critical Conservative amendment was defeated by 209 votes to 118, these 118 opposing votes constituted the largest Parliamentary protest at any time against the National Government's India policy. 'If the House had been given a free vote', Churchill told the *Evening News*, 'the Government proposal would probably have been defeated by a majority of the Conservative Party'. The Government's aim, he asserted, was 'to get support for its views and not to have an impartial investigation'.

Unknown to Churchill, Sir Samuel Hoare was indeed making substantial efforts to prevent any serious challenge to the Government's India proposals. News of these efforts was in due course to be leaked to Churchill, and to lead to uproar.

Chapter Four

'Stoats and weasels'

Sir Samuel Hoare's main concern as the Joint Select Committee was about to begin its investigation was that the textile industry would consider the Government's safeguards to be inadequate. In particular, he feared that the Manchester Chamber of Commerce would give evidence to the Committee critical of the extent of the economic powers to be transferred to Indian control; powers of tariff 'autonomy' which, once granted, could be used to the detriment of Lancashire, by Indian mill owners able to raise their own protective tariffs at will.

Constitutionally, the Committee was obliged to examine all the evidence submitted to it and to make up its mind on the basis of that evidence. A special rule of the House of Commons, Sessional Order No. 4, expressly forbad 'tampering with witnesses, or evidence to be offered to any committee'.

For Hoare, the Lancashire point of view was an embarrassment which it was essential to deflect. The Viceroy shared this view, and was relieved when Hoare wrote to him to suggest that Lord Derby, whose 'services' he had secured on the Committee, and who carried 'great weight in Lancashire', should be the member of the Committee to watch over the Lancashire interests.

On 5 May 1933 Hoare wrote to the President of the Manchester Chamber of Commerce, Richard Bond, informing him that the Government could not include any provision in the new Indian Constitution for restricting the powers of an Indian legislature to impose tariffs on British goods. Bond protested at this limitation, which amounted, he said, to the abandonment of the commercial interests of Britain, and with his letter of protest he enclosed an outline of the evidence he would put before the Joint Select Committee.

Hoare now knew the extent to which the Manchester Chamber of Commerce was critical of the India scheme. Realizing what this evidence was likely to mean, on 12 June 1933 the Viceroy wrote in alarm from India urging Hoare to induce 'our Manchester friends to keep their mouths shut'.

The Manchester men would not, however, be silenced, and within ten days of the Viceroy's letter, they completed the preparation of their evidence, and of their sustained quest for some definite economic safeguard against any unfair use of retaliatory tariffs. On 21 June 1933 the Board of Directors of the Manchester Chamber of Commerce approved the evidence unanimously, and a hundred copies of it were then printed, and sent to London to the Joint Select Committee.

Six days later the members of the India section of the Chamber of Commerce, including Thomas Barlow, who was both President of the Chamber of

Commerce and Chairman of the Lancashire Development Council, were invited to London by Lord Derby, to meet Sir Samuel Hoare at a private dinner party. Both Hoare and Derby were members of the Joint Select Committee, but no other members of the Committee were invited, or even informed. Derby's substantial wealth and influence had earned him the title 'king of Lancashire'. The Manchester men could not easily challenge his authority, should he choose to assert it.

Hoare informed the Viceroy on 7 July 1933 that serious opposition to the White Paper depended on getting a 'better feeling in Lancashire', and that Derby's help might accomplish this.

Hoare's efforts, however, went beyond mere presence at the Derby dinner, and the expression of pious hope. On his authority, the printed evidence sent from Manchester in the third week of June was never circulated to the Committee. Instead, the Chamber of Commerce was asked to change its conclusion and the evidence.

The thirty-two other members of the Joint Select Committee were never told of this procedure. Nor were they told that on 26 July 1933 Lord Derby informed the Secretary of the Manchester Chamber of Commerce, Raymond Streat, that what was needed were 'somewhat radical changes' in the Manchester evidence. But the India Section of the Manchester Chamber of Commerce had rejected the suggestion that it recall or change the evidence it had already submitted, and decided, on 28 July 1933, according to the minutes of its meeting, that they would not change their original submission, however much pressure was put on them.

Lord Derby was not deterred. Indeed, on the same day that he had written to Raymond Streat in Manchester, he also wrote to the India Office in London, to the Deputy Under Secretary of State, Sir Louis Kershaw, for help in preparing a revised memorandum. Five days later Kershaw sent Derby four pages of proposed alterations. On 9 August 1933 Derby sent these changes to Raymond Streat in Manchester, explaining that Kershaw, like himself, had been 'disturbed' by the wording of the original evidence. 'The notes I sent you', Derby explained, 'are really therefore the joint efforts of himself and myself.'

On 20 October 1933 Hoare wrote privately to the Viceroy to report his intention to postpone publication of the evidence of the Manchester Chamber of Commerce. It was likely, he warned to be both 'threatening' and 'provocative' in tone.

Hoare did not tell the Viceroy that the evidence had already been approved, printed, submitted, and withheld. Nor did he explain that the India Office itself, in the person of Sir Louis Kershaw, was helping Lord Derby totally to recast the evidence.

To the very last it looked as if Derby's pressure might fail, for on 23 October 1933 a telegram reached the Chamber of Commerce from its special fact-finding Mission to India, in which the Mission declared that they had never suggested that the original evidence should be withdrawn and could not understand where reference to withdrawal had come from.

This telegram came too late to turn back the tide of pressure. Lord Derby's influence was immense, for he combined his traditional authority as 'king of Lancashire' with his added authority as a member of the Joint Select Committee. On 25 October 1933, only two days after receiving the telegram from its Mission in India urging it not to withdraw the original evidence, and after a stormy meeting on October 24, the Manchester Chamber of Commerce called back that evidence from London.

The memorandum containing this evidence had been sitting in London for four full months, locked away at the India Office, and not shown by Hoare or Derby to any other member of the Joint Select Committee to whom it had been submitted. Now it was to be rewritten in its entirety. As one member of the Executive Committee of the Manchester Chamber of Commerce was to recall eight months later, the pressure which had been applied by 'responsible persons' in London had been passed back to Manchester 'in such emphatic terms that unfortunately it induced a majority of the Executive Committee to agree to alter a very excellent statement of what we required to one of no value at all'. It was only after a heated debate, and by a small majority, that it was agreed to bow to pressure, and then only after the President of the Chamber, Thomas Barlow, had threatened to resign.

On 3 November 1933 a revised Manchester memorandum was discussed in London by the Joint Select Committee. Only two members, Hoare and Derby, knew that this evidence was different from that which had originally been submitted. The other thirty-two members were entirely ignorant of the events of the previous six months. Asked by the Committee whether the Manchester Chamber of Commerce had any alterations to suggest in the Government's India White Paper, the Chairman of the India Section, Harold Rodier, answered in one word: 'No.' Pressed a second time, by two members of the Committee who were aware of the basic difference of view between the proposals of the White Paper and the interests of Manchester, Rodier repeated his succinct: 'No.'

That same day, Hoare, who had presided over the Joint Select Committee session, wrote privately to the Viceroy to tell him how Derby had succeeded in persuading the Manchester Chamber of Commerce to withdraw the 'dangerous and aggressive memorandum' which, he explained, 'fortunately I had prevented from being circulated'. The new Manchester evidence, Hoare added, was 'a very harmless document'.

This was indeed so. In their original submission the Manchester Chamber of Commerce had asked for binding economic safeguards to protect Lancashire against tariffs imposed by India. But in the re-submitted version there was no reference whatsoever to safeguards. Hoare's triumph was complete. The Ministerial head of an impartial inquiry had successfully prevented that inquiry from hearing evidence which argued against a proposal which the Government wished to see accepted.

Churchill knew nothing of the machinations of Hoare and Derby. But five months after the 'harmless' document had been submitted to the Joint Select Committee, a Manchester businessman, Harold Robinson, gave Churchill an outline of events of the past months, including details of the Derby dinner and a summary of the Derby-Streat correspondence. The rest was unknown. Hoare's letters to the Viceroy and Sir Louis Kershaw's involvement were both closely guarded secrets. But there was enough in the story to convince Churchill that a grave miscarriage of justice had taken place, and that evidence submitted to a quasi-judicial body, the Joint Select Committee, had been tampered with, against the specific rules of the House of Commons. 'I cannot conceive', Churchill reflected, 'that any fair minded man would approve of such behaviour.'

Churchill's first decision was to question the businessman who had produced the documents. This cross-examination took place on the afternoon of 8 April 1934 at a private room in the Savoy Hotel. Churchill was accompanied by Brendan Bracken, who on hearing the story for the first time was convinced that nothing could prevent it 'being brought out'.

Before taking further action Churchill went through the documents with his friend Sir Terence O'Connor, a distinguished barrister, and later Solicitor-General under both Baldwin and Chamberlain. O'Connor was convinced that Churchill had a powerful case, and after the two men had prepared a dossier of the material, Churchill sent the dossier to Lord Salisbury, one of the thirty-two members of the Joint Select Committee who had not been shown the original Manchester memorandum. In his reply Salisbury revealed that he had himself been uneasy ever since the Manchester delegation had appeared before the Committee. 'Of course,' he told Churchill, 'it was at once evident when the Manchester delegation appeared before us they had been got at. I was profoundly disgusted.'

In his letter to Churchill, Salisbury reflected that it was 'clearly the business of the Committee to get at the truth in this particular'. Nor did Salisbury regard this as an isolated incident, telling Churchill that he had no doubt that pressure had been applied to people in England as well as in India to give their support for the White Paper.

On 15 April 1934 Churchill made his move, writing to the Speaker of the House of Commons to say that he would raise the issue of privilege in the House the following day. It was a grave charge, accusing two members of a Parliamentary Committee of tampering with evidence, especially when one of the members, Sir Samuel Hoare, was a senior Cabinet Minister. And yet, as Churchill wrote to the Speaker, the evidence he had been shown revealed that 'grossly irregular and highly objectionable' methods had been used to bring 'influence to bear' on witnesses to alter evidence which they had already handed in officially.

Churchill's charges stunned Parliament, brought down upon him the bitter hatred of Sir Samuel Hoare, and led to two months of intense inquiry, speculation and ill-will. Yet Churchill was convinced not only that his charges were justified but that the whole fabric of honest government was at stake, telling the House of Commons on 16 April 1934, while he was setting out the case for a breach of privilege: 'These are not the days I think, when Parliament can afford to be too lax and easy-going on the assertion of its rights and responsibilities.' No man, Churchill declared, could be cited 'before all the country' as an independent and impartial arbiter, 'and then at the same time go round and manage and whittle down the evidence which is going to be presented to his colleagues and fellow-judges'. These two roles, he said, were 'absolutely irreconcilable'.

Having listened to the charges, the Speaker ruled that a case had indeed been made out 'for a breach of privilege', and that the Committee of Privileges would have to examine the evidence and give its verdict. The Committee Chairman would be the Prime Minister, Ramsay MacDonald. Other members were Clement Attlee, Stanley Baldwin, Austen Chamberlain, Sir Herbert Samuel, and the Attorney General, Sir Thomas Inskip.

Churchill himself appeared before the Committee of Privileges on 23 April 1934. The very fact, he said, 'that this Committee consists in the main of my political opponents and of Ministers of the Crown, whose respected colleague is attacked, will be sufficient to secure me all fair and reasonable consideration and facilities'.

Churchill's hopes were not realized. His plea to be allowed to question other witnesses was disallowed, and the documents which he wished to be produced from the India Office were never brought forward. As a result of these two Government decisions, Churchill's case was not as full as it might have been, and the extent of the links between Derby, Hoare and Kershaw was never revealed. Three days after Churchill had appeared before the Committee, Hoare discussed his evidence with Lord Hailsham, telling him of 'the difficulty of putting in all copies of the correspondence'. The crucial Derby–Kershaw letters were thus never presented to the inquiry.

During the course of the inquiry Hoare tried to protect himself by abusing Churchill and his role. 'This Winston business', he wrote to a friend, 'is really one of the most unscrupulous affairs that there has been in politics for a hundred and fifty years.' When Churchill had brought up his accusation in the House of Commons, Hoare added, 'I might have been a traitor being arraigned by the Star Chamber,' and he ended his letter: 'I should hope every decent person greatly resents this.'

A few days later Hoare wrote again: 'As a result of these outrageous proceedings my office, myself and three prominent members of the Government have been doing nothing but dealing with Winston's preposterous charges.' This, Hoare protested, had put 'an enormous amount of useless work' upon him.

Hoare's bitterness was deep. A few days later he wrote again that he hoped Derby would never forgive Churchill for, as he added, 'I certainly shall not.'

Later, Hoare was to send a friend an account of rumours that Churchill and

73

his son 'fight like cats with each other and chiefly agree in the prodigious amount of champagne that each of them drinks each night'.

Ramsay MacDonald went even further than Hoare and tried to silence Churchill. On 7 May 1934 MacDonald asked to see him at 10 Downing Street. Churchill reported the ensuing conversation to a friend, who recorded that MacDonald had 'harangued' Churchill on the duty of everyone pulling together at this difficult time 'in Europe and the East'. MacDonald had also suggested that as the situation in the Dominions was getting 'worse and worse' the Government were thinking of sending someone of standing to 'go and talk to them'. Churchill had sensed that this was a trap, telling MacDonald: 'If you are going to suggest that I should suppress the result of my inquiry, I tell you frankly that nothing will persuade me to do so.' At this, MacDonald had protested forcefully that he had had no such suggestion in mind.

In spite of MacDonald's pressure, Churchill persevered, and on 10 May 1934 he sent the Committee of Privileges a substantial memorandum, setting out his arguments in detail. One point which he was able to make from the documents at his disposal concerned Thomas Barlow, one of the most senior of the Manchester men who had been present at the Derby dinner. It was Barlow who, according to the minutes of the Manchester Chamber of Commerce, had threatened to resign unless the old evidence was withdrawn, and new evidence submitted. This threat had been successful. It had been made on 24 October 1933. Scarcely three months later, on 1 January 1934, Barlow had received a knighthood. 'It must however be remembered', Churchill wrote, laconically, 'that coincidence may afford a perfectly innocent explanation for his actions.'

There was another point which Churchill raised from a letter which was available to him to use as evidence. This letter had been sent by Lord Derby to Raymond Streat. In it Derby mentioned that 'I had a long talk with Sir Louis Kershaw on the subject'. This showed, wrote Churchill, that Derby was in fact 'concerting his action with Sir Louis Kershaw, who was giving him the views of the India Office'. It was difficult to believe, Churchill added, 'that the Secretary of State did not approve of the action of Sir Louis Kershaw, or that his subordinate acted contrary to his wishes and policy'.

The Committee of Privileges now began work on its report. On its decision would depend much of Churchill's credibility in the year of argument and debate that still remained until the India White Paper was accepted by Parliament, and the India Bill became law. The Committee of Privileges' report was drafted by a senior civil servant, Sir Maurice Gwyer, the man who had earlier drafted the India White Paper itself.

In the final stage of the inquiry another of Churchill's critics was involved: Sir Thomas Inskip, who, during Churchill's appearance before the Committee of Privileges had at one point asked him to answer the questions 'without rhetoric'. Many of Inskip's questions had been hostile in tone. Even more ominous, but unknown to Churchill, Baldwin, who was himself a member of the Committee of Privileges, told a friend that it was Inskip who 'had drawn up the report against Churchill'.

The report was made public on 9 June 1934. It was indeed 'against Churchill'. The combination of Gwyer and Inskip, both distinguished lawyers, and both opposed to Churchill's general attitude to India, was devastating. No breach of privilege had taken place, the report declared. The Joint Select Committee was 'not in the ordinary sense a judicial body'. It was therefore not subject to the ordinary rules applied to tribunals 'engaged in administering justice'.

According to this ruling, there could be no legal basis in accusing members of the Committee of applying 'wrongful pressure'. In any case, what had been called pressure was, the report concluded, 'no more than advice or persuasion'. The report also stated that none of the actual documents involved, and none of the documents set out by Churchill in his memorandum, were to be published. Publication, so the members of the Committee of Privileges wished to state 'unanimously and emphatically', would be 'harmful to the public interest'.

Churchill was defeated. The Joint Select Committee had not been a judicial body. Pressure was only 'advice' and 'persuasion'. Publication of the documents was to be forbidden. Bitterly, and against O'Connor's advice, he attacked the report when it was debated in the House of Commons on 13 June 1934. The report's ruling, he said, meant that in future any member of a Joint Select Committee could 'do anything in his power to endeavour to deter any witness from presenting evidence as he wished to present it'. Furthermore, he could do so without informing his fellow members and he could sit and listen to witnesses 'giving evidence contrary to what it was known was their original wish to give without informing the other members of the Committee'.

Churchill feared the wider use to which the report's endorsement of 'advice' and 'persuasion' could be put. 'Are these methods', he asked, 'quite blameless in personal honour, these methods of management and organizing, to be approved indiscriminately, and even applauded? Are they to be our guide in the future? Are they to be applied in every direction?'

The House must imagine the consequences, Churchill warned, if similar methods as were used for the Lancashire evidence were to be used 'over the whole vast field of the Indian case', wherever the views of the group giving evidence was at variance with the Government's proposal. 'I ask the House to pause long and to think deeply', he ended, 'before they blindly apply, to the methods revealed in this report, the seal of Parliamentary approbation.'

The mood of the House was against Churchill. One Conservative MP, John Morris, a member of the London Stock Exchange, made a personal attack on him. All Churchill's political life, Morris declared, 'has been notorious for changing opinions, just like the weathercock, which vacillates and gyrates with the changing moods'. Churchill was, said Morris, an 'extraordinary human being', with such a power that he constituted 'a definite menace to the peaceful solution of the many problems with which this country is confronted at the present time'. It was about time, Morris warned, 'that this House took notice of this menace'.

For a further year Churchill fought the Government's India White Paper, as finally upheld by the Joint Select Committee in November 1934, and then embodied in its India Bill. Again and again he was able to muster more than eighty MPs to join his challenge. But it was never enough. Adhering to his belief that Parliament must be persuaded by argument, or not at all, he accepted the verdict of the majority when, in June 1935, after so many debates and divisions, the India Bill finally passed into law. On the final reading the Government received 386 votes as against 122.

Of the opponents of the Bill, eighty-four were Churchill's Conservative supporters. Some were the 'die hards' and 'Colonel Blimps' of cartoon and legend. Others were young men. 'I should like you to know', the thirty-one-year-old MP, Patrick Donner, wrote to him, 'what a grand thing I count it and how much it has meant to me to be allowed to do battle on your side, and in your company.' Donner added: 'I would so much sooner lose a battle in your ranks, than win one on the side of the yes-men battalions.'

Churchill never regretted the time and energy which the India controversy had involved, or the comradeship which it had created. As he had written to his wife at the height of the Parliamentary battle: 'The odds are very heavy against us. But I feel that I am doing my duty, and expressing my sincere convictions.'

When the battle was lost, Churchill urged his constituents to accept defeat 'cordially'. To the Congress leaders themselves, Churchill held out the hand of reconciliation, telling one of Gandhi's closest supporters, G. D. Birla, who had come to visit him at Chartwell, that Gandhi had 'gone very high in my esteem since he stood up for the Untouchables'.

Churchill urged Birla not to give the former opponents of the India Act a chance to say that they had anticipated a breakdown. As for the Act itself, he believed the Government would never use their safeguards. He would be 'only too delighted' if the Reform were a success. As for his test of success, that, he said, was the improvement in the lot of the Indian masses, materially as well as morally. 'I do not care', Churchill added, 'whether you are more or less loyal to Great Britain.' In defence of British rule, Churchill told Birla that he had always felt that there are 'fifty Indias'. But it was the Indians who had control now: 'make it a success', he said, 'and if you do, I will advocate your getting much more'.

These thoughts led Churchill on to some of the practical problems which beset India. 'Make every tiller of the soil his own landlord,' Churchill told Birla. 'Provide a good bull for every village. Tell Mr Gandhi to use the powers that are offered, and make the thing a success.'

Churchill harboured no malice towards the man he had described four years earlier as 'a Middle Temple lawyer, now posing as a fakir . . . striding half naked up the steps of Viceregal Palace'. When Gandhi had come to England, he told Birla, he had felt it would be rather awkward to meet him. But Randolph had done so, and, Churchill added, 'I should like to meet him now. I would love to go to India before I die.'

Churchill's bitterness was not towards the Indians, but towards those who, during the Manchester Chamber of Commerce episode, had, as he believed, indulged in a gross impropriety, and then defended it deceitfully. 'I do not mind confessing to you', he wrote to a friend, 'that I sustained a very evil impression of the treatment I received.' He hoped some day 'to nail up this bad behaviour, as stoats and weasels are nailed up by gamekeepers'. Some of those involved, Churchill added, 'are dirty dogs and their day will come; though I thank God I am not a vindictive man'.

A single theme linked Churchill's dislike and opposition to the Government's India and defence policies. This was his belief that they represented a weakening of British resolve. He also felt that history had reached one of its 'unexpected turns and retrogressions', as he explained to a lifelong friend, Lord Linlithgow. Neither the 'mild and vague Liberalism' of the early years of the century, Churchill wrote, nor the surge 'of fantastic hopes and illusions' after the First World War, had led either to progress or fulfilment. Instead, they had already been superseded by what he called 'a violent reaction against parliamentary and electioneering procedure, and by the establishment of dictatorships real or veiled, in almost every country'.

At the very moment when Britain's Imperial links were being threatened and her trade and shipping were shrinking, the world was entering what Churchill described to Linlithgow as a period 'when the struggle for self-preservation is going to present itself with great intensiveness to thickly populated industrial countries'. It was no longer any use, Churchill argued, to go on 'mouthing the bland platitudes of an easy, safe, triumphant age which has passed away'. The tide had turned, and there was a danger of being 'engulfed' by it. England was at the beginning of 'a new period of struggle and fight for its life'.

It was the daily news from Germany that gave strength to Churchill's conviction that a struggle was imminent, and that national weakness would mean national ruin. On 10 May 1933, only six days after Churchill's letter to Lord Linlithgow, the Nazis organized in Berlin the public burning of tens of thousands of books of which they disapproved: books which had been written by Socialists, Communists, Liberals and Jews, books on philosophy and psychology, of protest and dissent.

These events in Berlin confirmed Churchill's deepest fears. The only means of keeping Nazism in check was, he believed, a vigilant defence policy. But unknown to Churchill, three weeks after the burning of the books in Berlin, the British Cabinet was told by the three Service departments – the Admiralty, the Air Ministry and the War Office – of what the official minutes described as 'our grave shortage of war supplies'.

Throughout July 1933 the Nazis extended their tyrannical hold on Germany by outlawing trade unions, by decreeing that all parties but the Nazi Party were illegal, and by sending thousands of people who might oppose the new regime or who had been associated with the government of the democratic Weimar Republic to prisons or concentration camps. Nobody could watch these events, Churchill told his constituents on 12 August 1933, 'without increasing anxiety about what their outcome can be'.

Churchill went on to point out that 'at present' Germany was only partly armed, so that 'most of her fury is turned upon herself'. But already her smaller neighbours, Austria, Switzerland, Belgium and Denmark, 'feel a deep disquietude'. There was 'grave reason' to believe that 'Germany was arming herself', in violation of the Treaty of Versailles.

In his speech of 12 August 1933, Churchill called upon the National Government, and especially the Cabinet Ministers in charge of the army, navy and air force, to make sure that the armed forces of the Crown were kept 'in a proper state of efficiency, with the supplies and munition factories which they require'. Those forces must be strong enough, Churchill warned, to enable Britain to work for peace or to decide freely whether or not to be neutral in the event of war.

Every indication which reached Churchill confirmed him in the view that the German danger was real and imminent. In September 1933 his friend Alfred Duff Cooper, who had just driven through Germany to Austria, wrote to him of how, throughout Germany, 'everywhere and at all times of the day and night there were troops marching, drilling, singing'. Everything that Duff Cooper had seen had convinced him that the Germans were preparing for war 'with more general enthusiasm than a whole nation has ever put before into such preparation'.

The evidence of German rearmament could no longer be ignored. But at an emergency meeting of the Cabinet on 20 September 1933, Ministers agreed that even if German rearmament became public, and was to be confirmed, Britain could accept 'no new responsibilities in the matter'. This meant that the sanctions provided for in the Treaty of Versailles, for joint Allied action against any German rearmament, could not be contemplated. The reason for this was weakness. 'Our ports were almost undefended', Lord Hailsham, the Secretary of State for War, told his Cabinet colleagues, 'and our anti-aircraft defences were totally inadequate'. As a result of the active disarmament policy since 1929, Britain's position had become 'most perilous' if there were to be any risk of war 'within the next few years'.

In spite of this warning, the Cabinet remained attracted to the continuing pursuit of European disarmament, and when, on 14 October 1933, Hitler withdrew Germany from the Disarmament Conference at Geneva, the Cabinet's first reaction was to increase pressure on France to make 'some concessions' to a renewed disarmament plan. Indeed, only nine days later, on 23 October 1933, the Cabinet took a deliberate decision to continue to work towards 'the limitation and reduction of world armaments'. Although secret, and inspired by the knowledge of existing defence weaknesses, this certainly seemed the popular course, for two days after this Cabinet decision, at a by-election in East Fulham, the National Government candidate was defeated by an independent socialist, on a platform which included disarmament.

Throughout October and November 1933 the Cabinet were faced with the question of what to do as a result of the breakdown of the disarmament talks. In spite of continued pressure from the Secretary of State for Air, Churchill's cousin, Lord Londonderry, who urged a speeding up of the still incompleted 1923 air programme, Baldwin continued to press for 'a scheme of disarmament which would include Germany'.

On 12 October 1933, in their annual report, the Chiefs of Staff warned the Cabinet that the international situation was 'steadily deteriorating', and following a further warning by Lord Londonderry a month later, MacDonald and Baldwin agreed to set up a special Defence Requirements Committee to prepare a programme designed to meet the 'worst deficiencies'. As Chairman, the Government appointed the Cabinet Secretary, Sir Maurice Hankey.

In a memorandum written on 24 October 1933 Lord Londonderry again warned his Cabinet colleagues that Britain's air strength was 'markedly inferior' to that of other great powers. This inferiority arose, he explained, as a result of the 1931 Armaments Truce, and the Government's continuing hopes since then for disarmament. Londonderry then told his colleagues that a 'substantial increase' in Britain's air strength was not only necessary, but would, he believed, 'command widespread support both in Parliament and in the country at large'. He would not, however, propose such an increase himself, hoping that it might still be possible to persuade foreign governments to reduce their air forces to the British level, 'rather than by our being compelled to build up to theirs'.

The Cabinet agreed that in the event of the final collapse of the Disarmament Conference, all States would be 'absolved from their obligations'; that is to say, that any State could rearm at will. But this lay in the future, and on 7 November 1933 the Government's continued committment to disarmament was reiterated in the House of Commons by Sir John Simon, who explained that he and his colleagues were still working to secure disarmament, including the abolition of specific types of offensive weapons. But Churchill, who also spoke, believed that such efforts were based upon a profound misunderstanding of the European scene, and were bound to fail; and that in failing they would prove disastrous for Britain. The 'great dominant fact', Churchill insisted, 'is that Germany has already begun to rearm'. The newspapers gave details, Churchill said, of imports into Germany 'quite out of the ordinary of scrap iron, and nickel, and war metals'. They also gave details 'of the military spirit which is rife throughout the country', showing that the 'philosophy of blood lust' was being inculcated into German youth in a manner 'unparalleled since the days of barbarism'.

Churchill then spoke out once more against the 'dangerous process' of disarmament. How lucky the French were, he said, not to have taken the advice pressed on them 'in the last few years' by Britain and the United States, advice, in the latter case, 'rendered from a safe position 3,000 miles across the ocean!' Had France disarmed then, 'war would be much nearer'. Churchill warned that Britain's disarmament already meant her security was gravely at risk, and he went on to insist that the only policy that could prevent war would be for the nations of Europe, acting through the League of Nations, to approach Germany as one body, not in order to 'haggle' about disarmament and thereby weaken themselves further, but to see if there might still be 'some redress of the grievances of the German nation', before the disarmament of the European States had reached the point when Germany could take action in her own hands.

Speaking in his constituency on 14 November 1933, Churchill pointed out that Germany was using the money she had been 'let off' in reparations payments in order to buy, on the international market, 'the means of rearming and making cannon, contrary to the solemn treaties of peace'. Once more, his source was the newspapers. But six days later he received further information from a private source, his friend Desmond Morton, the head of the Industrial Intelligence Centre, and the Government's highly secret watchdog of European armaments.

Morton did not write to Churchill on impulse. He had for some months been responding to Churchill's requests for comments on various books, articles and letters on defence matters which Churchill had received, and sent on to him. Morton always replied with a comprehensive analysis of whatever such materials Churchill sent him, and in his replies he almost always added extra, and sometimes highly secret material of his own.

In his letter of 20 November 1933 Morton commented on a document which Churchill had been sent by a Frenchman who described Germany's ability to supply a very large army within the span of a few months, with tanks and guns. Morton was sceptical about the actual rate of supply which the Frenchman forecast. But he did point out to Churchill one aspect which his correspondent had missed, that the present German civil aircraft used for heavy freight transport 'are believed to be built so as to be convertible into bombers by the unbolting and removal of certain sections and their replacement by others'.

Churchill amassed and absorbed all the information he could about German air strength, and above all about Germany's capacity to expand, arm and deploy its armed forces. It was the 'European quarrel', he wrote to Baldwin on 3 January 1934, 'that will shape our lives. There indeed you must feel the burden press.'

For a brief moment, shortly after his fifty-ninth birthday, Churchill's own burdens were lifted with the publication of the first volume of his biography of the Duke of Marlborough. Baldwin wrote to him: 'My dear Winston, I haven't enjoyed anything more in years than your Marlborough. I am about a third

LEFT Churchill on his way from 11 Downing
Street to the House of Commons on 24 April
1928, to deliver his fourth Budget. With him are
his eldest daughter, Diana, and his
Parliamentary Private Secretary, Robert
Boothby.
BELOW The Prime Minister, Stanley Baldwin, at
10 Downing Street with Churchill, his
Chancellor of the Exchequer from 1924 to 1929.

Churchill and Stanley Baldwin in Oxford, receiving honorary degrees: a photograph taken in 1925.

ABOVE Churchill inspects mechanized forces at Perham Down, Tidworth, Wiltshire, in 1927, while
Chancellor of the Exchequer.
BELOW Churchill with three Cabinet colleagues, on his way from Windsor Station to Windsor Castle,
to hand in his seals of office to the King, 7 June 1929.

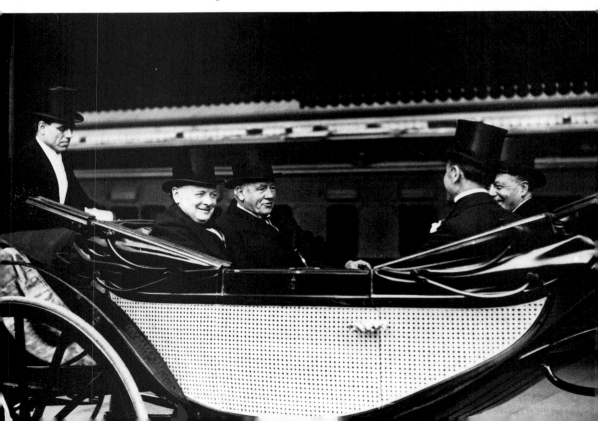

Clementine Churchill. 'What it has been to me to live all these years in your heart and companionship, no phrases can convey', Churchill wrote to his wife.

ABOVE The main entrance to Chartwell, Churchill's house at Westerham, Kent, bought in 1922, his treasured 'habitation' in which he lived until his death in 1965, at the age of ninety.
BELOW Churchill at Chartwell, building a house on the estate. In 1929 he had been invited to join the Amalgamated Union of Building Trade Workers and had received an 'adult apprenticeship' membership card.

FAR LEFT TOP Churchill at Calgary, Canada, inspecting the frost-covered pipes that conveyed oil from Home Wells to the separators in Turney Valley: a photograph taken on 9 September 1929.

FAR LEFT BELOW During his American visit in 1929 Churchill met Charlie Chaplin, and was captivated by him. This photograph was taken at the first-night party for *City Lights* at the Dominion Theatre, London, on 27 February 1931. In September 1931 Chaplin visited Churchill at Chartwell.

LEFT Bernard Baruch, the American Statesman and financier who had worked with Churchill during the First World War and who remained Churchill's friend throughout the inter-war years and after. This photograph was taken during a visit to Chartwell in 1949.

BELOW Churchill at his appointment as Chancellor of Bristol University in 1930.

'Prof' Lindemann, Churchill's close friend and confidant throughout the wilderness years.

ABOVE Churchill speaking against the Government's India policy at a meeting of the Indian Empire Society in a London hotel, 12 December 1930.
BELOW A scene at the House of Lords during the Indian Round Table conference in 1931: Churchill was a leading opponent of the Government's India policy, and for five years challenged it in Parliament and in a series of public speeches and newspaper articles.

ABOVE Churchill in his constituency on polling day, 27 October 1931. Clementine Churchill is sitting in the back of the car.
LEFT Neville Chamberlain, as Chancellor of the Exchequer, with Ramsay MacDonald, former Labour Prime Minister and, from 1931 to 1935, Prime Minister of the National Government.
RIGHT Churchill and his daughter Diana leaving Morpeth Mansions for St Margaret's Westminster for Diana's marriage to John Milner Bailey, 12 December 1932.

LEFT Lord Londonderry: Churchill's cousin, Ulsterman, coalowner, and Secretary of State for Air.
ABOVE LEFT A cartoon by Low on Churchill's call for a doubled, and then redoubled air force.
ABOVE RIGHT Desmond Morton, head of the Government's Industrial Intelligence Centre, responsible for collecting secret information about European rearmament; one of Churchill's closest advisers.
BELOW Adolf Hitler salutes, while two SS men hold back an excited crowd.

ABOVE Churchill speaking in his constituency, January 1933.
BELOW The Derby dinner on 25 May 1933: on Churchill's right is his friend Sir Abe Bailey (whose son had married Churchill's daughter Diana); on his left are Lord Derby, 'King of Lancashire', and Lord Camrose for whose newspaper, the *Daily Telegraph*, Churchill was to write a series of fortnightly articles in 1938 and 1939.

LEFT Sir Samuel Hoare, successively Secretary of State for India, for Foreign Affairs, and at the Home Office: one of Churchill's main political opponents during the wilderness years.
BELOW 'The Rival Screevers': Churchill and Sir Samuel Hoare, as portrayed by Bernard Partridge, and published in *Punch* on 1 November 1933. Churchill's view of Britain's role in India is contrasted with that of the Secretary of State for India who wished to transfer power more rapidly than Churchill believed was right.

THE RIVAL SCREEVERS.

Sam Hoare. "'ULLO, MATE! SO YOU DONE A ELEPHANT TOO?"
Winston. "AH! BUT MY COMPOSITION'S DIFFERENT—AN' I'VE MADE A LOT MORE O' THE BACKGROUND."

ABOVE Churchill at a shoot in Wales organized by his friend the Duke of Westminster. This photograph was published in the *Tatler* on 6 December 1933, with a caption describing Churchill as having the 'high distinction of being of those who are never averse from speaking their minds without fear or favour'.

RIGHT Churchill and his wife leave London for Paris on Imperial Airways, on their way to a Mediterranean holiday in 1934.

LEFT Churchill at the funeral of his cousin Sunny, the Ninth Duke of Marlborough.
ABOVE 'Air-Minded', a cartoon by Cecil Orr published in the *Daily Record and Mail* on 28 November 1934, at the height of Churchill's Parliamentary campaign to alert the Government to the extent of German air power, and British air weakness, a subject on which he was accused of having 'a bee in his bonnet'.
RIGHT David Lloyd George (right) and Sir Robert (later Lord) Horne, a former Conservative Chancellor of the Exchequer, and a supporter with Churchill of greater British rearmament in the 1930s.

LEFT Randolph Churchill speaking at a women's meeting on the eve of polling at Wavertree, 5 February 1935: during the 1930s he stood for Parliament – unsuccessfully – on three different occasions.

BELOW Churchill on the platform of the final meeting in Liverpool in support of his son Randolph on the eve of polling at Wavertree. Their friend 'Bendor', Duke of Westminster, stands between father and son.

RIGHT TOP Randolph Churchill and his father, together during Randolph's challenge to the Conservative Party at the by-election at Wavertree, 6 February 1935.

RIGHT BELOW 'An Embarrassing Position for the Parent at the Party!', a cartoonist's comment on the Wavertree by-election, published in the *Bulletin and Scots Pictorial* on 8 February 1935. In front of Churchill is Sir John Simon; on Simon's right, Stanley Baldwin; on Baldwin's right, Ramsay MacDonald.

AN EMBARRASSING POSITION FOR THE PARENT AT THE PARTY!

Why Not Mr. Churchill?

In an article in this page on Thursday last, Percy Cater, "Daily Mail" Parliamentary Correspondent, asked the question, "Why Not Mr. Baldwin?" and contended that he was the best leader of the country at the present time.

To-day F. G. Prince-White, "Daily Mail" Special Correspondent, retorts with "Why Not Mr. Churchill?"

IT has been said of William Pitt that he became Prime Minister at the moment when his leadership was a *tactical necessity.*

Great tasks awaited the hands of Chatham's brilliant son; there were vast responsibilities to be borne. England was soon to be shaken by the convulsions of a politically epileptic Europe. The timber for the tumbrils of the French Revolution was sea-

By

F. G. PRINCE-WHITE

soned; in Paris the Little Corsican was finishing his military studies, oblivious yet of his dazzling destiny.

At such a time no ordinary voice could speak the country's will — nor could a weakling's hand steady the State in the fast oncoming day of upheaval among the neighbour nations.

have been errors inseparable from the exercise of great gifts. And even Mr. Churchill's bitterest opponents cannot but own that he *is* uncommonly gifted.

To younger students of politics it is a most puzzling mystery that Mr. Churchill was not Prime Minister long ago. They look at his record and discover that he has occupied almost every other Government position.

In 1906, when he was only 32, he was given the post of Under-Secretary of State for the Colonies. Two years later he was President of the Board of Trade, and two years after that found him Home Secretary. From 1911 until 1915 he was First Lord of the Admiralty, from which office he passed to that of Chancellor of the Duchy of Lancaster.

In 1917 he followed Mr. Lloyd George in that supremely important Department, the Ministry of Munitions. Next he figured on the Governmental stage as Secretary for War and for Air, and after that as Secretary of State for the Colonies.

For five years—from 1924 to 1929—he was Chancellor of the Exchequer.

Here is no mediocre experience, but such as might well stand a Prime Minister in good stead.

Brilliant Oratory

IT has been Mr. Churchill's incomparable eloquence in the House of Commons that has crystallised most perfectly the nation's inmost thoughts and feelings in this prolonged season of international fear and distrust.

One could have believed, listening the other day to the climax of his speech on the Budget, that his voice belonged to one of the great masters of oratory and statecraft whose statues now stand silently amid Westminster Abbey's shadows:

" Either there will be a melting of hearts and a joining of hands between great nations, and they will set out on realising the glorious era of prosperity and freedom now within the grasp of millions of toiling people, or there will be an explosion and catastrophe the course of which no imagination can measure,

LEFT Churchill at Port Lympne with his host Sir Philip Sassoon, a close personal friend but for some years, as Under Secretary of State for Air, a political opponent.
ABOVE 'Why not Mr Churchill?': an article published in the *Daily Mail* on 11 May 1936.

A BAND OF HOPE.

(Left to right: Sir A. Ch——n, Lord W————n, Sir R——t H——ne, Mr. W——n Ch——ll.)

"WE DREAMT THAT WE DWELT IN MARBLE HALLS . . ."

'A Band of Hope', a cartoon by Bernard Partridge published in *Punch* on 3 June 1936, portraying Sir Austen Chamberlain (far left), Lord Winterton, Sir Robert Horne and Churchill at a time when all four men, although excluded from the Government, were urging greater vigilance in defence policy.

through it, savouring it as an epicure, and I shall finish it this week. It is A1. If I had – which God forbid – to deliver an address on you, I should say Read Marlborough and you may then picture yourself listening to Winston as he paced up and down the Cabinet room with a glass of water in his hand and a long cigar in the corner of his mouth. I can hear your chuckles as I read it.'

For the first six months of 1934 Churchill continued to put enormous efforts into his opposition to the Government's continuing disarmament policy, which Baldwin had confirmed in Cabinet, despite Lord Londonderry's advice to his colleagues that the Government ought to admit 'that we had disarmed to the edge of risk and had done it deliberately in pursuit of disarmament'.

In a radio broadcast on 15 January 1934, and in a speech in the House of Commons three weeks later, on 7 February 1934, in answer to the Government's White Paper on disarmament, Churchill spoke of the new situation created in the past four years 'by rubbing this sore of the Disarmament Conference until it has become a cancer', and then the 'sudden uprush of Nazi-ism in Germany', together with Germany's massive secret rearmament.

Churchill took note of the Government's declared policy that, having agreed to disarmament, they would not then agree to any future German demands for a larger navy, or for the return of her lost colonies. But he went on to ask whether Britain had either the military or the diplomatic arrangements with which to back up such declarations.

Unless Britain were in 'a proper state of security', Churchill argued, foreign threats and pressure would soon be applied. Then it would be the 'crash of bombs' on London which would reveal how the Government had allowed the weaknesses in aerial defence to continue. It was therefore essential, in his view, 'to begin the reorganization of our civil factories', so that when danger threatened they could be 'turned over quickly to war production'.

The Government White Paper was based on the British air force being restricted to a maximum of 500 aircraft. But Churchill was convinced that in 'the present state of Europe', Britain must adopt the principle of having an air force 'at least as strong as that of any power that can get at us'. In his reply to Churchill, Baldwin specifically stated that Britain's aim was to get 'an ordered armament limitation'. In the event of the breakdown of the Disarmament Conference, however, the Government would immediately take steps to look after the interests of the country.

For Churchill this was not enough. 'Security at home', he argued, should come before the world responded, or failed to respond, to the Disarmament White Paper. The Government, he went on to point out, commanded 'overwhelming majorities in both branches of the Legislature. Nothing that they ask will be denied to them. They have only to make their proposals, and they will be supported in them.'

Churchill was convinced that if the Government put forward rearmament plans 'with confidence and conviction', the nation would respond. He believed this even though public opinion seemed hostile to rearmament, as when he spoke to the Oxford University Conservative Association in the last week of February 1934. To his distress, a reference which he made to Britain's need for rearmament in order, as he phrased it, 'for us to be safe in our Island Home', evoked the meeting's derisive laughter.

Churchill believed that the Government was totally failing to give leadership to the country on the question of rearmament. In a radio broadcast on 16 January 1934 he declared: 'The hideous curse of war from the air has fallen upon the world,' and he went on to ask: 'Don't you think we ought to try to make ourselves as strong against attack from the air, as our Navy used to make us against invasion across the sea?'

The least Britain ought to do, Churchill told his listeners, was to have an air force 'as strong as that of the nearest power that can get at us', and he added: 'If we had that, I do not believe we should be attacked. And if we were, I do not think it would last long, or do us mortal injury.' But, he warned, 'till we have that, we are no longer the same kind of independent country that we used to be, that any of you were born into. We lie, with all our wealth and civilisation, exposed to the ferocious hatreds which tear the continent of Europe, and we have nothing to trust to for our life, and for our right to judge freely what course we will take, except our diplomacy and our good intentions.'

'I am for diplomacy and our good intentions', Churchill continued, 'but first of all we ought to make the island safe. Our finances are sound, we have the best credit in the world. No one can make better flying machines than we. We breed a type of young man nursed in freedom, intelligent and keen-eyed, who will do all that is required of them. And even if having a one-power standard in the air should make more work for builders, engineers and skilled men who are unemployed, I think we could put up with that.'

Churchill then urged upon his listeners the need for 'a clear, honest foreign policy, which anybody can explain and everybody can understand'. Only the week before, he pointed out, H. G. Wells had 'sneered' at the League of Nations. Churchill added, of Wells: 'He is one of those visionaries who are always talking about "a world state" and a "planned Destiny", and a "new order of society", and then when any practical steps are taken towards these remote ideals, are the first to point out their shortcomings and mock at them.'

Churchill also set out his faith in the need for a democratic society, telling his listeners: 'We do not want a violent plunge into Toryism, followed by a violent plunge into Socialism, followed by a violent plunge into Fascism; for that would be the end of our free, ancient constitution, and we should come down to the level of those unhappy countries where the ordinary people are simply the pawns and slaves of the Government and of the gang who are in the swim.' Churchill added: 'Please think this over very carefully because it will matter a lot to you and to your children.'

Following this broadcast of 16 January 1934 there was evidence that Churchill's efforts were beginning to be noticed, and to be appreciated. One young Conservative MP called the broadcast 'a clarion call to England', worthy of

Disraeli and Palmerston 'in their greatest days', while Desmond Morton wrote to say that it was 'a trumpet call, which cannot fail to stir your hearers to the very depths, unless they are already sunk in hopeless apathy and sloth beyond the reach of human sincerity and aid'. Even the Cabinet Secretary, Sir Maurice Hankey, wrote privately, in his own handwriting, to congratulate Churchill on such a 'stout-hearted' broadcast, and he noted: 'I nearly wrote to you to ask you to rub it in about our defences, but I felt sure you would do it and refrained.' Hankey added: 'We badly need some leadership on this subject just now, and it is a better horse than India I suspect. Thanks then for some real encouragement.'

In reply to Hankey, whose own influence over defence policy was thought by outsiders to be considerable, Churchill wrote to warn him of the 'frightful' risks that the Government were running, even more than before 1914. Hankey replied at once, his letter marked private and personal: 'I agree we are running great risks. I have been saying so for years.' What was important, Hankey added, was 'to get public opinion right. At present it is rotten.'

Hankey ended his letter to Churchill: 'You are doing yeoman work.' Encouraged by this, Churchill sent Hankey the document which he had already sent to Morton, about Germany's arms supply potential, seeking Hankey's comments. 'I can't reassure you much,' Hankey replied. 'There is little room for doubt that the Huns are going ahead.' But Hankey did send Churchill two 'reassuring' points: that the Germans could not at present produce aero-engines 'as fast as they want', and that the main German armaments industry was 'within easy bombing range' of French and Belgian aerodromes. In addition, Hankey wrote a few days later, his own son, just back from Berlin, had reported 'that every German, official and non-official, is terrified at the extent to which their heavy industry is exposed to attack from the air'.

Churchill did not share these hopes. Nor did Sir Robert Vansittart, the Permanent Under-Secretary of State at the Foreign Office, whom Churchill knew well, and with whom he was in regular if informal contact. Vansittart was a member of the Defence Requirements Committee, whose secret report, presented to the Cabinet on 28 February 1934, was based on the assumption that Germany would not be able to develop in the near future an air force sufficient to challenge Britain.

Vansittart rejected this conclusion. 'All who study Germany closely', he wrote to Hankey, the Committee's Chairman, saw clearly that Germany would not long remain 'inferior' to Britain in the air. Vansittart argued for 25 extra squadrons in addition to the 52 in the still incompleted 1923 programme. But Hankey rejected this, and it was decided instead that the air situation should be kept under 'close observation'.

Meanwhile, the British Government had decided, fourteen months after Hitler had come to power in Germany, that should the current disarmament talks fail, British air strength would have to be increased. This decision was made public in a Defence White Paper issued on 4 March 1934.

Four days later Sir Philip Sassoon, the Under Secretary of State for Air, announced in the House of Commons that Britain would build four new air squadrons. Sassoon explained that this decision had been made in order to satisfy the desire to 'pursue disarmament' and economy and also because it was no longer possible to postpone some increase in air rearmament, however small.

During the debate that followed Baldwin made a pledge of considerable importance. Britain, he said, would never allow herself to lose 'parity' with the dominant European air force, and would seek to promote an 'air convention' to establish air force sizes. The Labour Party rejected even this modicum of change. 'We deny the need for increased air armaments,' declared Clement Attlee. 'We deny the proposition that an increased British Air Force will make for the peace of the world, and we altogether reject the claim of parity.'

Some of those who denounced Churchill's advocacy of rearmament found it, as the Liberal leader, Sir Herbert Samuel, declared, a clarion call to anarchy and destruction. For supporters of disarmament the Air Estimates of 1934, which were even lower than the estimates for 1931, were admirable, showing as they did that the Government was still serious about disarmament. In secret the Cabinet had even decided on 28 February 1934 to sell 118 aeroplane engines to Germany: engines which, while naturally intended for civilian use, could in fact, as the secret Cabinet minutes noted, 'be used in small fighter planes'.

The Secretary of State for Air, Lord Londonderry, continued to express his 'grave perturbation' at the cut in expenditure. Other Powers, he pointed out, had almost without exception pursued, and were still pursuing far more rapid air rearmament. But even he accepted the Government's overriding theme that as the fate of MacDonald's disarmament proposals were still not known, more extensive measures should not be taken in the coming year.

Speaking for the Liberal Party, Churchill's friend Archie Sinclair denounced the slight air expansion as stupid and wasteful. A leading Socialist, Sir Stafford Cripps, went even further, accusing the Government of being pushed into action 'by the wild men like Mr Churchill'.

Churchill himself welcomed the parity pledge. He had indeed been to see Baldwin shortly before the debate, 'and in response to my appeal', as he wrote to a friend, 'he went much further than he has ever gone before'. But Churchill continued to urge vigilance, arguing that Baldwin's proposal for an air convention would be 'very dangerous indeed' if it delayed a review of Britain's air defences. Churchill told the House of Commons that he dreaded the day when the rulers of Germany would be able to threaten the heart of the British Empire. 'I dread that day', he repeated, 'but it is not, perhaps, far distant.' It was not a Party question, or a question between pacifists and militarists, he said, but a question 'of the essential independence of character of our island life and its preservation from intrusion or distortion of any kind'.

Even the killing of civilians by air bombardment, an aspect of air warfare raised by Baldwin as the greatest of all dangers, and described by Churchill as 'the shame of the twentieth century', could, Churchill argued, be avoided by a defence so strong that it would make it 'extremely unlikely' for Britain to be attacked. But the £130,000 earmarked in the White Paper for anti-aircraft defence would not enable the 'necessary measures' to be taken. Other speakers had said that Britain should not commit herself to further increases at that stage. 'But this', Churchill insisted, 'is the stage.' The turning point had been reached, 'and the new steps must be taken'.

Churchill was convinced that the hope of a reconciliation between France and Germany had gone. Germany was arming rapidly, 'and no one will stop her'. None of the grievances between the victors and the vanquished had been redressed. The spirit of 'aggressive nationalism' was rife. Long passed were the days when it looked as if it might be possible to achieve 'the laying in the tomb of that age-long quarrel between Teuton and Gaul of which we have been the victims in our lifetime'. That hope gone, it was essential to rearm, and to rearm rapidly. It was quite wrong for Baldwin to hesitate on the grounds of public opinion. He had only to make up his mind, 'and Parliament will vote all the supplies and all the sanctions which are necessary, if need be within forty-eight hours'. There need be no talk, Churchill declared, 'of working up public opinion. You need not go and ask the public what they think about this. Parliament and the Cabinet have to decide, and the nation has to judge whether they have acted rightly as trustees.'

Among those who listened to Churchill's speech was Lord Londonderry. Afterwards, when they met in the corridor, Londonderry told Churchill that Germany might actually have parity 'now' with Britain. Churchill was stunned by this admission, with its implication that Germany, with her small air force, was already as strong in the air as Britain. Acutely aware that all this had been withheld from Parliament, Churchill retorted: 'scandalous', and turned away.

Londonderry was offended by Churchill's behaviour. There was no need, he wrote to him in a private note, sent from the Air Ministry, 'to attack one of your oldest and certainly your best friends'. It was quite easy, Londonderry added, to make speeches in opposition, 'and some can be very helpful, as I thought yours was, but no great responsibility attaches to what you say and you have no knowledge of the difficulties I have had to contend with during the last two years here and at Geneva'. Nor, Londonderry added, was there any reason 'why you must be right and we must be wrong'.

Churchill replied at once. 'I am very sorry indeed', he wrote, 'to have been rough and rude in my manner to you. But what you said about our having Air Parity *now* seemed so monstrous and so dangerous that, without any other thought but the public safety, I turned upon you as I would have done in debate, or, may I add, as the House would have turned upon you if you had said it to them that afternoon.' Churchill's letter continued: 'I have always wished well to your career and I have done what I could to further it, but such complacency in such an office at such a moment will ruin it. It was this that stung me into using the word "scandalous", and into breaking off our talk.'

Churchill then set out his feelings about the part played by Londonderry as Air Minister in the whole defence story. 'You would do well', he wrote, 'to take stock of your position in relation to the public. The Air Ministry though usually a small office, has now become the key to national defence. A fierce light beats upon its holder. If my anger – which I do not excuse – should warn you of dangers, you have no real need to resent it. It was in no way personal to you.'

On 14 March 1934 Churchill again pointed out to the House of Commons the folly of holding on to hopes of continued disarmament: 'Why, it was only a little while ago that I heard Ministers say, and read diplomatic documents which said, that, rearmament is unthinkable.' But now the hope had become 'to regulate the unthinkable'. And Churchill added sarcastically: 'Regulated unthinkability, that is what the proposal is now; and very soon it will be a question of making up our minds to unregulate unthinkability.'

Churchill went on to say that he hoped Baldwin had not made his parity pledge 'to get round a Parliamentary corner on a particular occasion', and he warned that Baldwin's proposed air convention would be very dangerous if it delayed action on rearmament.

In reply to Churchill Sir John Simon declared that scepticism about 'regulated armaments' was unfounded. The alternative, he said, could only be 'un-regulated competition' in arms building, and this was an 'appalling prospect'. In the Cabinet five days later, Neville Chamberlain went so far as to revive the idea of a general disarmament scheme under the aegis of the Disarmament Conference, as an alternative to the extra military expenditure proposed by the Defence White Paper.

While the Cabinet delayed committing itself to the necessary expenditure involved in the parity pledge, Churchill suggested the establishment over the next few years of a Ministry of Defence.

Churchill's proposal, although dismissed by both Londonderry and Hankey, was taken seriously elsewhere. Desmond Morton hoped that Churchill's speech had done something to undermine the Government's efforts to convince the House of Commons that all was well. Both Morton and Churchill were convinced that if public opinion was, as Hankey had described it, 'rotten', the Government's confident assertions that everything necessary was being done and that all was well would be unlikely to enlighten it. There was indeed an element of confusion in certain sectors of society.

There was even pro-German feeling, such as that expressed by Sir Arnold Wilson, a Conservative MP who returned from a lecture tour in Germany in May 1934. In a broadcast over the BBC he spoke of 'German youth displaying in work and play an energy and an enthusiasm which, because it is wholly unselfish is wholly good'. Wilson continued: 'Whatever be the aims of their leaders, I believe that the temper of the people is peaceful. They rejoice to feel and believe that they are again a united nation – able to look the world in the face.' Wilson's broadcast ended: 'Our task is to do what we can individually to make it easier for them to shake hands with their neighbours.'

Churchill was fully aware of such opinions as those of Sir Arnold Wilson, writing to Lord Rothermere to say how 'deeply anxious' he was about the situation. His anxieties were caused, he explained, not only by Britain's defence weakness but also by the cumulative evidence of the true nature of Nazism. He was receiving much information about this and the Nazis' efforts to dupe sections of opinion in England as to their true intentions and behaviour. Desmond Morton wrote to him in March 1934: 'I dined with four young Nazi students a week ago. They had been sent over to tell England what the Hitler movement was doing for the youth of Germany. It all sounded very unpleasant, though they seemed to like it. They make no secret of their belief that within three or four years time Germany would be at war.'

The war which these young men talked about was against Russia. But Churchill was convinced that the German army would ultimately be turned against France, and that German power would be used to dominate Austria and Czechoslovakia – even Poland.

Churchill constantly sought to fight German propaganda by pointing out the unbridgeable differences between the democratic and totalitarian ways of life. 'I believe', he wrote to George Bernard Shaw at the end of May 1934, 'that freedom for the individual to succeed or fail, in spite of all the resulting irregularities, gives the best climate for culture, happiness and material well-being. I think', he added, 'the English constitution and Parliamentary system, expressing the English character, has produced results superior to those now existing in any country, and I hope I shall die before it is over-turned.'

In a magazine article published two days later, Churchill set out in full the reasons for his deep hostility to Nazism. The German people, he wrote, 'the most powerful and the most dangerous in the western world', had reverted to the conditions of the Middle Ages, 'with all the modern facilities and aggravations'. In Nazi Germany, Europe was confronted 'with the monstrosity of the totalitarian state'.

Churchill then examined the different facets of Nazism, where all were to think alike, no one was to disagree, and where any criticism of the regime was to be judged 'heresy and treason'. Then there was the Nazi racial policy. 'Jews must be baited for being born Jews,' Churchill wrote. 'Little Jewish children must be insulated by regulation and routine on particular days of the week or month, and made to feel the ignominy of the state of life to which the Creator has called them.'

Throughout Germany, Churchill wrote, 'Venerable pastors, upright magistrates, world famous scientists and philosophers, capable statesmen, independent minded manly citizens, frail poor old women of unfashionable opinions, are invaded, bullied and brutalised by gangs of armed hooligans, to resist whom is a capital offence.' To be thought disloyal, he went on, 'or even unenthusiastic to the regime which only yesterday was unknown, warrants indefinite bondage in an internment camp under persecutions which though they may crush the victim, abase also the dignity of man'.

What a fate this was, Churchill reflected, for Germany, Europe's 'strongest, most industrious and most learned son'. And he went on to ask: 'Is there anything in all this which should lead us, the English speaking world, to repudiate the famous chain of events which has made us what we are? – to cast away our Parliament, our habeas corpus, our rights and many freedoms, our tolerances, our decencies?'

On the contrary, Churchill declared, 'ought we not betimes to buttress and fortify our ancient constitution, and to make sure that it is not ignorantly or lightly deranged?' What a 'lamentable result' it would be, he reflected, if the British and American democracies, with their recent democratic franchises, 'squandered in a few short years, or even between some night and morning, all the long-stored hard-won treasures of our island civilisation'.

Churchill ended defiantly: 'It must not be.'

Despite his political and Parliamentary isolation, Churchill determined to fight the apathy which he believed had been created by a combination of active German propaganda and British Government weakness. He resolved to use his considerable powers – of speech and expression – to try to avert the catastrophe to civilization which in his view would be inevitable if Nazi dictatorship were allowed to dominate Europe.

Chapter Five

'Leaderless confusion'

On 7 July 1934 Churchill set out in his constituency the basic formula which he was to refer to later as the only hope for averting disaster: 'A large vote of credit to double our Air Force, – and a larger vote of credit as soon as possible to redouble the Air Force.' It was to be nearly a year before anything resembling such a policy was initiated. But at the time he urged it Churchill was ridiculed, so much so that the Liberal statesman, Sir Herbert Samuel, stated publicly that Churchill's exhortation about doubling and redoubling the air force was the language 'of a Malay running amok'.

Meanwhile, the Cabinet continued to discuss the report of the Defence Requirements Committee, without coming to any conclusion. On 2 July 1934, more than four months after the report had been submitted, and after pressure from Neville Chamberlain, it was decided that the Committee's estimate of the money needed to be spent to put 'our worst deficiencies' in order was, as Baldwin phrased it, 'a counsel of perfection' and too expensive.

Guided by his Treasury officials, Neville Chamberlain now stressed Britain's economic problems, which made even these minimum proposals 'impossible to carry out'. As to Baldwin's suggestion that the Government issue a special Defence Loan, this, Chamberlain told his colleagues, was in his opinion 'the broad road that led to destruction'. When the air force chiefs asked for funds to provide reserves of planes and pilots as an essential back-up to Britain's first-line air strength, Chamberlain said that there was simply not the money available – an extra £10 million pounds – and suggested 'dispensing' with reserves altogether. Yet even as Chamberlain spoke, only five of Britain's air squadrons, scarcely sixty planes, had any reserves at all.

In order to cut down even on the minimum figures proposed by the Defence Requirements Committee, Chamberlain suggested concentrating, as a first priority, on the air force. But in order to do this, the existing recommendations were referred to yet another committee. This new body, working under Chamberlain's reiterated warning of the need for economy, discussed the possibility of the air force dispensing with its reserves. These reserves were very expensive, but without them, according to the Air Staff, it would be impossible for the air force to fight for more than a week or two.

On 18 July 1934 the Cabinet accepted a substantially revised air programme, Scheme A. This scheme was based on the Air Staff's calculation of absolutely minimum needs. Under it, the Royal Air Force was to be expanded to 960 planes for home defence by 1939. But this was to be at the expense of the army and navy. Indeed, on Chamberlain's insistence, the total minimum expenditure originally advised by the Defence Requirements Committee four months before was to be cut by £26 million.

The decision to expand the Royal Air Force even to the minimum requested by the Air Staff, and at the expense of the army and navy, has often been referred to as 'air panic' on the part of Ministers. Several historians have been tempted to ascribe this so-called 'air panic' to Churchill's alleged 'exaggerations'. But 'air panic' was, in fact, the beginning of a new and deliberate Government policy of moving away from disarmament, while at the same time being unwilling, because of Chamberlain's worries about finance, to adopt the assessments and recommendations of the Government's own experts. This dichotomy persisted until 1939, with the experts making repeated recommendations for an increase in spending to meet minimum defence needs, and with the Chancellor's fears of a budget deficit causing those needs to be rejected or whittled down again and again. Thus it was that in July 1934 the disarmament against which Churchill had so inveighed gave way to an air rearmament whose scale was stated to be inadequate, not only by Churchill, but by successive Air Ministers with all the resources of intelligence and inside information at their disposal.

Churchill again argued on 13 July 1934, in the House of Commons, that German rearmament was now the main concern. But the Labour leader, Clement Attlee, disagreed with Churchill's view of Hitler's warlike intentions, arguing that his dictatorship was 'falling down'. Anthony Eden not only denied Churchill's contention that nations must be 'heavily armed' in order to create an 'effective world consultative system', but also stated, with considerable emphasis and support, that 'general disarmament must continue to be the ultimate aim'.

After Churchill's speech, his friend Terence O'Connor wrote to congratulate him, and to point out how pleasant it was to see that the failure of Churchill's Committee of Privilege challenge had not weakened 'the position you hold in the House and in public opinion'. It was clear, O'Connor added, from the response of the Commons, that there was 'no lessening of your hold on affairs'.

A major air debate was held in the House of Commons on 30 July 1934. The focus of the debate was a Labour Party motion of censure, brought by Attlee, against the Government's proposed increases in air construction. For the Liberals, the motion of censure was supported by Sir Herbert Samuel. Baldwin defended the Government's increases. Since 1929, he pointed out, Britain had, in effect, been practising 'unilateral disarmament', and no new squadrons had been built as part of the 1923 programme for the past two years. But Britain must now consider her frontier, not at the cliffs of Dover, but on the Rhine.

To cries of dissent from both the Labour and Liberal benches, Churchill argued in favour of a yet larger air budget. Germany's air production, he declared, would reach, by 1936, a thousand planes a year, and by the end of 1936 the German air force would not only be larger than Britain's, but Britain, with her lower productive capacity, would not then be able to catch up.

Churchill's figures and forecasts came direct from Desmond Morton, who was also supplying them, officially, to the Government. Morton's Intelligence estimates made clear that the 500 aircraft which Germany would have by the end of 1935 would include aerodromes, ground staff, and reserves.

Basing himself on the details Morton had given him, but not revealing his source, Churchill asserted that Germany, in violation of the Treaty of Versailles, had already created a military air force 'nearly two-thirds as strong as our present home defence force'. This claim had already been admitted to him privately by Lord Londonderry, when he had told Churchill during their quarrel in the lobby of the House of Commons that Germany probably had parity with Britain in the air.

German civil aviation, Churchill pointed out, was 'three to four times' as large as British civil aviation. But whereas British civil aviation was purely commercial in character, with machines which could not be converted to military purposes, the German machines had been 'deliberately and scientifically planned by the Government for the express purpose of being converted into war machines'. The whole scheme of conversion had been minutely worked out and organized.

Churchill then spoke of the important detail of the plans to convert German civilian planes to military purposes. 'I am informed', he said – drawing upon Morton's information, but not revealing his source – 'that the bomb racks which would be substituted for the passenger accommodation in a great number of these fast German civil machines have already been made and delivered, and it would be a matter of only a few hours to unbolt the one and fasten in the other.'

In a letter to Lord Rothermere, Churchill repeated the figures he had given in the House of Commons. He had received them, he wrote 'from a source that ought to be well-informed, and which I have found trustworthy'. Churchill added that the Government itself had not denied the acts which 'convict' their new air scheme 'of hopeless inadequacy'. He hoped, he said, to galvanize the Government to greater action by moving an amendment in Parliament that November, for he felt 'a deep and increasing sense of anxiety'. Even November 1934, he thought, might be 'too late'.

Churchill's forecasts were the opposite of exaggerated, as events were to show. But these forecasts were widely dismissed as alarmist. One Labour MP, the Clydesider, Jimmy Maxton, criticized Churchill's 'cynical, sarcastic words', which were, he declared, taken even more seriously abroad than Churchill took them himself. Terence O'Connor, however, continued to try to encourage Churchill when he wrote to say how 'gallant' he thought Churchill's speech had been. 'You fill a place in many people's lives', O'Connor added, 'and your own fortunes and happiness are the concern of more people than you can guess.'

Throughout the summer and autumn of 1934 Churchill continued with the writing of his biography of the Duke of Marlborough. In June he was much saddened by the death of his cousin, 'Sunny' Marlborough. The two men had known each other since 1879, when Churchill was five and Sunny was eight. In 1899 they had been together in South Africa, as soldier colleagues on the march to Pretoria. Later, they had often ridden and hunted together, and between Churchill's marriage in 1908 and the move to Chartwell in 1923, the Churchill family had nearly always spent Christmas at Blenheim.

Sunny Marlborough had died of cancer. 'It is only a month ago', Churchill wrote in *The Times*, 'that he was riding out to watch his horses at Newmarket or preparing a speech for the House of Lords. Suddenly that fell disease which commands and baffles the highest efforts of modern science laid hands upon him. His sons and friends looked forward with dread to months of hopeless agony. But cancer is sometimes merciful, and the end was swift and painless.'

Sunny had known that he was about to die. 'He faced this universal ordeal', wrote Churchill, 'with dignity and simplicity, making neither too much nor too little of it. He always had the most attractive and graceful manners and that easy courtesy we have been taught by the gentlefolk of a bygone age. At a tea party, to some of those who cared about him on the last night of his life, when strength had almost ebbed away, he was concerned with the entertainment of his guests, and that his conversation had not been wearisome to them.'

Together with F. E. Smith, 'Sunny' Marlborough had been Churchill's intimate friend for almost all their adult lives. Churchill's other friends understood his deep pain now that both were dead. Archie Sinclair realized how irreparable the losses were, writing that no-one could replace 'the two whom you have so recently lost'. Churchill's sadness and sense of growing old was noticed by all his friends, one of whom wrote: 'Please do not talk of yourself as a very old man. You are letting us all down by doing so.'

In August Churchill went on holiday with Randolph and 'Prof' Lindemann. Their base was the Château de L'Horizon, a villa on the French Riviera owned by an American actress, Maxine Elliot, a friend of Churchill's late mother. Maxine Elliot's home was to provide Churchill with a summer haven for four consecutive years. With him on this first visit Churchill took his devoted secretary, Violet Pearman, and each day that he was there, dictated to her a little more of his third Marlborough volume. At the same time his mind ranged over another possible subject for his historian's pen, and he wrote to Clementine that he would like to write a life of Napoleon 'before I die', although he wondered how he would find the 'time and strength' to get through all the work he had to complete.

Driving back from the south of France to Chartwell, Churchill and Lindemann made a short but important stop at Aix-les-Bains, where Stanley Baldwin was spending his own annual summer holiday. Together the three men discussed Britain's ability to put up an effective air defence.

Lindemann's criticism of the existing scientific research into air defence methods was well-known, and in a letter to *The Times* three weeks earlier he had called for a greater focus on research and experiment to meet the challenge of air attack. During their meeting with Baldwin at Aix, both Churchill and Lindemann had reiterated that a special effort was needed, even if it involved increased expenditure.

On 16 November 1934 Churchill broadcast over the BBC, in its series 'The Causes of War'. To an audience of at least a million people, Churchill stressed what he described as the 'most brutish' of all the evils of Nazism, the possibility of compelling the submission of races 'by terrorizing and torturing' the civilian population. Churchill warned that Britain would soon be faced with the same 'grim choice' she had been faced with before: 'whether we shall submit or whether we shall prepare', submit to the will of a stronger nation, or 'to defend our rights, our liberties and indeed our lives'.

Were Britain to submit, Churchill added, then her submission should be 'timely'. Were she to prepare, then her preparation 'should not be too late'. Submission would involve at the very least the end of the British Empire and acceptance of whatever future any small power could hope for 'under the Teutonic domination of Europe'. Preparation, on the other hand, would involve substantial expense, statesmanship, and national exertion.

Peace, Churchill asserted, 'must be founded on preponderance'. If the adversaries were evenly matched, five or six on each side, 'there might well be a frightful trial of strength'. But if the collective armed forces of one side were three or four times that of the other, 'then there will be no war'.

Churchill now announced that he would be speaking about German air rearmament, and the British response, in the House of Commons on 28 November 1934. Throughout the week before the debate, a flurry of activity marked both Churchill's preparations, and the Government's anticipation of them. Unknown to Churchill, the Government itself had become aware that its complacent attitude was no longer being accepted by the public. Churchill's cousin Lord Londonderry had already written to Ramsay MacDonald earlier that November to warn that German rearmament meant that it was no longer possible to discuss disarmament, and that it would be well to 'take some steps to meet the inevitable consequences'. In the third week of November Sir Samuel Hoare had written to Baldwin, to urge the Government to make a 'frank' statement in the debate about German rearmament, as this was after all the reason behind the Government's air expansion plans. It was, Hoare added, 'the German menace' that was stirring up the grave anxiety in the minds of most of their supporters.

A week before the debate Lord Londonderry sent his Cabinet colleagues a secret estimate of imminent German air superiority which tallied exactly with Churchill's earlier warnings.

For four months before the air debate of November 1934 the Government had known the detailed facts of German rearmament. Within the Foreign Office the facts themselves and the Government's response to them were causing consternation not only to Sir Robert Vansittart, but also to the officials who had to deal with Germany from day to day – Ralph Wigram, the head of the Central Department and Michael Creswell, his deputy.

Ralph Wigram was a remarkable man; within the Foreign Office he was considered to be, as one of his junior officials wrote of him, 'the genius of the place, the personification of the department, the authentic deity'. This junior official, Valentine Lawford, was so struck by his senior when he came to the Central Department that he gathered all the past history of Ralph Wigram that he could. His first impression of Wigram was 'gentleness, young looks, shyness, modesty, economy of language'. Although Wigram possessed these qualities, Lawford was to learn how much more there was in the hard taskmaster, so deeply concerned for his country's future.

Like Lawford, Churchill was soon to fall under Wigram's spell. The main impression which Wigram made on both of them was of enormous courage. Wigram had been the victim of infantile paralysis at the age of thirty-six when he had been First Secretary at the Embassy in Paris. 'For months', Lawford later recalled, 'it seemed unlikely that he would survive, even when at long last, to the bewilderment of the doctors, his strength of will and his wife's nursing achieved the impossible, and he was once more installed in Chancery, he was a semi invalid to whom further illness would be fatal, for a while little more than a ghost of himself, often in great pain, and permanently deprived of the normal use of his feet'. All the more cruel, Lawford added, to someone who always ran and was a good athlete and tennis player. 'But far from repining, he now taxed his brain and body harder than ever, and to his juniors seemed even more of a perfectionist than ever. Still leaner now and continuously limping, but robust and rapid as ever in mind, with eyes and ears missing nothing, he was again seen all over Paris when there was anything to be learnt.'

Lawford also recalled the impression which Wigram had made on him when first they had met inside the Foreign Office: 'leaning slightly backwards, with a bunch of papers in one hand and a stick in the other, he stood at his own door as I passed, and asked me how I was getting on. After a mumble, he had signalled me to go ahead and said a curt goodnight.' Lawford did as he was asked, but 'not before I had seen (as I couldn't help feeling, against his wishes) with what an infinite unfair handicap he moved: head down and to one side, forelock hanging perpendicular, white knuckles pressing heavily on a stick for support – as it were his stick and head and hand alone, with a laborious, manifold motion, dragging first his back, then his thigh, then his foot along the echoing corridor behind them.'

The main impression that Wigram made on those who worked with him was that of an outstanding colleague who possessed an extraordinary memory, a formidable intellectual grasp and a great capacity for hard work. Lawford recalled how Wigram dictated his letters and papers, hardly ever correcting himself and rarely using notes unless to quote something verbatim. Vansittart wrote of Wigram's 'astonishing ability and fertility that came to him so naturally from the complete mastery of every subject that he ever touched'.

Since Hitler's accession in 1933 both Vansittart and Wigram had been alert to the upheaval in Europe. During July 1934, together with Vansittart, Wigram had decided that the only hope of avoiding war was to find a system which would prevent the Germans 'trying their luck from 1938'.

By October 1934 the Central Department was gravely concerned about German intentions. On 26 October 1934 Wigram wrote that Germany was 'working for an army of offensive strength' and a front-line air strength of 1,000 planes by 1936. The Germans would, he wrote 'have to be mad . . . to try any games in the immediate future' but by 1938, he believed, 'we shall be faced by a very, very much stronger Germany'.

On 19 November 1934 Wigram prepared a memorandum detailing Germany's great advances in military strength. The regular army was now 300,000 and the reserves were being prepared. Indeed the German Government were now strong enough to 'come into the open at any time and confront the Powers' with their rearmament. In the air the expansion planned for 1935 was complete and a further expansion was immediately beginning under 'emergency conditions'. The Air Ministry now believed, Wigram pointed out to his colleagues, that the Germans were building aerodromes which would threaten France as well as targets in the East.

In his November memorandum Wigram urged that 'consideration should also be given to the industrial and commercial aspects of the matter, i.e. the transformation of factories, and accumulation of stocks of raw material'. Wigram did not consider that Germany would only become a danger when she was prepared 'to wage an aggressive war'. Before that, Germany would feel herself 'sufficiently armed to secure compliance with the sort of demand which she is likely to make upon individual powers'. Germany's attitude would, he believed, become 'increasingly arrogant and definitely aggressive. Instead of emitting protests and airing grievances Germany will make demands and assert rights.'

Once Germany had thrown off the shackles of the Treaty of Versailles, Wigram suggested, she would then turn 'her attention to the absorption of Austria and the penetration of central Europe'.

In this memorandum Wigram clearly forsaw the potentially dangerous courses which the British Government was likely to adopt. He feared a tacit acceptance of German rearmament and the consequent alienation of France. Believing that 'the whole principle of international cooperation' was based on Anglo-French cooperation, he advocated an immediate arrangement with France to 'arraign' Germany before the League of Nations for her violation of the Treaty of Versailles. This, Wigram argued, would 'give us an opportunity for informing public opinion clearly of the nature of German rearmament'. If Germany became defiant, Wigram believed that an Anglo-French alliance with special arrangements for the defence of Belgium and Holland would force Germany to back down, as her military and economic reorganization was not yet complete.

In this memorandum Wigram clearly forsaw both the dangers and what the British Government's response to them would be. He therefore continued to prepare material on German rearmament and endeavoured to make it known. His junior colleague, Michael Creswell, recalled forty years later that Wigram was in communication with Desmond Morton at this time. Morton passed on Wigram's material to Churchill. Both Wigram and Morton were concerned that the knowledge they acquired with such care and difficulty was failing to influence Government policy.

Creswell also recalled that it was felt in the Central Department that their political chief, Sir John Simon, the Foreign Secretary, did not really want to know 'uncomfortable things', nor did the rest of the Cabinet. At the briefing box in the House of Commons, Creswell added, 'One felt again and again that for them the important thing was to get through the debate; that what was happening in the world wasn't in the forefront of their mind.'

This was certainly the Government's attitude on the eve of the debate on 28 November 1935, a debate which was discussed three times by the Cabinet in advance. At the second of these discussions, Simon had reminded his colleagues that in winding up the debate in July he had 'evaded' Churchill's questions. But he felt that the Government could no longer deny that Germany was rearming in the air, and that if German rearmament were now to be admitted, the Government 'must also be prepared to state what further steps they contemplated'.

Three days before the debate, the Cabinet discussed how to deal with Churchill's charges. It was Sir Samuel Hoare who, in spite of his own fears and concern, suggested that it should be made clear, as the records of the Cabinet recorded, that Churchill was exaggerating and that Britain would be stronger than Germany in the air for eighteen months. It was also decided at this meeting that the Government should say there was a programme 'for a large expansion', although in fact, as the secret records phrased it, the Government must actually 'wait to see how the situation develops', before any substantial expansion scheme was put into operation.

Two days before the debate the Cabinet met again. At this meeting the Air Staff urged that the whole of Britain's air programme should be speeded up, and asked that all the aircraft already agreed to under Scheme A – 960 aeroplanes in all for home defence, including 480 extra – should be ready, not in March 1939, as planned, but by the end of 1936. Neville Chamberlain, however, told the Cabinet that information coming from Germany in no way justified such an acceleration. In addition, he argued, the March 1939 deadline was all that could be achieved without inefficiency or waste. The economic situation was such that he felt bound to warn his colleagues 'against incurring fresh commitments'.

As a result of Chamberlain's arguments, the Air Staff proposal that all 480 extra planes would be ready at the end of 1936 was overruled. Only 264 of the extra planes would be brought forward to the earlier date. For the Air Staff, this meant that Britain would by then have fallen behind the projected German air strength.

The debate of 28 November 1934 marked Churchill's most sustained attempt to accelerate British aircraft production, and to set out the nature of Germany's growing air strength. Armed with the material from Desmond Morton, some of which had undoubtedly come through Ralph Wigram, Churchill made a devastating attack on Government policy. 'To urge preparation of defence is not to assert the imminence of war. On the contrary, if war was imminent, preparations for defence would be too late.' But time was running out and, he said, 'if we do not begin forthwith to put ourselves in a position of security it will soon be beyond our power to do so'.

'What', Churchill asked, 'is the great new fact which has broken in upon us during the last eighteen months? Germany is rearming. That is the great new fact which rivets the attention of every country in Europe.' Germany, he warned, 'already has a powerful, well-equipped army'.

German factory production, Churchill pointed out, was geared increasingly to war materials. 'Much of it is undoubtedly in violation of the treaties of 1919. Germany is rearming on land, she is rearming at sea. But what concerns us most of all is the rearmament of Germany in the air.' And he added: 'It is no exaggeration to suppose that a week or ten days intensive bombing upon London would leave thirty or forty thousand people dead or maimed, a civilian population in grave panic and millions driven out into open country. The flying peril is not a peril from which one can fly. It is necessary to face it where we stand. We cannot possibly retreat.'

Churchill then made three assertions, which he challenged Baldwin to 'confirm, correct or contradict', and which, he explained to the House, he had already sent to Baldwin a week earlier. The three assertions were: that Germany 'already, at this moment' possessed a military air force, illegal, but 'rapidly approaching equality with our own'; that by this time next year, if the British and German air programmes both proceeded according to plan, the German air force would be in fact 'at least as strong as our own, and it may be even stronger'; and, thirdly, that on the existing programmes, by the end of 1936 the German air force would be 50 per cent stronger than the British, and by 1937 'nearly double'. To meet this danger, Churchill urged an acceleration of British air production to create a striking force capable of the 'only direct measure of defence on a great scale', the power to inflict on the enemy as much damage as the enemy himself could inflict, and to do so 'simultaneously' with any enemy attack. Churchill also warned the Government not to neglect scientific research into anti-aircraft defence. And he suggested offering 'good wages' to 20,000 or 30,000 unemployed, now working on unessential relief projects, to construct the earthworks needed for the 'proper protection' of British aerodromes.

It was what Churchill regarded as the slow pace and insufficient scale of British aircraft production that lay at the centre of his appeal.

Baldwin's reply disappointed Churchill, and those who had provided Churchill with his material. While stating: 'I think it is correct to say that the Germans are engaged in creating an air force', Baldwin went on to say that Germany's 'real strength' in the air 'is not 50 per cent of our strength', and that if both air programmes were to continue on their existing course, 'so far from the German military air force being at least as strong as, and probably stronger than, our own, we estimate that we shall still have a margin in Europe alone of nearly 50 per cent'.

Speaking of Churchill's charges, Baldwin told the House that he believed 'that his figures are considerably exaggerated'. As for the spectre of German air superiority, Baldwin pledged that the British Government, 'are determined on no condition to accept any position of inferiority with regard to what air force may be raised in Germany in the future'.

This renewed 'parity' pledge made a strong impression, blunting the edge of Churchill's criticisms. But writing about the debate in a private letter to the Viceroy of India, Sir Samuel Hoare admitted that had the Cabinet decided to answer the technical service questions which Churchill had raised, then Churchill 'would have scored heavily'.

The debate of 28 November 1934 ensured that German air rearmament was now an accepted fact. But Churchill's attempt to set out clearly the imminent German advantage had been frustrated by Baldwin's confident answer, and by the parity pledge. Nor was the pledge itself accompanied by any clear Government policy as to what steps would be taken to ensure that the promised parity would be maintained.

From Berlin, the British Ambassador, Sir Eric Phipps, sent the Foreign Office a full report of how the debate of 28 November 1934 had been covered in the German newspapers. 'The Press generally', Phipps noted, 'is not disposed on a second perusal to take the debate tragically.' While to the Press in Berlin, Churchill himself was 'dismissed as the incorrigible Germanophobe of pre-war days'.

It was also noted in the German press that Baldwin 'did not upbraid Germany with violating the Treaty. Indeed he did nothing calculated to wound or to hinder further discussions.' In Paris, as the Foreign Office learned from the British Embassy, there was disappointment that Baldwin had let the Germans off 'too leniently' by underestimating German rearmament and also for not condemning it.

Already the fears that Wigram had expressed on the eve of the debate were being fulfilled. On 4 December 1934 he wrote in a departmental note that the Germans were under the impression that the debate had 'legalised German rearmament', and 'that Germany can now proceed with her plans without the danger of intervention'. Wigram urged that a question should be asked in the House so that the Government could publicly repudiate the idea that Germany was free to break her Treaty obligations 'by unilateral action'. His suggestion was rejected because the Government were afraid that such a statement in

Parliament would 'encourage the French to adopt an uncompromising attitude'.

The result of the debate of 28 November 1934 showed, therefore, that the Government would not adopt the measures advocated either by Churchill or by the Foreign Office: greater rearmament and a close working partnership with France designed to prevent Germany from taking the initiative. Ralph Wigram clearly saw the extent to which the Government was opposed to a policy of rapid rearmament and closer relations with France. Henceforth, he was to fight as hard as he could from his restricted position, and also to help Churchill to fight, to change Government policy.

Two days after the air debate of 28 November 1934, Churchill celebrated his sixtieth birthday. To mark the event, Randolph arranged a dinner-dance at the Ritz. 'There never was a party', wrote one of his aunts, 'that went with such a swing from first to last.' The whole Churchill family, she added, was resplendent and beautiful, 'and dearest and noblest of all, your beloved Papa, who certainly didn't look sixty'.

Shortly after the birthday party, Clementine Churchill left on a cruise to the Dutch East Indies, aboard a splendid yacht belonging to Lord Moyne, who acted as her host. Churchill and his children wished her well on her long adventure, as they themselves prepared to spend Christmas at Blenheim, with the new Duke of Marlborough and his wife. While at Blenheim Churchill divided his time between cards and working on yet another volume of his Marlborough biography. Then he returned to Chartwell, writing to his wife on the last day of the year: 'My darling one, I felt so sad when I got home the other day after seeing the last wave of your dear white hand out of the carriage window. It will be four months before we meet again, and to see you vanishing away like that was a melancholy thing.' 'I miss you very much', Churchill added, 'and feel very unprotected.'

That night, at Chartwell, Churchill sat down to his New Year's dinner alone. As he prepared to begin his solitary meal, he noticed that a second place had been laid. It was for his daughter Diana, who at that very moment, as he wrote to Clementine, walked in 'looking absolutely lovely'. She had come down on her own, he wrote, 'to keep me company'.

The pleasure Churchill derived from his daughter's company was in stark contrast to his discomfort two weeks later, when Randolph decided to stand for Parliament, and to do so as an independent Conservative, challenging the official candidate, and the official India policy. The occasion was a by-election at Wavertree. 'This is', Churchill wrote to his wife, 'a most rash and unconsidered plunge', which could only split the Conservative vote, and lead to a Labour win. 'All together I am vexed and worried about it,' Churchill admitted. 'Randolph has no experience of electioneering', he added, 'and does not seem to want advice, and the whole thing is amateurish in the last degree.' Yet, with a father's natural concern, Churchill finally agreed to give his son a helping

123

hand, and sent him much sympathetic advice in the last days of the campaign. 'I should be less than human', he told the Press Association, 'if, in all the circumstances of these critical times, I did not wish him success.'

Churchill was caught up in the lively and controversial atmosphere generated by Randolph's campaign, telling Clementine that because 'popular enthusiasm' was undermining the workings of the 'machine' the meetings he was going to attend on Randolph's behalf would be crowded out. When, on 5 February 1935, Churchill spoke at Randolph's eve-of-poll meeting, the expressed his deep anxiety about current events. His speech ended with a reassertion that Britain's destiny was still in 'our own hands' but that Britain must now proclaim her 'will to survive as a great nation'.

In spite of Wavertree, Churchill wrote to his wife at the height of the campaign, 'Ministers are extremely civil,' and he added: 'They see the terrible difficulties into which they are plunging.'

The voting at Wavertree took place on 6 February 1935, and, as Churchill had foreseen, his son did split the Conservative vote, so that the Labour candidate was elected. 'Randolph beaten', Churchill telegraphed to Clementine 'after magnificent battle. No harm done.' Two days later, however, *The Times* denounced both father and son for seeking to destroy the system of National Government out of self interest. They would achieve only one success, *The Times* added, and that was 'the success of suicide'.

Such hostile comments did not deter Randolph. One 23 February 1935 he decided to put up his own candidate at yet another by-election, at Norwood, in south London, against his father's wishes. Churchill wrote to Clementine that it was impossible to reason with his son, that they had exchanged 'sharp words' when Randolph had come to dinner. Indeed, Randolph had left the table in violent anger. Churchill was becoming more and more worried about the unfavourable repercussions that Randolph's behaviour would have upon his interests, but he hoped that it would do Randolph some good personally as he believed he was in for 'a thoroughly bad flop'. Randolph had chosen a poor candidate, Richard Findlay, a member of the British Union of Fascists, and was getting no support either from members of Parliament or from the Press. Churchill added that he was viewing the situation dispassionately as he believed that when one could not control events there was 'no use worrying'.

The hostility generated by Randolph's two ventures into politics, first at Wavertree and then at Norwood, did not deter Churchill from pressing ahead with two parallel campaigns, first, to try to force the Government to adhere to Baldwin's pledge that Britain's air force would never fall behind that of Germany, and second, to press for greater Government scientific research into the techniques of air defence. Indeed, scarcely two weeks after the Wavertree result, Ramsay MacDonald saw Churchill, Lindemann and Austen Chamberlain and promised them the Government would soon set up a special sub-committee of the Committee of Imperial Defence, devoted entirely to air defence research.

Churchill's concerns, and those of the Foreign Office, were now almost identical. Within the Central Department of the Foreign Office, Ralph Wigram and Michael Creswell, having studied the Air Ministry's most recent intelligence reports, were staggered to discover that in respect of aircraft production, Germany's superiority over both Britain and France was already substantial. On 28 February 1935 Creswell prepared a detailed memorandum for Wigram, stressing that the Air Ministry's most recent figures made it clear 'that the real criterion of strength in the air' lay not so much in any particular figures of existing air strength, 'as in the present manufacturing capacity of a country', and that by this method of analysis the German superiority over both France and Britain was 'immeasurably great'. The German factories, Creswell noted, were 'already practically organized on an emergency war-time footing'.

As a result of this organization, Creswell pointed out, it seemed probable that before October 1936 the German air force would have 'a larger number of machines' in each of the war categories 'than either our Home Defence air force or the French metropolitan forces', as well as possessing the additional advantage of 'entirely new material throughout'.

Having read Creswell's memorandum, and studied these charts, Ralph Wigram noted on 8 March 1935 that the facts that Creswell had assembled were 'most alarming' as they showed a 'vast German superiority over our own forces by October 1936'. Four days later, on the day of the Defence White Paper debate, the Central Department discussed Creswell's memorandum in detail. During this discussion Wigram stressed that the facts that Creswell had so carefully assembled showed beyond any doubt that the German air force would exceed France's by 1936 and would also exceed 'very greatly' Britain's own air strength. Germany, Wigram added 'is out for superiority'.

On 4 March 1935 the Government published a special Defence White Paper, admitting 'serious deficiencies' in all the Defence Services. An extra £10 million was to be spent on defence in the coming year. The Germans, angered by this announcement, cancelled Sir John Simon's planned visit to see Hitler. 'This gesture of spurning the British Foreign Secretary from the gates of Berlin', Churchill wrote to his wife, 'is a significant measure of the convictions which Hitler has of the strength of the German Air Force and Army.'

All the 'frightened nations', Churchill told his wife, were at last beginning 'to huddle together', and he was glad that this was so. 'There is safety in numbers', he wrote, and added: 'There is only safety in numbers.' If war broke out again, Churchill reflected, it would be 'the end of the world. How I hope and pray we may be spared such senseless horrors.'

Within the Foreign Office, Vansittart, his deputy Sir Orme Sargent, and Wigram saw Hitler's 'rage' in refusing to see Sir John Simon as the first fruits of a weak Government policy.

But in the House of Commons, on 11 March 1935, when the Labour Party brought a vote of censure against the Government, Clement Attlee attacked the proposed increases in defence spending as being both 'nationalist and imperialist'. War could not be averted, he said, 'by national defence', but only by a new world policy based on 'the abolition of national armaments'.

The Labour vote of censure was defeated. Five days later Hitler announced the introduction of compulsory military service throughout Germany. Under the Treaty of Versailles, Germany's army had been restricted to 300,000 men. Now, he declared, he already had 500,000 under arms.

It was with these facts newly before it that the House of Commons began its Air debate of 19 March 1935. During the debate Churchill made many of the points which had already been made so emphatically, in secret, by both Creswell and Wigram. Churchill boldly challenged Baldwin to repeat his statement of the previous November that Britain would have a margin of 50 per cent by November 1935.

During the course of his speech, Churchill warned that 127 of the aircraft included in Baldwin's figures were auxiliary aircraft and not comparable to 'whole-time regular units of the Royal Air Force'. And he went on to question the actual amount being spent on increasing the air force – a million pounds on new construction which could only produce a further 150 military aircraft. Churchill pointed out that it was impossible to forecast how quickly the Germans would push ahead in the same period. But he believed that if the figures of German defence spending were known they would 'stagger us'. Certain things could be discerned, however, such as the vast increase in the population at Dessau, one of the main factories of the Junker aeroplane works. The work being done at Dessau, Churchill said, 'consists in a rapid assembly line, like a jig-saw puzzle or Meccano game, with the result that aeroplanes are turned out with a speed incomparably greater than in our factories, where a great deal of the earlier stages of the work is done on the spot'.

Churchill calculated, as the *Daily Telegraph* had recently suggested, that the Germans could now produce at least 100 military aircraft every month. Furthermore, Churchill told the House, 'they have, of course, made preparations for converting the whole industry of Germany to war purposes by a single order, of a detail and refinement which is almost inconceivable'.

Had the necessary British preparations been made two years before, Churchill asserted, at a time when the danger was already 'clear and apparent', Britain might have retained a clear lead. But now that lead was in doubt, and Britain had entered 'a period of peril'. From being 'the least vulnerable of all nations', Churchill warned, 'we have, through developments in the air, become the most vulnerable. And yet, even now, we are not taking the measures which would be in true proportion to our needs.'

In answer to Churchill's challenge, the Under Secretary of State for Air, Sir Philip Sassoon, admitted that the situation had deteriorated since the previous November. But he repeated the Government's assertion that by the end of 1935 there would still be a British margin of superiority over the Germans, and called Churchill's actual figures 'conjectural'.

One Labour MP, William Cove, the Chairman of the Welsh Labour

Parliamentary group, called Churchill's speech 'scaremongering'.

It was the Government's continued inadequate response that made Wigram so angry and frustrated that he now arranged to go to see Churchill personally, on 24 March 1935. But at the last moment he was unable to go. Wigram's wife, Ava, went instead. As soon as she returned to London, she wrote to Churchill to urge him to keep the information to himself.

On the day after Ava Wigram's visit to Chartwell, Hitler announced that his air force was now as large as that of Britain's, as the Foreign Office had long since known. Because the British Government had stated only six days earlier, in the Commons debate, that Britain's front-line air strength was 690 aircraft, this meant that Hitler, likewise, must have at least 690. But as Churchill had warned in the debate of 19 March 1935, the actual British front-line strength was not really 690; for this figure included Fleet Air Arm and Auxiliary craft which the Air Ministry did not consider as front-line aircraft. This brought the actual British figure down to 453.

Hitler's statement, Churchill wrote to his wife on 5 April 1935, was a 'political sensation' and 'completely stultifies everything that Baldwin has said'. It also, he continued, 'incidentally vindicates all the assertions I have made'. In fact, Churchill ventured, it was most likely that Hitler was 'really much stronger than we are'.

This was indeed so, and on 5 April 1935 Sir Christopher Bullock of the Air Ministry informed the Foreign Office of the precise numerical situation, a maximum of 453 front-line British aircraft, without reserves, as against a minimum of 690 German first-line, together with the German immediate reserves of a further 160 aircraft. In addition, Bullock's letter laid stress, as Churchill had in the debate of 19 March 1935, on the high organization of the German air industry, which could change rapidly from peace to war production, and thus make good her initial battle losses 'in a much shorter space of time than can countries whose industry is less well organized'. This meant, according to Bullock and the Air Ministry's calculations, 'that Germany, after the first clash and consequent losses, would be in a stronger position than her opponents during the period in which they were organizing their aircraft industry to meet war wastage'.

When Sir Robert Vansittart read the correspondence he declared that Germany's now acknowledged superiority in the number of her service aircraft should be made known 'to every member of His Majesty's Government'.

Vansittart's note was dated 6 April 1935. On the following day Ralph Wigram himself went down to Chartwell. Three weeks earlier he had written in an internal Foreign Office note that the main problem, once the strength of Germany was finally recognized, was how to make the British public realize the need for defence. He believed that the British people would endure any inconvenience if they were aware of the need to defend themselves. The problem was, as Wigram wrote, how to 'grapple with 15 years of "unreality" brought on by the apparent weakness of Germany'.

After so many months of trying to influence the Government by means of his trenchant memoranda, Wigram had now thrown aside any inhibitions, and had already decided that he must go direct to Churchill. Henceforth, Wigram and his wife were often to visit Churchill at Chartwell, or to entertain Churchill at their house in London, only a few minutes walk from the House of Commons. 'He was a charming and fearless man', Churchill later wrote, 'and his convictions, based upon profound knowledge and study, dominated his being.'

Wigram's visits to Chartwell brought Churchill into contact with the most recent diplomatic dispatches from Germany, and with specific material: the full texts of Hitler's speeches, reports of German military and industrial developments, and secret information about Germany's foreign policy intentions. Often, as soon as some secret document reached him, Churchill would give it to Lindemann, who would drive at once to Oxford – a journey of over three hours – photograph it and develop a copy in his own dark room, helped by his faithful valet, Mr Harvey, and then drive back immediately to Chartwell, so that Churchill could have the copy, and so that the original could be returned to its place in the Foreign Office files.

There were times when Churchill went to the Foreign Office. One day Valentine Lawford had been asked by Wigram to bring some documents to Vansittart's room. Outside the room, as he later recalled, he saw 'an odd-looking hat and stick' and smelt 'a whiff of cigar smoke under the door'.

Vansittart encouraged these contacts. Although, as he later wrote, Churchill was always 'miserable' without office, 'he suited me much better outside, for my information on German trends would at least be voiced. He certainly made good use of it.' Vansittart also recalled in his memoirs how, at this time, 'little Ralph Wigram, made desperate by our danger, asked leave to leak some of my figures to select publicists'. Vansittart, so he recalled, 'pondered and agreed'.

On 9 April 1935 the British Ambassador in Berlin confirmed that the German first-line air strength was between 800 and 850 aeroplanes. This led Michael Creswell to note within the Foreign Office that the Germans had now, in fact, a 55 per cent superiority over Britain's home defences, rather than the Government's so recently announced British 'margin' of superiority over Germany. Wigram commented on this situation: 'these are grave and terrible facts for those who are charged with the defence of this country', and he added that not only British Foreign policy and diplomacy depended upon this question, but 'our very existence'. Urged to do so by his civil servants, Sir John Simon now brought the matter before the Committee of Imperial Defence, warning MacDonald on 10 April 1935 both of the German air force's growth and the development of its manufacturing capacity. The danger was such, Simon added, that he doubted Britain's ability to regain 'a level of parity'.

After his first talk with Ralph Wigram at Chartwell, Churchill had written to Clementine pointing out an ominous fact: 'There is no doubt', he explained to her, 'that the Germans are already substantially stronger than us in the air and that they are manufacturing at such a rate that we cannot catch them up.'

Churchill also informed his wife that Lord Londonderry had telephoned him to try to dissuade him from speaking in the next Air debate, offering to give him the 'true' figures. But Churchill had replied that, considering how completely the Government had misled the country, 'no confidence' could deter him from what he saw as his public duty. Londonderry then told Churchill that Mac-Donald himself had offered to show Churchill 'all the real figures', to which Churchill replied tersely that he thought his own were better. 'It is a shocking thing', Churchill commented to his wife, 'when a Government openly commits itself to statements on a matter affecting the public safety which are bound to be flagrantly disproved by events.'

In his letter to Clementine, Churchill added: 'I have been sometimes a little depressed about politics, and would have liked to be comforted by you.' But he had not grudged her the long cruise, which he realized had been a 'great experience and adventure' for her. He also told his wife that he had been upset when he had visited Randolph, who had been extremely ill with a severe but undiagnosed infection, to find that his son had grown a beard which made him look to Churchill 'perfectly revolting'. Churchill explained that although Randolph himself was saying that he looked 'like Christ', to Churchill, Randolph looked in fact 'very like my poor father in the last phase of his illness'. Lord Randolph's dying months, forty years earlier, had been a period of deep unhappiness for the young Churchill, and now his son's striking similarity was a painful reminder of those distant, sad days. Nevertheless Churchill was amused to see Randolph in his sick bed 'visited by youth and beauty', and was relieved that he was recovering.

Returning to the political scene and commenting on the personalities at home, Churchill wrote that Baldwin, with all the cards in his hand, had become a 'power miser', with the utmost skill and industry, gathering together 'all the power countries, without the slightest wish to use them, or the slightest knowledge how!' Meanwhile, Lord Rothermere was telephoning Churchill every day. 'His anxiety is pitiful', Churchill wrote. 'He thinks the Germans are all powerful and that the French are corrupt and useless, and the English hopeless and doomed. He proposes to meet this situation by grovelling to Germany. "Dear Germany, do destroy us last!" I endeavour to inculcate a more robust attitude.'

Churchill still hoped that although Germany was now 'the greatest armed power in Europe', the threatened States would still combine in self-defence, and would do so in such a way that Germany would not even attempt to make war. But Wigram and Creswell were afraid, as they wrote in a letter which Sir Robert Vansittart then sent to the Foreign Secretary, that Britain's present air inferiority would 'increase the difficulty of conducting an independent and effective foreign policy'.

Wigram's one hope was that Hitler's actions would at last galvanize the Government to act. On 16 April 1935 he wrote to Churchill to say that he could not get away to continue their discussions at Chartwell as there had been developments and that it looked at last as if the Government were going to deal with the situation seriously. Wigram was referring to Lord Londonderry's approach to the Cabinet, seeking authority for further air force expansion. But when the Foreign Office did finally see the new proposal they were even more appalled, for it only aimed at air parity by 1940.

Sir Robert Vansittart was angered by the Air Ministry's scheme, which accepted British inferiority for five years. He himself had always stated that 1938 was the year of maximum danger. 'If a clear foreign policy is adequately backed', Vansittart wrote, 'there need be no fear of the future.' But, he added 'There is much to fear if this is not the case; and it cannot be the case on these dates and figures.'

Wigram now asked to see Churchill again, and on 28 April 1935 he returned to Chartwell. During this visit, Churchill and Wigram went through a comprehensive memorandum which Churchill had prepared, in part using Wigram's own materials. Churchill now repeated his Parliamentary accusation of the previous month that the Government had misled the public. In his memorandum he warned Baldwin that he would repeat the charge in the forthcoming Air debate. Churchill also referred to an article in the *Daily Telegraph* which, he commented, 'evidently comes from some official source', and which confirmed his own figures.

Churchill sent his memorandum to Baldwin, and to several other Cabinet Ministers. 'I fear', he wrote to Baldwin in a covering letter, 'they have got ahead of us not only in actual power, but even more in the momentum their air industry has now acquired.'

This industry was already organized in such a way, Churchill warned, that it would produce 'under war conditions' a steady flow of aeroplanes and engines. Britain had, as yet, no such capacity.

The conflict between Churchill and the Government was paralleled by a conflict within the Government itself. The Government's Ministerial Committee set up to consider the new situation discussed the Londonderry scheme which had so angered Vansittart. At the meeting Sir John Simon read out Vansittart's opinion that Germany would be able to dictate her wishes to Europe, from early in 1938. Lord Londonderry retorted, however, that this 'was the non-professional point of view', and that Vansittart had ignored 'considerations' which the 'professional' had to take into account.

During the meeting Simon, the Foreign Secretary, and Vansittart's chief, pointed out, as Churchill had in his memorandum, that Baldwin's 'parity' pledge had not meant that one day Britain would be on a level with any potential enemy, but that *'at no time* should we have an inferior force'. The Air Ministry's proposals, therefore, Simon argued, did not fulfil Baldwin's pledge. Indeed, he said, a 'rather curious feature' of the new air scheme seemed to be that 'the longer the expansion went on, the further ahead would Germany get'.

During this discussion it was generally agreed that what Simon said was true. Then Neville Chamberlain suggested that parity should be dealt with, not in terms of the number of aeroplanes, but 'in terms of air power'. This the Cabinet agreed to. It was also agreed that in the next Air debate it would be announced that the Government intended to maintain the pledge. Thus on 2 May 1935, although Ramsay MacDonald told the House of Commons that the German air force had been expanded 'to a point considerably in excess of the estimates' which had been given to the House the previous year, he went on to state that Baldwin's parity declaration still stood.

Churchill was not impressed by MacDonald's assurance, and challenged Baldwin to repeat his previous statement that Britain had a 50 per cent superiority in the air. On the contrary, Churchill argued, by the end of 1935, the German air force would be 'between three and four times' as strong as that of Britain.

During the debate, Churchill told his fellow MPs: 'when the situation was manageable, it was neglected, and now that it is thoroughly out of hand we apply, too late, the remedies which then might have effected a cure'. There was, he added, nothing new in that story: it was as old as the Sibylline books of classical legend. It fell into what Churchill now called 'that long dismal catalogue of the fruitlessness of experience, and the confirmed unteachability of mankind'.

Angered that his warnings, as well as his suggestions in 1933 and 1934, had been dismissed as alarmist and ignored until too late, Churchill told the House of Commons: 'Want of foresight, unwillingness to act when action would be simple and effective, lack of clear thinking, confusion of counsel until the emergency comes, until self-preservation strikes its jarring gong, these are the features which constitute the endless repetition of history.'

Churchill ended his speech, however, with words which foreshadowed his oratory of the Second World War, telling the House of Commons: 'Never must we despair, never must we give in, but we must face facts and draw true conclusions from them.'

Among the many letters of congratulations which Churchill received was one from Ralph Wigram. 'I read your speech of yesterday with the greatest pleasure and interest,' he wrote, 'and I am sure that it will have a great effect in Parliament and in the country, and I hope that it will make the Government push on all the faster with the Air Programme.' Speeches such as Churchill's, Wigram added, were 'far more likely to lead to the preservation of peace than all the "imploring" of Germany with which I regret to see even the debate of yesterday was ended'.

Wigram encouraged Churchill to speak again as soon as possible, and to do so 'in the same style' during the next defence debate. Meanwhile, in a series of internal Foreign Office memoranda, Wigram stressed his fear that current talk of a five-power Air Pact might weaken the Government's resolve to expand the air force and achieve parity. Wigram wrote on 10 May 1935 that he felt that the French proposal for 'a Franco–British military agreement' should be given 'serious consideration'. He thought that the need for a plan for 'common air defence' was even more necessary than that of naval defence had been before the First World War.

On 15 May 1935 the *Daily Telegraph*'s Air correspondent gave a detailed report of the Government's Air expansion plans, involving a total of 1,460 planes by April 1937. In his article the correspondent pointed out that: 'It is known that Germany will have an equal strength in the near future, if she does not possess it already.' On the very day that this article appeared, the Cabinet discussed what measures should be taken to counteract such a 'serious leakage of information.'

Despite such Cabinet disapproval of leaks, Wigram continued to give Churchill whatever documents and information he felt would strengthen Churchill's public speeches. One such document was a seven-page Foreign Office memorandum of 30 May 1935, which contained a detailed critique of Hitler's speech earlier that month, in which Hitler had made a sustained attack on the 'dictated' Treaty of Versailles. 'Yet what peace in history', Wigram asked, 'was not dictated to or imposed upon the vanquished by the victor, at least where the victor was strong enough to do so?' The real German objection, Wigram commented, was not that the Treaty of Versailles was a dictated peace, 'but that it was dictated to her and that she herself had not dictated it'.

One of the main themes of Hitler's speech had been that Germany had scrupulously fulfilled the disarmament clauses of the Treaty of Versailles. But Wigram pointed out in his commentary that in 1929 alone Germany had spent 'on artillery, small arms ammunition and anti-gas material £2 million more than the British army', while the British Ambassador in Berlin in 1929, Sir Horace Rumbold, had described in his annual report how 'the necessary jigs and patterns and gauges for the manufacture of modern weapons are being prepared and stocked in various factories all over Germany'.

Wigram also set out evidence to show that Germany had never intended to abide by the territorial changes of the Treaty of Versailles: that the return of Danzig, the Polish Corridor and eastern Upper Silesia, as well as future joining of Austria to Germany, had been permanent features even of Weimar policy, which Hitler had taken over as his own.

The efforts of the Central Department to make the truth about German preparations known to the public through Churchill were not unsuccessful: indeed, on the day after Churchill's Parliamentary challenge of 2 May 1935, Sir Maurice Hankey had warned Ramsay MacDonald that Parliament itself now believed there was virtually 'a state of emergency'. But this was not enough to make the Government adopt adequate measures with regard to defence. On 21 May 1935, the day before Baldwin was to answer Churchill's charges in the House of Commons, the Cabinet accepted a new Air expansion scheme, which became known as Scheme C, in which German potential superiority was accepted as a fact of future policy.

Churchill probably knew from Wigram of this ominous development. At the same time he wrote to Colonel Pakenham-Walsh, who had accompanied him to the Blenheim battlefields three years before, that he was 'astounded' at the indifference with which the Press and public seem to view the fact that 'the Government have been utterly wrong about the German air strength'. Even worse was the fact that Britain was 'substantially outnumbered and must continue to fall further and further behind for at least two years'. In fact, Churchill added, 'we can never catch up unless they wish it'.

On 22 May 1935 Churchill's claims and alarms of the past two years were fully vindicated, for on that day Baldwin finally made his admission to the House of Commons: 'First of all, with regard to the figure I gave in November of German aeroplanes, nothing has come to my knowledge that makes me think that figure was wrong. Where I was wrong was in my estimate of the future. There I was completely wrong. We were completely misled on that subject.'

Baldwin continued that there was no need for 'panic', and he sought to reassure the House by saying: 'I would not remain for one moment in any Government which took less determined steps than we are taking today.' As for criticisms that the Air Ministry was pursuing 'an inadequate programme', Baldwin added, such a situation was the responsibility 'of the Government as a whole, and we are all responsible and we are all to blame'.

After Baldwin's admission that he had been 'completely wrong' about German rearmament, Churchill's role was no longer just to reveal the extent of German preparedness, but to try to ensure continued vigilance in the pace and scale of rearmament and research. With no more than the resources of a private person, but with a growing circle of officials, friends and admirers willing to help him, he watched what Germany was doing, and pressed for an adequate response. In foreign affairs, encouraged by Vansittart and Wigram, he stressed the need for collective security and support for the League of Nations, and also for a careful scrutiny of what was happening inside Germany, so that Britain would not be caught unawares. Although he regarded 1933 and 1934 as 'locust' years that could never be retrieved, and lamented the fact, in a letter to a friend, 'that they did not take my advice in time', he still believed that the democratic powers, once alerted to the dangers, could and must still try to maintain their strength and independence.

The predominant question throughout 1935 remained that of Hitler's intentions. When Hitler offered, during May, to outlaw all air bombing, if the other European powers would agree, both Eden and Attlee welcomed his appeal, while Sir Herbert Samuel for the Liberals declared that Hitler's plan could lead to what he called 'an appeasement in western Europe'.

Churchill did not believe in the sincerity of Hitler's plan. Desmond Morton had already sent him, a few days earlier, notes about German aircraft manufacture. According to Morton's Intelligence, there were more than twenty-four factories in Germany making airframe components, and 'considerably more' than eight further factories making aeroplane engine components. Organizing all this, Morton explained, was a 'great Trinity' of Junker, Heinkel and Dornier, 'on whose behalf the majority of other factories are working'.

Shortly after Hitler's offer of an air treaty, Ralph Wigram sent Churchill a twelve-page memorandum on Hitler's territorial claims. The theme of this memorandum was that Nazi Germany had no intention to abide by her existing eastern frontiers with either Poland or Czechoslovakia, or to respect the independence of Austria.

Speaking in the House of Commons on 31 May 1935, Churchill drew on the material which Wigram had sent him, without of course revealing his source, to warn of a German threat to Czechoslovakia, where a Nazi Party had been created among the Sudeten German minority. All over Europe, he noted, Nazi ideologies were beginning to win admirers and adherents, and the growing German power was making an impression on many individuals inside Austria, Hungary, Bulgaria and even Yugoslavia. Inside Germany itself, he pointed out, a 'tremendous propaganda' was at work, enforced by brutal repressive measures.

Eden, Attlee and Samuel had spoken hopefully of the future. Churchill did not deny that the lines of hope and 'paths of peace' should be followed. But, he warned: 'do not close your eyes to the fact that we are entering a corridor of deepening and darkening danger'. Furthermore, Churchill ended, Britain would pass through that corridor 'for many months and possibly for years to come'.

On 7 June 1935 Stanley Baldwin succeeded Ramsay MacDonald as Prime Minister. It was Baldwin's third premiership. Neville Chamberlain remained Chancellor of the Exchequer, Sir Samuel Hoare succeeded Simon as Foreign Secretary, and Anthony Eden entered the Cabinet as Minister without Portfolio, responsible for League of Nations affairs.

Asked the same day to write a magazine article about the personalities of the new Government, Churchill declined, telling the editor who had asked him: 'they are pretty small people, though called upon to deal with momentous issues and play large parts'.

Churchill also spoke in the House of Commons on the first day of Baldwin's premiership, telling an attentive chamber about his unease at the slow pace of air defence research. The special Air Defence Research Committee, recently set up by the Government, had met only twice in the three months since its inception: 'a slow-motion picture', as Churchill called it. If funds had been provided and efforts had been made, he declared, 'twenty important experiments would be under way by now', any one of which might decisively affect Britain's means and ability to defend herself.

His sole aim in raising this question in public, Churchill said, was to spur on the work of the Committee.

The Government was now worried about the part Churchill would play, and the ideas he would put forward in the forthcoming election. The new Lord

Chancellor, Lord Hailsham, who had formerly been Secretary of State for War, wrote to Churchill of his wish 'to have a talk about the world in general, and ourselves in particular'. Soon, Hailsham explained, there would be a General Election, and it was 'essential for the Empire and our own national existence that we Conservatives should be thinking and working together'.

Another of Churchill's friends who had been promoted was Sir Philip Cunliffe-Lister – soon to become Earl of Swinton – the new Secretary of State for Air. He invited Churchill to the annual Air Review at the end of June 1935, and agreed to Churchill's suggestion to send on to the Air Ministry the letters which now reached Chartwell in increasing numbers from members of the public, enclosing ideas and inventions about air defence.

As the election approached, Churchill was asked by Baldwin to join the Committee of Imperial Defence's Air Research sub-committee, of whose sloth he had recently been so critical. 'If you think I can be any use upon it', Churchill replied, 'I shall be very glad to serve', and to add to it 'a few ideas which, if of any value, would be quite unfit for publication'.

Churchill insisted, however, that his membership of this technical body should in no way inhibit his criticisms of the Government's air policies, and Baldwin agreed. 'Of course', he wrote in reply, 'you are as free as air (the correct expression in this case!)' to debate 'the general issues' of air policy. The invitation, Baldwin explained, 'was not intended as a muzzle, but as a gesture of friendliness to an old colleague'. In his reply, Churchill warned the new Prime Minister of his responsibilities for the public safety. 'You have gathered to yourself', Churchill wrote, 'a fund of personal goodwill and confidence', which should be used to preserve Britain's safety during the forthcoming period 'of strain and toil'.

Henceforth as a member of the Air Defence Research sub-committee, Churchill was to urge that only continuous large scale experiments, fully financed and energetically pursued, would yield results in time. But three years later, when the whole pace of experimentation seemed to him in retrospect to have been far too slow, Churchill was to feel that his membership of the committee had served only to muzzle him over this essential area of defence preparedness.

In 1938 he was to write, to the then Secretary of State for Air, Sir Kingsley Wood: 'I regret Professor Lindemann and I accepted Baldwin's invitation to take part in these studies.' He was sure, he added, that with the support he had in the House of Commons he could have successfully focused more attention on the subject than they had achieved 'by being members of these committees'. Churchill concluded: 'The secret information to which we became parties, although going very little further than what we knew ourselves, imposed silence.'

In a private letter to Cunliffe-Lister in August 1935, Churchill noted the enormous German military expenditure for that year alone of £1,000 million 'on military preparations, direct and indirect'. Although he did not say so, he had received this figure from a leading businessman, Sir Henry Strakosch, with whom he was on terms of increasing friendship. 'Can you doubt', Churchill asked Cunliffe-Lister, 'what this portends?' Churchill himself had no doubts. 'We are moving into dangers greater than any I have seen in my lifetime', he wrote, 'and it may be that fearful experiences lie before us.'

Churchill stressed in this letter to Cunliffe-Lister that 'time may be so short', and, remembering 'the intense efforts made' before the last war, he expressed his anxieties about 'our present leisurely procedure, and woeful inferiority'. No-one, he wrote, wished the new Air Minister better than Churchill did in the key office he had undertaken. That is why he sent 'this word of alarm'. And he added: 'Pray do not resent it from an aged counsellor.'

Churchill had further cause for continuing anxiety. On 22 June 1935 a Peace Ballot, organized by the League of Nations Union, gave 10,400,000 votes for international disarmament, with only 870,000 against. This vote, Churchill later wrote, acted as 'a heavy deterrent' to Baldwin to take what Churchill was convinced was the 'necessary action' in both military preparations and foreign policy. Less widely noticed were the 6,750,000 votes cast *in favour* of using military sanctions against an aggressor, with 2,360,000 votes against, scarcely more than a third. It was the answer to the first question, disarmament, which made the national, and international, impact.

Abroad, the Peace Ballot was interpreted as a sign of British pacifism pure and simple. 'It must be observed', Churchill later wrote, 'that the British people in the ebb and flow of their party politics and public opinion are often too capricious, changeable and inconsequent for foreigners to understand.' It was a period, Churchill later reflected, 'of leaderless confusion', and he went on to ask: 'How could Hitler and Mussolini discern in the Britain of 1934 and 1935 the Britain of 1939 and 1940?'

The signature of the Anglo–German Naval Agreement in July 1935 was a source of further 'confusion' in Hitler's favour. The Agreement abolished the Versailles restrictions on German shipbuilding, and did so without France having been consulted.

Speaking in the House of Commons on the 11 July 1935, Churchill deprecated the new Naval Agreement whereby 'we condoned this unilateral violation of the Treaty' without consulting any of 'the other countries concerned'. 'In the name of what is called practical realism', he argued, 'we have seemed to depart from the principle of collective security in a very notable fashion', while Europe's great hope was 'the gathering together of Powers' who are afraid of the 'rearmed strength of Germany'. The new Agreement cut across this divide, isolating France, but providing Britain with no real protection.

Churchill's criticisms of the Anglo–German Naval Agreement were unwelcome to Neville Cha berlain, who had high hopes of it, and to Samuel Hoare, the new Foreign Secretary, who had helped to negotiate it. Without naming Churchill in the debate, Hoare spoke disparagingly of people who seemed to take 'a morbid delight in alarms and excursions' and went on in similar vein to tell a tale of a child who, when asked by her nurse why she had so many balloons had replied: '"I like to make myself afraid by popping".' Hoare drew a moral from the tale, telling the House of Commons: 'That may be a harmless habit in the case of a child, but it is a dangerous habit in the case of the many alarm-mongers and scare-mongers who now seem to take this delight in creating crises, and, if there is a crisis, in making the crises worse than they otherwise should be.' The Naval Agreement, Hoare ended, would prove profitable alike 'to peace, and to the taxpayer'.

Despite his direct clash with Churchill over the Anglo–German Naval Agreement, Sir Samuel Hoare sought Churchill's advice just over a month later, when Mussolini threatened to invade Abyssinia. After their talk, Hoare noted how 'deeply incensed' Churchill was at the Italian threat.

It must be made perfectly clear to the world, Churchill told Hoare, that Britain was prepared to carry out its League obligations 'even to the point of war', under the condition that other members of the League were prepared to take the same action. Although the issue today was Italy, tomorrow it would be Germany. 'If the League collapsed now in ignominy', Churchill warned, it would mean 'the destruction of the bond that united British and French policy', and also of the one instrument that might in the future be chiefly effective 'as a deterrent to German aggression'.

Churchill was greatly relieved three days later when the British Government announced that if Italy attacked Abyssinia, Britain would uphold its obligations under the League of Nations. But, with his fears of an inadequate response, and of its repercussions, he wrote to Hoare on the day after the declaration to urge him to make sure that British diplomacy was based upon the existence of adequate naval strength to give effect to it. 'I am sure you will be on your guard', he added, 'against the capital fault of letting diplomacy get ahead of naval preparedness.'

Hoare responded sympathetically to Churchill's letter, telling him that he considered the Indian chapter 'closed', and welcoming any further 'suggestions' or 'warnings'. A month later, however, on 1 October 1935, Churchill wrote to Austen Chamberlain that he was 'very unhappy' about the necessity to 'smash up Italy' at this juncture, as it would later 'cost us dear'. Churchill regretted that Hoare and the Government had not as he had urged built up the navy that summer in the Mediterranean, as a warning to Mussolini. For the Italian dictator was now convinced of Britain's weakness and saw no potential barrier or opposition to his invasion of Abyssinia.

On 1 September 1935 Churchill left Chartwell for the south of France, for a two-week holiday at Maxine Elliot's villa on the coast near Cannes. Most of his time was spent painting, and swimming, but in a letter to Clementine he told of how he was also enjoying the 'general optimism and contentment engendered by old Brandy after a luncheon here alone with Maxine'.

But even while Churchill was enjoying the sun and relaxation of the French

Riviera, he could not put the state of Europe out of his mind. If only the League of Nations could stop Italian aggression against Abyssinia, he wrote to his wife, 'we should all be stronger and safer for many a long day'.

One day, during lunch at the villa, an elegant French woman argued that England had no right to object to Mussolini's invasion of Abyssinia, since Britain had profited from that 'kind of thing' often enough in the past. 'Ah', Churchill replied, smiling benevolently across the table, 'all that is locked away in the limbo of the old, wicked days. The world progresses. We have endeàvoured, by means of the League of Nations and the whole fabric of international law, to make it impossible for nations nowadays to infringe upon each other's rights.'

What Mussolini was doing by his attack on Abyssinia, Churchill warned, was to invoke a 'dangerous and foolhardy' attack on the whole established structure. 'Who is to say', he asked, 'what will come of it in a year, or two, or three? With Germany arming at breakneck speed, England lost in a pacifist dream, France corrupt and torn by dissension, America remote and indifferent – Madame, my dear lady, do you not tremble for your children?'

Churchill expressed these fears publicly at the Conservative Party Conference at Bournemouth on 4 October 1935, when he moved an amendment seeking to pledge the Conservative Party to a greater defence effort, and the speedy conversion of industry to meet these requirements. His amendment was carried unanimously.

At one point during his speech, Churchill's reference to the great volume of confidence and goodwill which Baldwin now enjoyed led to prolonged cheering. In response to it, Baldwin welcomed Churchill's 'generous gesture' of reconciliation, and rejoiced that the differences of the past two years were 'at an end'.

As soon as Baldwin had returned from Bournemouth to Downing Street, he wrote personally to Churchill of the 'great pleasure' which Churchill's Conference remarks had given him. Replying from Chartwell on the following day, Churchill reflected that when 'things are in such a state' it was 'a blessing to have at the head of affairs a man whom people will rally round'. But, Churchill warned, 'if your powers are great, so also are your burdens – and your responsibilities'.

In this letter to Baldwin, dated 7 October 1935, Churchill offered his services to the Prime Minister to help in the election campaign. Four days later, he wrote formally to the Conservative Central Office offering to speak outside his constituency. Central Office responded with pleasure and alacrity.

Churchill now prepared a major speech, in which he hoped to focus the electorate's attention on German rearmament and the European danger. The occasion was the last debate, on 24 October 1935, before Parliament was dissolved. Material came, as before, from Desmond Morton, Ralph Wigram and Sir Henry Strakosch. But the speech itself, the emphasis, and the clarity, were Churchill's own. 'When we separated in August', Churchill recalled, 'the

House was concerned about the scale and rapidity of German rearmament,' and he went on to ask: 'What has happened in the interval? The process has continued remorselessly. The incredible figure of more than £800,000,000 sterling is being spent in the currency of the present year on direct and indirect military preparations by Germany. The whole of Germany is an armed camp. Any Member of the House who has travelled there can add his corroboration of that statement. The industries of Germany are mobilized for war to an extent to which ours were not mobilized even a year after the Great War had begun. The whole population is being trained from childhood up to war. A mighty army is coming into being. Many submarines are already exercising in the Baltic. Great cannon, tanks, machine-guns and poison gas are fast accumulating. The Germans are even able to be great exporters of munitions as well as to supply their own enormous magazines. The German air force is developing at a great speed, and in spite of ruthless sacrifice of life. We have no speedy prospect of equalling the German air force or of overtaking Germany in the air, whatever we may do in the near future.'

Churchill then referred to a recent speech by Lloyd George, likewise warning of the new German military strength. Such a speech, Churchill commented, coming from so senior figure as Lloyd George, was 'a very welcome episode'. And yet, Churchill added, 'I must remind the House that he was very slow to recognize these tremendous developments in Germany. When I pointed out two or three years ago what was then beginning, he derided the idea; and he was not the only one. But neither he nor His Majesty's Government will, I imagine, disagree to-day with the statement that Germany is already well on her way to become, and must become, incomparably the most heavily armed nation in the world and the nation most completely ready for war. There is the dominant factor; there is the factor which dwarfs all others, and affects the movements of politics and diplomacy in every country throughout Europe.' It was, Churchill added, 'a melancholy reflection in the last hours of this Parliament that we have been the helpless, perhaps even the supine, spectators of this vast transformation, to the acute distress of Europe and to our own grievous disadvantage'.

Churchill again appealed to the House of Commons to put its trust in two factors: British rearmament, and the League of Nations. In proposing sanctions against Italian aggression in Abyssinia, the League had proved that it was 'alive and in action'. It was fighting for its life. 'Probably', Churchill added, 'it is fighting for all our lives.' And he ended by urging the British Government to use the machinery of the Covenant of the League in order to challenge aggression: 'The League of Nations has passed from shadow into substance, from theory into practice, from rhetoric into reality. We see a structure always majestic, but hitherto shadowy, which is now being clothed with life and power, and endowed with coherent thought and concerted action. We begin to feel the beatings of a pulse which may, we hope and we pray, some day – and the sooner for our efforts – restore a greater measure of health and strength to the whole world. We can see these difficulties and dangers for ourselves, but if we confront them with a steady eye, I believe the House and the country will reach the conclusion that the case for perseverance holds the field.'

This then was to be Churchill's election call, 'Arms and the Covenant': continued and accelerated rearmament at home and support for the League of Nations Covenant in opposition to aggression abroad. On this platform he was prepared actively to campaign for a Conservative victory.

The German Government reacted violently against Churchill's speech. The Nazi Party newspaper declared that it was his friendship with 'the American Jewish millionaire', Bernard Baruch, which had led him to expend 'all his remaining force and authority' against Germany. The German Ambassador in London protested to the Foreign Office, and Ralph Wigram sent Churchill the full text of the protest. But Churchill's friends were sure that he had been right to speak out as he had done, despite the hostile German reaction. 'It is right', Desmond Morton told him, 'that Germany should realize that we are not all lulled into weak-livered complacency.'

Six days after his speech of 24 October 1935, Churchill published an article in the *Strand* magazine in which he again focused attention on the 'ferocious doctrines' of Nazism, and of the enforcement of these doctrines 'with brutal vigour'. He was particularly scathing about Hitler's anti-Jewish measures. 'No past services', he wrote, 'no proved patriotism, even wounds sustained in war, could procure immunity for persons whose only "crime" was that their parents had brought them into the world'. Every kind of persecution, Churchill noted, was practised, and 'glorified', on the Jews of Germany, from world-famous scientists, writers and composers, down to 'the wretched little Jewish children'. Similar persecution had fallen upon Socialists, Communists, Trade Unionists and liberals. 'The slightest criticism', he pointed out, 'is an offence against the State.'

Side by side with the training grounds of the new armies, and the great aerodromes, Churchill noted, 'the concentration camps pock-marked the German soil'. In these camps thousands of Germans were being 'coerced and cowed into submission to the irresistible power of the Totalitarian State'.

Churchill then drew attention to Hitler's book, *Mein Kampf*, written ten years before, full of hatred of France and vitriol against the Jews, who were to be declared 'a foul and odious race'. And yet, Churchill pointed out, many Englishmen who had met Hitler had found him competent, cool and agreeable. Might Hitler not become, Churchill asked, 'a gentler figure in a happier age'. Churchill believed he would not, for even as Hitler spoke his words of reassurance to western Europe, arms of all sorts continued to pour out of Germany's factories at as great a rate as ever: rifles, cannons, tanks, bombs, poison gas, aeroplanes and submarines, in 'ever-broadening streams'.

Once more, the German Government protested officially about Churchill's attack on the Head of the German State. The tone of his article, so the British Ambassador reported from Berlin, 'is much resented here'. Wigram again sent

Churchill the text of the German protest, including Hitler's own angry question: 'What is to be the fate of the Anglo–German Naval Agreement if the writer of this article is to be the Minister of the British Navy?'

Many political commentators assumed that Churchill would indeed receive Cabinet office after the election. Some spoke of the Admiralty, as Hitler had done. Others looked to some specially created Ministry of Defence.

As the election campaign developed, however, Churchill's hopes of a Cabinet post were dampened by a speech which Baldwin made, in answer to the Labour Party's accusation, in its manifesto, that a Conservative victory would be a danger to peace as it was pledged to 'a vast and expensive rearmament programme'.

Answering this charge at the Peace Society on 31 October 1935, Baldwin pledged: 'I give you my word there will be no great armaments.' And he went on to speak indirectly but hopefully of Germany itself. It may be, he said, that there were Governments 'deliberately planning the future, leading reluctant or unsuspecting peoples into the shambles'. But in his own experience, he had not encountered Governments 'possessed of all these malevolent qualities'.

In order to counter such attitudes, Churchill wrote a long article in the *Daily Mail*, in which he stressed the war-making intentions of Nazi Germany, and expressed his fears that people were unaware just 'how near and how grave are the dangers of a world explosion'.

The General Election took place on 14 November 1935. Randolph who had stood as an official Conservative at West Toxteth, was only narrowly defeated by the sitting Labour member. Churchill increased his own majority at Epping. The National Government returned to power, with the Conservatives winning 432 seats, the Labour opposition 154 and the Liberals 21 seats.

As the election results became known, Churchill went to Lord Beaverbrook's house off Piccadilly. Greeting Churchill at the door, Beaverbrook said to him, cruelly: 'Well, you're finished now. Baldwin has so good a majority he will be able to do without you.'

Churchill returned to Chartwell, to await a letter or telephone call, offering him a Cabinet post. But no such summons came. Baldwin explained to a friend that Churchill should not be given a job 'at this stage'. He should be kept 'fresh' in case war did break out, in which case he would become 'our war Prime Minister'. When the first list of Ministers was published in the newspapers, Churchill's name was not in it. Some years later he recalled that he had felt a 'pang', because of what was 'in a way, an insult'. This discomfort was made worse by the ensuing mockery in the Press. 'I do not pretend', he wrote, 'that, thirsting to get things on the move, I was not distressed.'

Churchill remained at Chartwell, writing the third of his four Marlborough volumes, and preparing the groundwork for yet another major literary venture, a four volume history of the *English-speaking Peoples*, which he intended to finish by the end of 1939. But he knew that it might not be easy to complete so ambitious a project. 'The future is still very uncertain for me,' he wrote to a friend, 'indeed if the truth were realized, for all of us.'

The secret information reaching the Government from inside Germany confirmed all Churchill's fears. On 4 December 1935 the Foreign Secretary, Sir Samuel Hoare, who in July had spoken so disparagingly of those who were worried about Germany, told the Cabinet that the dispatches from the British Ambassador in Berlin 'fully justified' the concern of the Foreign Office over German war preparations. These dispatches, he added, would surely convince his Cabinet colleagues 'that there was no time to lose in the preparation and completion of our own defensive arrangements', and Hoare stressed that he himself was 'somewhat depressed at the slowness with which progress was being made', as exemplified by the production of anti-aircraft ammunition.

Hoare also told the Cabinet that he could not urge 'too strongly' the importance of pressing ahead with rearmament, as Germany, even if not yet completely ready, 'might easily take some action if satisfied that the defences of other countries were even further behind'.

Churchill knew nothing of Hoare's warnings, which were so much in line with what he himself had been saying publicly, and Vansittart and Wigram had been saying secretly, for so long. But he did know of the Berlin dispatches on which these warnings were based; at the very moment when Hoare was circulating copies of them, at Vansittart's suggestion, to the Cabinet, Ralph Wigram was giving Churchill a set, under seal of secrecy.

On 10 December 1935 Churchill and his wife left England for a short holiday in Majorca. While they were away Sir Samuel Hoare came to a tentative arrangement with the French Prime Minister, Pierre Laval, to allow Mussolini a substantial territorial slice of Abyssinia, some twenty per cent in all. This 'Hoare–Laval Pact', as it became known, was leaked to the Press. In England there was an outcry. Baldwin at once renounced the Pact, and Hoare resigned. The man in the street, Desmond Morton wrote to Churchill, 'does not look on this business as a great national crisis, but as a very nasty stink'.

On learning of the Hoare–Laval Pact, Anthony Eden had nearly resigned from the Cabinet. But Baldwin persuaded him to stay, and now he was appointed as Hoare's successor. Churchill, who had gone on to Marrakech, with Mrs Pearman and his Marlborough notes, wrote to his wife of how Eden's appointment did not inspire him with confidence, and he added: 'I expect the greatness of his office will find him out.'

Churchill still hoped that, as the crisis passed, and the paramountcy of the German danger reasserted itself, there might be a place for him in the Cabinet. When Randolph proposed writing an article attacking the Government over Hoare–Laval, and especially the motives of Baldwin and Eden, Churchill wrote to his son from Morocco that it would be 'very injurious' at this juncture if Randolph were to launch such an attack. If such an article were to appear, Churchill added, he would no longer be able to feel confidence in Randolph's 'loyalty and affection' towards him. These were stern words. But Churchill regarded the times as too dangerous for personal or even political vendettas, or even for the public expression of private doubts, such as his own about Eden.

Clementine Churchill returned to England to spend Christmas at Blenheim. Then she crossed back to Europe with her daughter Mary, to go skiing in Switzerland. Churchill, meanwhile, had remained in Morocco, writing to his wife on 30 December 1935, that Britain was getting in the most terrible position, as she was 'involved definitely by honour and by contract in almost any quarrel that can break out in Europe, our defences neglected, our Government less capable a machine for conducting affairs than I have ever seen'. The Baldwin–MacDonald regime, he added gloomily, 'has hit this country very hard indeed, and may well be the end of its glories'.

Contemplating the Abyssinian crisis, Churchill wrote to his wife about the Italians: 'They are throwing away their wealth and their poor wedding rings on an absolutely shameful adventure.' Of the international situation he wrote: 'The world seems to be divided between the confident nations who behave harshly and the nations who have lost confidence in themselves and behave fatuously.' Churchill also revealed to his wife how much he hoped for a Cabinet post, pointing out to her that Baldwin had been 'greatly weakened over Abyssinia' and would want 'a strong reconstruction'.

Writing books, preparing newspaper articles, and painting were a solace for Churchill. 'Luckily', he told his wife, 'I have plenty of things to do to keep me from chewing the cud too much.' One piece of personal news which he sent his wife on New Year's Eve was that he had just turned down a private offer from Lord Rothermere of £2,000 – more than £25,000 at today's values – if he gave up both spirits and wine in 1936. 'I refused', he explained, 'as I think life would not be worth living.' He had, however, accepted a second bet of £600, not to drink brandy or any other 'undiluted spirits' for twelve months. 'So tonight', he confided, 'is my last sip of brandy.'

As 1935 drew to a close, Churchill viewed the future with foreboding, writing to Sir Samuel Hoare, in congratulating him on the 'dignity' of his resignation speech: 'We are moving into a year of measureless perils.'

Chapter Six

Appeasement:
'This long retreat'

During the first weeks of 1936 Churchill still hoped to be asked to serve in the reshuffled Cabinet. But to his amazement and horror, Randolph suddenly announced his intention to challenge the National Government's candidate at a by-election at Ross and Cromarty, in Scotland. The official candidate was none other than Ramsay MacDonald's son Malcolm, who had just been appointed Secretary of State for Dominion Affairs, but had been defeated in the General Election.

It was essential that a Parliamentary seat be found for Malcolm MacDonald, if he were to remain in the Cabinet. The mere act of Randolph standing against MacDonald, would, as Churchill explained to his wife, 'put a spoke in my wheel'. Even if the young MacDonald were to win, Churchill added, it would make it difficult for Baldwin to offer him the Admiralty or the 'coordinating job', and then for him to 'sit cheek by jowl with these wretched people'.

Churchill told his wife that he was thinking of uttering 'the following "piece"': "I wish Mr Baldwin would tell me the secret by which he keeps his son Oliver in such good order."' However, Churchill added, for the time being he would remain 'completely mum'.

As Randolph's by-election campaign proceeded, Churchill's embarrassment increased. 'I should think', he told his wife, 'that any question of my joining the Government was closed by the hostility which Randolph's campaign must excite.' But on personal grounds, his anger with his son quickly abated. In the modern world, Churchill told Lord Rothermere, grown sons are responsible for their own actions and consequently parents cannot be held responsible for their sons' behaviour. In any case, political disagreements between fathers and sons were not a bar to 'affection and sympathy'.

It was the future of Europe that dominated Churchill's thinking even during Randolph's escapade. For Churchill was deeply concerned, as he wrote to his wife on 17 January 1936, that Hitler would soon march his troops into the Rhineland. Although this area was an integral part of Germany, it had been 'demilitarized' under the Treaty of Versailles which forbad Germany to have either troops or forts in the western border zone along the frontier with France and Belgium.

If Hitler were to remilitarize the Rhineland, Churchill told his wife, the League of Nations would have to declare Germany guilty of aggression. France would then be entitled to demand Britain's 'specific aid' in enforcing sanctions.

'So', he wrote, 'the League of Nations Union folk, who have done their best to get us disarmed may find themselves confronted by terrible consequences.' As for Baldwin and MacDonald, Churchill wrote, 'guilty of neglecting our defences in spite of every warning', they might well feel anxious 'not only for the public but for their own personal skins'.

Churchill also mused about possible changes in the Cabinet, writing to his wife that Hoare would probably become First Lord of the Admiralty, and telling her: 'Evidently the reason Hoare made no complaint of his treatment was because of some promise of early reinstatement.' But in any case, he wrote, he did not believe that the Government would take serious action in coordinating the defence measures and suspected that 'some Minister without portfolio may be assigned some of the duties'.

On 20 January 1936 King George V died at Sandringham. The *News of the World* at once asked Churchill, who was still in Morocco, to write an article on the late King for their issue on the following Sunday, six days later. Churchill agreed to do so, and at once dictated the article to Mrs Pearman as they packed up their Marlborough notes and Churchill's own paintings, and prepared to travel back to England.

As soon as Churchill's train reached Tangier from Marrakech, his article was telegraphed to London. It earned him £1,000, the equivalent of two years salary for an MP. The publication of the article made a considerable impact, for in it Churchill made a strong defence of constitutional monarchy, tracing its evolution and adaptation to modern times since the King had come to the throne a quarter of a century before. Since the end of the First World War, Churchill noted, over much of the rest of Europe, 'with a savage shout, not only the old feudalisms but all liberal ideals have been swept away'.

Returning to England, Churchill was angered by a newspaper report that Randolph was only challenging Malcom MacDonald because his father had put him up to it. 'As a matter of fact', Churchill wrote in protest to the paper's owner, 'I strongly advised him to have nothing to do with it.' Naturally, he added, 'as a father, I cannot watch his fight, now that it has begun, without sympathy'.

From Ross and Cromarty itself Randolph wrote to his father of how the local Scotsmen thought it a 'scandal' that Churchill was not in the Government. Unknown to Churchill, Neville Chamberlain's half brother Austen, who had never been particularly close to Churchill politically, had written to his sister about a possible Minister of Defence: 'In my view there is only one man who by his studies, and special abilities, and aptitudes, is marked out for it, and that man is Winston Churchill.' But Austen Chamberlain realized that Baldwin would not offer Churchill the job of Minister of Defence, and Neville Chamberlain would not wish to have him back in the Government. 'But they are both wrong', Austen Chamberlain continued. Churchill was in his view 'the right man for that post, and in such dangerous times, that consideration ought to be decisive'. The Government, however, were still not prepared to create a

Ministry of Defence, nor to organize industry for war production, even though the defence chiefs continued to press for 'a far more effective standard' of defence preparedness.

Churchill was increasingly aggravated by the Government's sloth and frustrated by his own inactivity. As one young Conservative MP, a friend of Baldwin, noted in his diary after supper with Churchill, 'he is obviously very irritated and unsettled, furious at not being in Government, contemptuous of present regime, and overwhelmed with German danger – very unbalanced, I thought'.

Randolph's defeat at Ross and Cromarty on 10 February 1936 did not help Churchill's chances. One newspaper wrote that the defeat seemed above all to emphasize 'the unpopularity of the Churchillians', and to be regarded widely 'as another nail in the political coffin of Mr Winston Churchill', as far as any Cabinet post was concerned, either at the Admiralty, or in charge of the coordination of all three service ministries. Churchill sensed this mood clearly. It was evident, he wrote to his wife, that Baldwin 'desires above all things to avoid bringing me in. This I must now recognize.'

Churchill's instinct was correct. After Baldwin had discussed the possibility of further Cabinet changes with Hoare, the former Foreign Secretary reported to Neville Chamberlain that 'on no account' would Baldwin contemplate Churchill's return to the Cabinet. The chief reason, Hoare explained, was 'the risk that would be involved' in having Churchill in the Cabinet when the question arose of choosing Baldwin's successor as Prime Minister.

Pressure on Baldwin to make Churchill Minister of Defence, or Minister for Coordination of Defence, continued in the press. Harold Macmillan was among those who had, as the newspapers reported, 'whispered' to Baldwin that 'Churchill is the man'. The *Daily Telegraph* reported on 3 March 1936 that Churchill's name was being widely suggested as the most likely candidate.

In Parliament, there was also great pressure to make Churchill Minister of Defence. After a motion in the House calling for such a Ministry, Sir Maurice Hankey wrote that he was afraid that the Government would have to make a concession in the matter of the Defence Ministry and must therefore try to arrange something that would 'not upset the psychology of the machine'. A few days later Baldwin said to a friend of Churchill's that he could not only think of his own interests, but had also to think of 'the smooth working of the machine'. Neville Chamberlain was reported as saying: 'of course if it is a question of military efficiency, Winston is no doubt the man.' Churchill himself surveyed the field in a letter to his wife, explaining to her why two of the various contenders would not want the job: Neville Chamberlain 'because he sees the Premiership not far away' and Sir Kingsley Wood, later Secretary of State for Air, 'because he hopes to be Chancellor of the Exchequer then and anyhow does not know a Lieutenant-General from a Whitehead torpedo'.

'So at the end', Churchill concluded, 'it may all come back to your poor Pig.' But he added: 'I do not mean to break my heart whatever happens. Destiny plays her part. If I get it, I will work faithfully before God and man for *Peace*, and not allow pride or excitement to sway my spirit.'

Churchill was under no illusions as to what the new Ministry would mean. 'It would be the heaviest burden yet,' he told his wife. 'They are *terribly* behindhand.'

As the speculation continued, the Government published a Defence White Paper, whereby munitions factories would be extended, and civilian industry organized in such a way as to enable it eventually to be turned over to war production. A new air programme, Scheme F, was also made public, adding 224 aeroplanes to the earlier Scheme C, and aiming at a total of 1,736 aircraft by 1939. But unknown to the public, the new Air Minister, Lord Swinton, recorded for the Cabinet his anxiety with regard to the forecast of German air expansion on which the British plan had been based. The German capacity to produce aeroplanes was, Swinton warned, 'enormous'.

When the House of Commons debated the White Paper, Clement Attlee attacked the proposals as being too bellicose, but Churchill urged that industry should be prepared for war production so that it would be ready 'to turn from peace to war production at the pressing of a button'. Because this had not been done three years earlier, he warned, and at the first signs of danger, there would now be 'two horrible years of hiatus', when Germany would be prepared and able to do as she liked. In urging that a new Ministry of Munitions was needed to supervise the necessary conversion of industry, Churchill recalled his own years as Minister of Munitions in 1917 and 1918 and told the House of Commons: 'Here is the history of munitions production: first year, very little; second year, not much, but something; third year, almost all you want; fourth year, more than you need.' Britain, he warned, was only at the beginning of the second year while 'Germany is already, in many respects, at the end of the third.'

Churchill went on to warn the House of Commons of the general public impression that Britain was making up for lost time and every month the relative position was improving. 'That', Churchill said, 'is a delusion. The contrary is true. All this year and probably for many months next year, Germany will be outstripping us more and more.' Even air parity could only be achieved if Germany herself were to slow down, or even 'arrest' her present air expansion.

From the Air Ministry, Sir Christopher Bullock wrote to thank Churchill for the 'keen interest' he was taking 'in all questions bearing on the very difficult problems of war production, of which you have such unrivalled experience'.

On 7 March 1936 Hitler shocked all Europe when he ordered his troops into the Rhineland: 35,000 men crossed into the demilitarized zone and occupied all its main towns. Churchill considered Hitler's action to be a clear and grave warning and in his memoirs referred to the 'hideous shock' that had been felt particularly in France. Churchill also recalled how Hitler, 'in order to baffle

147

British and American public opinion', had declared that the action was 'purely symbolic' and had accompanied it with a proposal for a twenty-five-year pact demilitarizing both sides of the Rhine frontier and limiting air forces, together with a non-aggression pact. This proposal, Churchill recalled, 'provided comfort for everyone on both sides of the Atlantic who wanted to be humbugged'.

Among those who sought such comfort was *The Times*, which referred to the events as 'a chance to rebuild'. 'British opinion', its editorial read, 'will be really unanimous in its drive to turn an untoward proceeding to account. The old European structure of European peace, one-sided and unbalanced, is nearly in ruins. It is the moment not to despair, but to rebuild.'

There was a body of opinion which was in agreement with *The Times*. On 8 March 1936, at a weekend house party at Lord Lothian's house at Blickling, Sir Thomas Inskip, Nancy Astor and Tom Jones prepared an analysis of the crisis which they telegraphed to Baldwin. All three welcomed Hitler's declaration 'whole heartedly' and, in condemning the entry of German troops into the demilitarized zone, urged that the action should not be treated tragically, in view of the peace proposals which accompanied it. They urged that the 'entrance to the zone' should be treated as an 'assertion, demonstration, of recovered status of equality and not as act of aggression'. Rearmament should be pursued but Hitler's declaration should be accepted as being made 'in good faith'. Tom Jones noted in his diary that his aim was to convince Baldwin to accept Hitler's proposal at its face value before he discussed the crisis in Cabinet.

The Cabinet met on 11 March 1936 to discuss the re-militarization of the Rhineland. Baldwin told his colleagues that the British Government would have to tell the French that their demand for a League pronouncement of military measures under the Locarno Agreement would only result in another world war which would in its turn result in Germany going Bolshevik. In addition, Baldwin was not sure that the Germans would back down if they were opposed.

The Air, Navy and Army Ministers told the Cabinet that 'our position at home and in home waters was a disadvantageous one, whether from the point of view of the Navy, Army or Air Force or anti-aircraft defence'. It was then agreed by the Cabinet that although failure to support the French was 'fraught with grave issues for the future of the League of Nations and the principles of collective security' there was no alternative but to tell the French that this was the position. One Minister pointed out that 'public opinion was strongly opposed to any military action against the Germans in the demilitarized zone'. Furthermore, many people were saying 'openly' that they did not see why the Germans should not 're-occupy the Rhineland'. It was agreed that in these circumstances 'it was worth taking almost any risk' to escape from having to take action.

Anthony Eden tried, as Foreign Secretary, to put forward another view. He said that the French were very 'pacifist' and were worried that if Germany were not stopped now, war would break out 'in three years' time' when Germany was rearmed. Eden shared this French concern, which was also the concern of his advisers, Vansittart and Wigram.

In reply to Eden, Baldwin explained, however, that when Britain had agreed to help France eleven years ago at Locarno there had been no risk, as Germany had been 'totally disarmed'. As a result of the failure of the Disarmament Conference and the time it had taken to 'educate public opinion', Britain was now 'caught at a disadvantage' in her defence preparations. It was, therefore he said 'very unfriendly' of France to 'put us in this present dilemma'. They should, he said, 'welcome our coming rearmament rather than expose us to the present embarrassments'.

The French Foreign Minister, Pierre Étienne Flandin, whom Churchill had met on a number of occasions, and who was a good friend of the Wigrams, hurried to London where the League of Nations Council was to discuss the Rhineland crisis. Ralph Wigram attended the League Council meeting, which was held at St James's Palace, and was seen at Eden's side 'inwardly increasingly disillusioned and depressed'.

During the crisis, Wigram called the Press to his house in Lord North Street in an effort to alert public opinion. There Flandin told the members of the Press: 'If you do not stop Germany now, all is over,' and he continued: 'France cannot guarantee Czechoslovakia anymore, because that will become geographically impossible.'

On the evening of 11 March 1936 Wigram went specially to Chartwell to tell Churchill the full story of Flandin's mission. Early on the following morning Churchill drove up to London, to his flat in Morpeth Mansions, near Victoria Station, where he received Flandin, and wished him 'all success' in persuading the British Government to join the Allies of the last war in concerted opposition to Hitler. It was evident, Churchill later wrote, 'that superior strength still lay with the Allies of the former war. They had only to act, to win.'

That evening Churchill set out this view to the Foreign Affairs Committee of the House of Commons, telling MPs of all parties that he believed that if the smaller nations of Europe were to support France and Britain against Germany, then Germany would back down. 'We must fulfil our obligations under the Covenant', he told them; and it seemed, as one observer recorded, that a 'substantial proportion' of those present were prepared to go to war.

Churchill's presentation of the case for collective action was answered by the former Foreign Secretary, Sir Samuel Hoare, who had just been brought back into the Cabinet as First Lord of the Admiralty, and who stressed that the nations of Europe which Churchill had mentioned were totally unprepared for war. This speech had its effect on the MPs, who became, even as Hoare was speaking, less excited.

That night, Churchill gave a dinner in London for Flandin, in order to introduce him to some of his friends. Flandin then met Baldwin, at both Wigram's and Churchill's suggestion. During the meeting, Baldwin told the

French Foreign Minister that the Cabinet had already agreed that Britain could not be committed to any policy involving 'policing' operations, as Britain was in no state to go to war.

Flandin reported Baldwin's remarks to Churchill, who was deeply concerned about the Government's negative policy. If no lawful redress could be found for France and Belgium, he wrote in the *Evening Standard*, the 'whole doctrine of international law' would lapse. Peace could only be preserved, he wrote, if both moral and physical force were employed to support the reign of law in Europe. Nothing else could stop 'the horrible, dull, remorseless drift' to war in 1937 or 1938.

On the day after this article was published, as Ribbentrop returned in triumph from the League Council in London to Germany, and Flandin with broken spirit returned to France, the British Government announced the creation of a Ministry for Coordination of Defence. The new Minister was not to be Churchill, as more and more people had urged, nor indeed any other of the obvious candidates, but Sir Thomas Inskip, the Attorney General, and the man who had been responsible for the Committee of Privileges' rejection of Churchill's charges against Hoare and Derby. This appointment, Lindemann told a friend, was 'the most cynical thing that has been done since Caligula appointed his horse as Consul'.

On learning of Inskip's appointment, Desmond Morton sent Churchill a long and sympathetic letter. 'It is a horrible job awaiting the uncertain,' he wrote, 'as you and I learnt to recognise in the war.' Of Inskip's appointment, Morton wrote: 'I do regret what appears to me to be the intention of the Government to shelve really effective defence measures. There is a feeling abroad little short of dismay.' Of Inskip's personality, Morton told Churchill: 'I hear from legal friends of his, that he is bad at conducting crown cases in the Courts, and that he revokes at Bridge more frequently than any professed player of the game.'

Churchill himself recalled in his memoirs how Inskip's appointment was 'a heavy blow' as it seemed to exclude him finally from any share in defence preparations. In all the debates and discussions that followed, Churchill later recalled, he had to be 'very careful' not to lose his 'poise'. 'I had to control my feelings and appear serene, indifferent, detached.' He was also certain that Baldwin believed he had dealt him a 'politically fatal stroke', and at the time Churchill himself believed this to be so.

In his diary Neville Chamberlain confided that it was Hitler's remilitarization of the Rhineland which had produced 'an excellent reason' for denying the new Ministry to both Churchill and to Hoare. Both, he wrote were too well known in Europe to be given the Defence Ministry during such a crisis. Inskip, on the other hand, 'would create no jealousies. He would excite no enthusiasm, but he would involve us in no fresh perplexities.' And on 17 March 1936, three days after Inskip's appointment was announced, the Cabinet justified Baldwin's Rhineland policy, as having been based, as the official – and secret – minutes recorded, on the desire 'to utilize Herr Hitler's offers in order to obtain a permanent settlement'.

Suddenly, the gulf had widened between those like Churchill, who were convinced that no 'permanent settlement' was possible with Nazi Germany, and those like Neville Chamberlain who were convinced that 'Hitler's offers' could be the basis of long-term agreement.

The Government's refusal to support France during the Rhineland crisis forced every thinking person to decide where he stood in this division. Within the Foreign Office, those who regarded the abandonment of France as a disaster turned increasingly to Churchill for encouragement and to help him lead the unofficial opposition.

For Wigram himself, the effect of the Rhineland crisis was traumatic: 'a mortal blow' as Churchill later recalled. And Ava Wigram was later to write to Churchill of how, after he had accompanied Flandin to Victoria Station on his return to France, Wigram had gone back to his house in Westminster 'and sat down in a corner of the room where he had never sat before, and said to me, "War is now *inevitable*, and it will be the most terrible war there has ever been. I don't think I shall see it, but you will. Wait now for bombs, bombs on this little house."'

Ava Wigram added, in her letter to Churchill: 'I was frightened at his words, and he went on, "All my work these many years has been no use. I am a failure. I have failed to make the people here realize what is at stake. I am not strong enough, I suppose. I have not been able to make the people here understand. Winston has always, always understood, and he is strong and will go on to the end."'

Many years later one of Wigram's juniors, Valentine Lawford, noted that Wigram's words to his wife had been interpreted 'as breaking his heart'. But Lawford, who had watched Wigram so closely, commented: 'I think he would have been surprised, even a little piqued, to hear it. Sensitive as he undoubtedly was, he was of all men surely one of the least inclined to allow discouragement, however deep, to distract him for long, much less pull his spirit permanently down. The purely physical demands of those twelve days had been almost intolerable; and they had still further enfeebled the frail organs of a body that thanks to his constant habit of overwork, had never even halfway recovered from its brush with death in Paris ten years before.'

There was no evidence at all, Lawford added, 'of anything resembling a defeated heart' in Wigram's behaviour after the Rhineland crisis. He had in any case a capacity 'to accompany deadly seriousness with a kind of mischievous music that prevented him in real life from ever seeming grim or priggish', and after the Rhineland he continued his daily work, 'the habits of half an official lifetime', of compiling detailed accounts of events and developments in Germany.

Wigram also continued after the Rhineland crisis to send Churchill material on German intentions, and on British foreign policy. 'Dear Mr Churchill', he wrote on 26 March 1936, in a typical letter, 'I send you one or two papers which may help you. The note of September 1932 (it was published), a note on Hitler's 25 points (October 1930, before he came into power), a note of my own on the speech of May 1935, the White Papers about disarmament in case you haven't got them all, a despatch of Rumbold's on Mein Kampf – the quotations you can evidently use – though the despatch is confidential.' Wigram added: 'The only thing I can find on the Hitler–Papen talk in 1932 to which you and Lindemann referred. Our records for the period are not very good. A White Paper is coming out early next week containing all the important German correspondence between June 1934 and March of this year – it may be of a certain help to you.' In a postscript Wigram wrote: 'Thank you so much for our delightful and interesting weekend. It made us both feel much better in every way. It is such a privilege and encouragement to me to hear your views. I wish and wish they were the views of the Government.'

Churchill was undeterred by the rejection of what he believed ought to be the Government's correct line of action. He therefore continued to try to alert public opinion to the mounting danger. In an article in the *Evening Standard* on 3 April 1936, he argued that all threatened nations must act immediately and in concert in order to avoid a war which would not only destroy homes and lives, but reduce 'such civilisation as we have been able to achieve' to 'primordial pulp and squalor'. His article continued: 'Never till now were great communities afforded such ample means of measuring their approaching agony. Never have they seemed less capable of taking effective measures to prevent it. Chattering, busy, sporting, toiling, amused from day to day by headlines and from night to night by cinemas, they yet can feel themselves slipping, sinking, rolling backward to the age when "the earth was void and darkness moved upon the face of the waters".'

Churchill's article ended: 'Surely it is worth a supreme effort – the laying aside of every impediment, the clear-eyed facing of fundamental facts, the noble acceptance of risks inseparable from heroic endeavour – to control the hideous drift of events and arrest calamity upon the threshold. Stop it! Stop it!! Stop it now!!! NOW is the appointed time.'

This article, and all Churchill's subsequent articles on international affairs for the next three and a half years, were to be syndicated throughout the world. 'Stop it Now' was published in the leading newspapers of fourteen different countries.

Within three weeks of the publication of 'Stop it Now', and at the explicit suggestion of Vansittart, another senior Foreign Office official, Rex Leeper, also made contact with Churchill, and asked to speak to him privately.

It had been Rex Leeper who, as head of the News Department of the Foreign Office, had at the height of the Rhineland crisis been called, together with Wigram and Vansittart, to Eden's room at the Foreign Office to discuss the implications of Hitler's 'pacific' proposals. All three officials had expressed their scepticism about Hitler's offer. But when Eden had asked Leeper what he thought the newspaper reaction would be, Leeper had told him: 'I think they will say that Germany is in her own territory.' That, Eden had replied, was what he was afraid of.

Rex Leeper's great fear was that while the German people were being indoctrinated with the philosophy of racialism, the people of Britain and the western democracies were being given 'little or no guidance' from their Governments as to the underlying gulf between the two outlooks.

Leeper wanted a nation-wide campaign, to educate the British people on the realities of their situation, in order to give them determination to rearm, and to 'abandon an attitude of defeatism vis à vis Germany'. It was a campaign which, in his view, must bring together the Press, the BBC, the League of Nations Union, and even the Churches. Public speakers would have to be found, he told Vansittart, who were willing to make 'bold and frank speeches, not hesitating to call a spade a spade and not shirking from unpleasant truths'.

Vansittart endorsed Leeper's proposal. He too believed that the need for action was most urgent. He also believed, as did Leeper, that war could only be avoided if the democratic countries made it quite clear that they would look after themselves within the League. 'If we are to succeed', Vansittart wrote 'we must *all* be ready to the best of our ability not only in word but deed; and we must eventually go *in practice* as far as we are prepared to go in *theory*, otherwise we must fail.'

Both Leeper and Vansittart now realized that there was little hope that the Government would follow this policy, or educate the public to accept it. They therefore turned to Churchill to lead their campaign behind the Government's back.

Churchill, so recently excluded by Baldwin, readily agreed to help when Rex Leeper visited him at Chartwell on 24 April 1936. Together, the two men worked out a plan, using Churchill's personal standing, to bring together all those who were concerned about the threat to democracy posed by the Nazi system, but who had no means of influencing public opinion.

Faith in democracy was the base, the need to defend democracy by united action was the theme, and Churchill was the focus of the new movement. Its organizational framework was a group, already in existence, known as the Anti-Nazi Council, whose President was the Trade Union leader, Sir Walter Citrine, and whose slogan was: 'Nazi Germany is the enemy of civilization.'

Within a month of Leeper's visit to Chartwell, Churchill was present at the first of a series of private luncheons given by the Anti-Nazi Council, and intended to create an active and informal leadership. Among those present at the first of these luncheons was the Chairman of the National Executive of the Labour Party, Hugh Dalton. In the course of his speech, Churchill urged those present to work to make it clear that all men of all classes, from 'the humblest workman' to 'the most bellicose colonel', could and must work together to resist danger, aggression and tyranny.

Churchill now embarked upon an intensive campaign of public speaking and of private exhortation. To one of those working in the Anti-Nazi Council who sought his advice, a life-long Liberal, he outlined the policies he believed that the Government should adopt: all the countries including Soviet Russia, from the Baltic southwards to the Aegean coast, should, he wrote, be brought together to agree to 'stand by any victim of unprovoked aggression'. Each of Germany's neighbours should be persuaded to guarantee 'a quota of armed force' in order to create such a united front. Germany would then be invited to join this system, and herself receive firm guarantees of support in the event of any unprovoked aggression against her. Such a plan, Churchill believed, 'would either ensure the peace of the world, or an overwhelming deterrent against aggression'.

Churchill also sought to counter the growing pro-German, and in places even pro-Nazi, sentiment. To his cousin Lord Londonderry, who was convinced that no united front against aggression was needed, and who criticized Churchill for his 'strong anti-German obsession', Churchill explained: 'I certainly do not take the view that a war between England and Germany is inevitable.' But, he added, he feared 'very gravely' that unless something were to happen to the Nazi regime in Germany, 'there will be a devastating war in Europe'. The only chance of stopping such a war, he believed, was to have 'a union of nations, all well-armed and bound to defend each other, and thus confront the Nazi aggression with overwhelming force'.

As to his alleged 'anti-German obsession', Churchill told his cousin, this simply did not exist. What he did have was a sense of the continuity of British policy, which, for 400 years, had been 'to oppose the strongest power in Europe by weaving together a combination of other countries strong enough to face the bully'. Sometimes, he pointed out, this 'bully' had been Spain, 'sometimes the French Empire, sometimes Germany. I have no doubt who it is now.' If France were to set up the over-lordship of Europe, Churchill would, he said, endeavour to oppose her in the same way. It was thus, he explained, that Britain had maintained her freedom and independence through the centuries.

His own reading of the future, Churchill told his cousin, was that Hitler's Government would confront Europe 'with a series of outrageous events and ever-growing military might'. It would be these events, he said, which would show Britain's dangers, 'though for some the lesson will come too late'.

Churchill worked throughout the summer of 1936 to bring this lesson home to as many people as possible. In the House of Commons he asked whether Austria might not be Hitler's next victim, now his forces were installed in the Rhineland. To Desmond Morton he confided his fear that even in the Air Ministry there were those who 'still woefully underrate the German power'. In a further debate in the Commons he noted that the remilitarization of the Rhineland had brought German troops right up to the French and Belgian borders, bringing the danger to Britain's own security 'very much nearer'. No further negotiations should be conducted with Germany by individual States, he advised, but only through the League of Nations, where a large number of

States 'who individually are helpless' were collectively powerful.

Churchill was also worried about continuing anti-French feeling, which was being stimulated by France's new defensive pact with the Soviet Union. Churchill himself approved this development, and at the beginning of April 1936, with Sir Robert Vansittart's encouragement, he made contact with the Soviet Ambassador, Ivan Maisky, and continued to see Maisky at regular intervals until the outbreak of war. On 19 April 1936, following his first meeting with Maisky, Churchill suggested to Sir Maurice Hankey that the Government should 'collect all the evidence, official and otherwise, that there is about Russia, in order to determine whether she is an ally worth having or not'.

In public and in private Churchill continued to urge greater rearmament. In the House of Commons he again pressed for the establishment of a Ministry of Supply, to lay down a clear structure for the evolution of industry from preparatory, to precautionary, and then to emergency conditions. If such plans could not be made under peace conditions, he said, then conditions must be created 'which would impinge upon the ordinary daily life and business of this country', and the Government must explain to the people why this change had to be made. He also urged the Government to make arrangements with the Trade Unions, and to take action to avoid profiteering in the event of war.

Baldwin's response to Churchill's appeal was cynical. 'One of these days', he told his friend Thomas Jones, a former Deputy Secretary of the Cabinet, 'I'll make a few casual remarks about Winston.' Baldwin said that he had already prepared his remarks. He was going to say 'that when Winston was born lots of fairies swooped down on his cradle gifts – imagination, eloquence, industry, ability, and then came a fairy who said "No one person has a right to so many gifts", picked him up and gave him such a shake and twist that with all these gifts he was denied judgement and wisdom'. That was why, Baldwin added, 'while we delight to listen to him in this House we do not take his advice'.

Although dismissed by Baldwin and Chamberlain, Churchill's suggestions for greater Government action were supported, in secret, both by the new Minister for the Coordination of Defence, Sir Thomas Inskip, and by the Cabinet Secretary, Sir Maurice Hankey, who told Inskip that the defence reconditioning programme was not showing great efficiency and might have to be dealt with 'on a war basis'. The existing peace conditions on which Britain's preparations were based, Inskip told the Cabinet, were not perhaps compatible with the increasing tensions of the European situation. But in reply to Inskip, Neville Chamberlain expressed his doubts as to the urgency of the situation, and argued, successfully, that the question of Government directives to manufacturers, as Inskip had suggested, should be deferred.

At Chartwell Churchill worked on his speeches and correspondence with Ministers, reading voraciously, and receiving information from an ever-increasing circle: from Wigram at the Foreign Office, from a number of Government armament contractors, from several senior army and naval officers, from an ever-widening group of industrialists and bankers, from one of the leading personalities of the League of Nations Union, Viscount Cecil of Chelwood, and from many private citizens. The information which came his way spanned every aspect of national defence, or its neglect. 'I do not pose as an expert on these matters', Churchill told the House of Commons early in May 1936, in raising one such issue, the state of the Fleet Air Arm, 'but as one who is accustomed to judge the opinion of experts.'

Churchill did not have to judge alone. At his side, with slide-rule and eagle eye, 'Prof' gave him constant guidance. In mid-May Churchill wrote to Austen Chamberlain from Chartwell, that Lindemann and he were together preparing a case to encourage the Government to speed up experiments in aircraft defence. As a result of Lindemann's briefing on this particular aspect of defence policy, Churchill wrote direct to Inskip, urging him to give the matter his personal attention. 'You will be shocked', Churchill added, 'to see how slow, timid and insignificant is the progress made.'

Churchill's main complaint was that experiments were being made on a haphazard basis, whereas he and Lindemann wanted each idea tested at once and thoroughly, until proved either useful or useless. 'Accustomed as I was to see how things were done in the war', Churchill told Inskip, 'and how orders can be given for large scale experiment and supply, I have been deeply pained by the dilettante futility which has marked our action.'

Even as he was writing this letter, a further cause for concern was about to be brought to Churchill's attention. For some months his secretary, Mrs Pearman, had been seeing something of an air force officer, the Director of the Training School, whose worries about the state of the Royal Air Force were acute. The officer's name was Torr Anderson. In the First World War he had served first as an infantryman on the western front, where he had been badly wounded, and then with the Royal Flying Corps, receiving the Distinguished Flying Cross. Now he was forty-years old, and full of zeal to set things right.

In a tea shop at Westerham, only a few miles from Chartwell, Torr Anderson poured out his worries to Mrs Pearman, and asked her what he should do. He was a serving officer, in a responsible position, with access to much secret information. He knew of deficiencies and neglect throughout the air service, and he was in contact with other officers, some senior, some in important specialist positions, who were likewise concerned, and who were continually bringing him information.

It was clear to Mrs Pearman, with more than six years experience of politics and secrets, that Anderson was a patriot, and a man of courage. It was also clear that he was wracked with worries about the weakness of the air force, and also about the danger of revealing these weaknesses, even to Churchill. Understanding Anderson's fears, Mrs Pearman suggested that he go to see Churchill, who would certainly listen sympathetically, and would at the same time respond with the utmost discretion to all he had to tell.

The first meeting between Anderson and Churchill took place, at Churchill's

London flat, on 25 May 1936. Henceforth, for more than three years, Anderson was to give Churchill information of the utmost secrecy, and to introduce him to other airmen with similar secrets to reveal, in the hope that Churchill would stir the authorities to action. Churchill seldom revealed what he was told in public, as the matters were so sensitive, but he applied whatever pressure he could behind the scenes, through his personal correspondence and contacts with Ministers.

Churchill listened carefully to all that Torr Anderson told him: at this first meeting it concerned the paucity of training facilities for observer-navigators, and the lack of plans to extend those facilities.

The information available to Churchill was also available to the Government. But the Government still refused to adopt emergency measures, even when, on 11 June 1936, Inskip himself warned the Cabinet that the three- to five-year period of preparation was too long, and that the increasing danger of the situation might make it necessary to work to an earlier date and take emergency powers.

Sir Robert Vansittart, who had been invited to attend this particular Cabinet meeting, supported Inskip's view that peace in Europe could not be guaranteed for five or even three years. Vansittart also told the Cabinet of what he considered to be a 'distinctly sharper' tone in German policy. This comment drew an immediate response from Neville Chamberlain, who suggested that Germany's 'next forward step' might not necessarily 'lead us into war'. Vansittart was not deterred by Chamberlain's comment, begging to disagree, and warning the Cabinet that Germany's next aggressive move 'would probably be against Czechoslovakia'.

Inskip and Swinton both stressed the need for emergency powers. But Sir Samuel Hoare opposed them, saying that such powers would be a 'shock' to the country and might harm industrial production. Neville Chamberlain agreed with Hoare, and went on to warn the Cabinet of the dangers to financial stability of any such emergency measures, which could not be justified, in his view, until there was further 'over powering' evidence of the need for them. Vansittart's warning had fallen on stony ground.

On the day after Inskip's unsuccessful pleas to his Cabinet colleagues about the need for emergency powers, the inventor of radar, Robert Watson-Watt, saw Churchill privately to seek 'urgent' help against what he called the Air Ministry's 'unwillingness to take emergency measures' for the proper testing of radar. He also complained that he had been unsuccessfully recommending that he coordinate experiments to improve ground communication between the Observer Corps, and aircraft whose job would be to intercept the raiders once they had been located. Thirteen weeks had already passed, Watson-Watt told Churchill, since it had been recommended officially that he coordinate all such research. But still nothing had been done.

Churchill listened sympathetically to Watson-Watt, and passed on his complaints to the Air Minister, Lord Swinton. 'I fear', Churchill wrote to Swinton in a covering letter, 'that a similar slowness and intermittance characterizes other lines of research in this field.' Unknown to Churchill, a parallel unease was being expressed yet again by Sir Maurice Hankey, who wrote direct to Baldwin, not long after Watson-Watt had been to see Churchill, that he had 'received a certain rumour of evidence' that the 'realization of the need for push and drive' in the Defence programmes had not penetrated very far below those who hold immediate responsibility'. One result of this disturbing situation, Hankey reported, was the 'interminable delays involved by the bandying about of minutes and correspondence between the Service Departments and Technical Experts'.

In spite of the fact that the experts were as concerned as Churchill, there was increasing Cabinet resentment at what was considered interference by him and at his constant appeals to Ministers and civil servants for greater vigilance. A dispute arose in June when Churchill wrote a memorandum to his Air Defence Research sub-committee, arguing that Germany's accumulated reserves would soon enable the German Air Force to make a rapid expansion of its first-line strength. Churchill pointed out that at least 330 military planes already in squadrons and with their pilots were not included in the Air Ministry's estimates of German first-line strength, but were credited with a training role only.

The Air Ministry and the Foreign Office were in fact in agreement with Churchill on several major principles: that these extra aeroplanes would be a force to reckon with in eighteen months time; that the German airframe and aero engine production was far ahead; that German industrial preparations for war meant that the Germans needed far fewer reserves than did Britain, and that the French and Germans themselves regarded all twelve machines housed with the squadrons as first line, not just the nine machines hitherto counted by the Air Ministry. But in spite of so many agreements in principle, Lord Swinton was by now angered by the correspondence, and decided to bring it to an end, and to stop sending Churchill secret papers.

In fact, eighteen months later, as Churchill had anticipated, the Air Ministry was forced to recognize, in a secret reassessment, the massive expansion of German first-line strength and the corresponding British weakness; a weakness which was to give Hitler the diplomatic free hand which Churchill, Vansittart and Wigram had each forecast, and dreaded.

There were those who now advised Churchill to curtail his criticism of the Government, in order to be received back into the Conservative Party hierarchy, and to groom himself as Baldwin's successor. But Churchill declined to take this course, and during a speech to his constituents he explained that following his conscience was more important to him than political office. 'I have done my best', he said, 'during the last three years and more to give timely warning of what was happening abroad, and of the dangerous plight into which we were being led or lulled.' It had not, Churchill said, been 'a pleasant task. It has certainly been a very thankless task.' It had, he said, brought him into conflict 'with many former friends and colleagues'. He had been 'mocked and censured as a scare-monger and even as a warmonger, by those whose complacency and inertia have brought us all nearer to war and war nearer to us all'. But at least, he concluded, he had the 'comfort of knowing' that he had 'spoken the truth' and done his duty.

At the end of June 1936 a former Foreign Secretary, Sir Austen Chamberlain, asked Baldwin for a secret session of the House of Commons, in order that Britain's defence policy could be debated without any public report being made of the discussion. Churchill supported this move, which would, he believed, enable the defence position to be debated with greater freedom than had become possible in such dangerous times.

The Cabinet, however, were not in favour of such a course, and Ramsay MacDonald, now Lord President of the Council, asked his Cabinet colleagues whether they were prepared to face answering Churchill's criticisms in detail in the House of Commons.

Parliament was about to break up for the summer, and in its final debate of the session, Inskip tried to alleviate concern when he spoke with assurance of developments in the defence programmes, including 'a swelling tide' of production, regular sources of supply having reached capacity, and forty new aerodromes having been acquired.

During the debate that followed Churchill drew the House's attention to Inskip's argument that had the Royal Air Force expansion begun three years earlier 'we should be cumbered with a mass of inferior machines'. Churchill used powerful irony to dismiss this unfortunate statement. If it were true, he said, then there had been no need for Baldwin's confessions of blame, 'because apparently this was not an oversight; it was not an accident: this was some deep design, a truly Machiavellian stroke of policy, which enabled us to pretend that miscalculation had been made while all the time we were holding back in order to steal a march on other countries'.

Unfortunately this was not true, Churchill said, for had the factories been put to work three years ago, the apprentices trained, and the plant and staff extended, then the new types of aeroplanes could have been put into production much more easily and far earlier, than was now possible.

Churchill said that times had 'waxed too dangerous' to make his case in public or to make detailed criticisms of Inskip's speech. However, he did have many searching questions, and he wanted them answered, even though the Parliamentary holiday was about to begin. 'Jaded Ministers,' he commented, 'anxious but impotent members of Parliament, a public whose opinion is more bewildered and more expressionless than anything I can recall in my life – all will seek the illusion of rest and peace.'

As soon as the debate was over, Baldwin agreed to receive a private deputation of senior political figures, to discuss the defence situation. Churchill hoped that it would be possible to put together this Defence Deputation on an all-Party basis, but the Labour leader, Clement Attlee, and the Liberal leaders Sinclair and Lloyd George, refused to join it.

Upset in particular by the Labour Party's refusal, and by continuing Labour Party opposition to British rearmament, Churchill told an audience in Sussex on 23 July 1936 that he could understand how 'some circles of smart society', or 'groups of wealthy financiers', or others who would like the Government to be 'strong enough to keep the working classes in order', as well as all those who 'hate democracy and freedom', might be able to accommodate themselves to Nazi tyranny. But he did not believe that British Trade Unionists or Socialist and radical intellectuals could bear it, any more than 'the ordinary British Tory'. It would, he said, 'be intolerable'.

Churchill now began to prepare his material for the Defence Deputation. Both Desmond Morton and Torr Anderson helped to provide him with the most secret recent facts and figures of German industrial production, and the British air response. Unknown to Churchill, at Baldwin's suggestion no Service Ministers were to be present at the meeting. To do so, Hankey explained to Swinton, would give the discussions too much importance and would make it difficult to avoid responding to the Deputation's questions.

The Defence Deputation was received by Baldwin on 28 July 1936, with Lord Halifax and Inskip as the only other Ministers in attendance. In strictest secrecy, eighteen senior Conservatives, led by Lord Salisbury, Sir Austen Chamberlain and Churchill, put their detailed points of criticism for several hours. Churchill's theme was a stark one. 'The months slip by rapidly,' he said. 'If we delay too long in repairing our defences, we may be forbidden by superior power to complete the process.' Churchill ended his statement: 'I say there is a state of emergency. We are in danger as we have never been in danger before.'

There was a second meeting of the Deputation on the following day. Churchill now spoke of the urgency of turning a large part of British industry over to war production. Complaint was made, he said, 'that the nation is unresponsive to the national needs', but Churchill argued that as long as the Unions and the Labour Party were 'assured by the Government that there is no emergency', then it was clear that 'obstacles will continue'. Churchill still believed, however, that all these obstacles would 'disappear if the true position about foreign armaments' were set before the British public, not by words or 'confessions', but in the form of action.

After each member of the Deputation had voiced his concern at the slow pace of rearmament and preparation, Baldwin spoke of how he had been unable to rearm before the 1935 election as the country might have rejected such a policy. Furthermore, he said, he had several times discussed with Neville Chamberlain the adverse 'effect on trade' of turning the peace-time economy even half-way towards war conditions. As a result of their talks, both he and Chamberlain had come to the conclusion that any disturbance of peace-time production 'might throw back the ordinary trade of the country perhaps for many years', seriously damaging the financial strength of Britain 'at a time when we might want all our credit'.

Baldwin also had another reason for rejecting the Deputation's sense of urgency. Hitler, he said, 'wanted to move East, and if he should move East, I should not break my heart'. But he did not believe Germany wanted to move West because, as he expressed it, 'West would be a difficult programme for her.' He was not, he added, going to get Britain into a war with anybody 'for the League of Nations or anybody else, or for anything else'. If there were to be any fighting in Europe, Baldwin declared, 'I should like to see the Bolshies and Nazis doing it.'

Although Churchill did not know it, low priority was given to considering the Deputation's points. At Hankey's suggestion it was decided that even when the various Ministries' replies were ready, they should not be shown to the members of the Deputation, as this would involve what Lord Swinton called a 'waste of time'.

Churchill did not share Baldwin's view that if there were to be fighting in Europe, it would be good 'to see the Bolshies and Nazis doing it'. Indeed, with the outbreak of the Spanish Civil War, he was afraid that Conservative sympathies, veering as they did to Franco and anti-Communism, would go too far, and move closer to Germany. 'I do not like to hear people talking of England, Germany and Italy forming up against European Communism,' Churchill wrote to the French Ambassador.

In whatever way the Spanish Civil War ended, Churchill wrote in an article in the *Evening Standard*, the violence, and cruelties and the drawing in of outside forces, could only help the ever-increasing Nazi power.

Churchill spent much of the late summer of 1936 at Chartwell. He was now in the very last stages of the third of his four Marlborough volumes, and had acquired a new research assistant, Bill Deakin, a young Oxford don who was to remain with him until the outbreak of war, and was then to return to his side in the post-war years to work on the war memoirs.

Deakin was only twenty-three years old. But he shared Churchill's deep dislike of Nazism, and while at Oxford had helped to organize a small group of like-minded university people to come to the aid of the ever-growing stream of refugees from Nazi persecution. At Chartwell, Deakin was quickly drawn in to the intense and lively atmosphere. 'I felt very shy and nervous at first', he later recalled, 'but once Churchill accepted you, he was very considerate.' There was never a 'wasted' moment: correspondence, dictation and work in the morning, a real break at lunchtime with guests and 'magnificent' conversation, a short rest in the afternoon, more correspondence or work before dinner, dinner itself 'the event of the day' with laughter and wit ranging over every subject, and then, at midnight, when the guests had left, the hard literary work. 'Work on Marlborough would go on to three or four in the morning,' Deakin recalled. 'One felt so exhilarated. Part of the secret was his phenomenal power to concentrate – the fantastic power of concentrating on what he was doing – which he communicated. You were absolutely a part of it – swept into it.'

At the end of August 1936 Churchill left England for a short painting holiday in France. His work on Marlborough went with him, and half-way through the holiday Bill Deakin was summoned to Paris by telephone. Not work, but politics, greeted the young assistant on his arrival, for in Paris he and Churchill lunched with the French politician, Georges Mandel, who told them that as a result of the Rhineland crisis, the British and French had 'lost everything'. Later Churchill and Deakin saw General Georges, whom Churchill had known during the First World War, and who reiterated that 'too much had been given away' already for a decisive stand to be made in the future.

From Paris, Churchill went on to Cannes, to paint at his favourite Château de l'Horizon, and from Cannes, when his painting holiday was over, he went as the guest of the French Government to French army manoeuvres. A week later he visited the Maginot Line, France's eastern fortress defence system, before returning to Chartwell. But his return was only for a short while, as he intended to go back to France for a major speech. He had been invited by the Press Secretary at the Paris Embassy, Charles Mendl, a personal friend, and also a friend of Rex Leeper. As Leeper had hoped, Churchill wished to take the opportunity to assert the supremacy of western democracy, seek to create a sense of Anglo–French common purpose, and set out the dangers which threatened both that common purpose, and democracy itself.

It was on the morning of 24 September that Churchill returned to France, flying to Paris with Clementine, and lunching with President Herriot. That evening he made one of the most important speeches of his long career, appealing to all Englishmen and Frenchmen for the utmost vigilance in defence of parliamentary democracy and liberal civilization.

Democracy, Churchill declared, was a precious heritage enjoyed by Britain, France, the United States, Switzerland, Belgium, Holland and the countries of Scandinavia. In these countries 'thought is free; speech is free; religion is free; no one can say that the Press is not free'. Such were the hallmarks of liberal societies. 'Moreover,' he said, 'and this is what really matters, although we French, English and Americans have differences among ourselves and wrangle about our internal affairs, and although we are very much aware of the short-comings of our civilisation, and the need of continual social betterment, we believe fervently that our institutions are such as to enable us to improve conditions and correct abuses steadily, and to march every year and every decade forward upon a broader front into a better age.'

These advantages, Churchill continued, were 'a great treasure to guard': they were also 'a great cause' which had to be defended. 'Now this is the question I ask my countrymen repeatedly', he said, 'and have come here to ask you: are we taking every measure within our power to defend that cause? This is the solemn question we must ask each other, and ask ourselves.'

There were many people, Churchill told his Paris audience, who believed that the only choice for Europe was between the 'two violent extremes' of Communism and Nazism. And yet, he said, 'between the doctrines of Comrade Trotsky and those of Dr Goebbels there ought to be room for you and me, and a few others, to cultivate opinions of our own'.

Churchill denied that there was any virtue whatsoever in the totalitarian systems of Right or Left. How could those who had been bred in the democratic tradition bear, he asked, 'to be gagged and muzzled; to have spies, eavesdroppers and delators at every corner; to have even private conversation caught up and used against us by the Secret Police and all their agents and creatures; to be arrested and interned without trial; or to be tried by political or Party court for crimes hitherto unknown to civil law. How could we bear to be treated like schoolboys when we are grown-up men; to be turned out on parade by tens of thousands to march and cheer for this slogan or for that; to see philosophers, teachers and authors bullied and toiled to death in concentration camps; to be forced every hour to conceal the natural workings of the human intellect and the pulsations of the human heart? Why, I say that rather than submit to such oppression, there is no length we would not go to.'

Not good defences alone, Churchill argued, but generous motives and high ideals were also needed if democracy was to survive in the 'modern, grim, gigantic world', and he declared, amid considerable applause: 'We must trust something to the power of enlightened ideas. We must trust much to our resolve not to be impatient or quarrelsome or arrogant. We seek peace. We long for peace. We pray for peace. We seek no territory. We aim at no invidious monopoly of raw materials. Our hearts are clean. We have no old scores to repay.'

'Another Great War', Churchill warned 'would extinguish what is left of the civilisation of the world, and the glory of Europe would sink for uncounted generations into the dark abyss.' And in a final peroration he declared: 'No one can read the inscrutable riddles of the future, but of this I am sure, that if we do our duty, every one of us fearlessly and tirelessly in whatever station we may stand, the strength and splendour of the French Republic and the British Empire will not easily be trampled down, nor will the lights which they offer to mankind be quenched in barbaric gloom.'

Churchill's Paris speech of 24 September 1936 marked a high point of his advocacy of democratic ideals, and his concern that those ideals should be understood, and defended. In Berlin this speech, and those that followed it on the same theme, were met with mounting abuse.

The Foreign Office, which had so encouraged Churchill to speak out, approved his outspokenness. 'It is good', wrote a younger member of the British Embassy in Paris, 'that the Germans should realize that there is one English statesman who, instead of apologizing for democracy stands up for it.'

Returning to Chartwell, Churchill had a few brief moments of domestic calm. His third Marlborough volume was being published, with all the pleasures which that brought of signing more than a hundred copies, including 'number one' to the King, Edward VIII, whom he had helped from time to time with drafts of speeches for ceremonial occasions. Baldwin, Neville Chamberlain and Sir Maurice Hankey were likewise recipients of Churchill's generous delight in sending out his books. 'You put all other historians into the shade', wrote Hankey, 'because you tell us the things we really want to know.'

An unhappy personal interlude for Churchill was the intense Press gossip which surrounded his daughter Sarah's friendship with the Austrian-born concert pianist, Vic Oliver. For some months Churchill himself had been worried about his daughter. Vic Oliver was sixteen years older than Sarah. He had been married twice before, and it was not at first certain whether his second divorce had been valid: when Churchill telegraphed to a lawyer friend in New York to examine all the relevent documents, he added: 'Paramount object is to prevent hasty marriage.'

Sarah Churchill prepared to give up her career as a dancer in London, in order to join Vic Oliver in America. Before she left, Churchill asked to see her at Morpeth Mansions. 'He was looking very serious,' Sarah later recalled. 'I sat down at his bidding. He spoke to me for about half an hour. He pointed out every conceivable reason why he feared my marrying. I could not really disagree with him. I completely saw his point of view – a point of view any parent might voice.'

During their talk together Churchill asked his daughter: 'Are you not betraying your own dedication to the work you have already struggled so hard for, by marrying so soon?' Sarah did not know how to answer. Her father's encouragement of her stage career had meant a great deal to her, and she hated having to disappoint him. There was a long silence. Her father looked at her, she later recalled, 'with his extraordinary eyes – slightly prominent, pale blue eyes, capable of so many impressions of subtlety and passion. I said nothing. There was nothing I could say.'

Suddenly Churchill sprang up from his chair, and from his desk took Sarah's passport, holding it dramatically in front of him. 'One thing I ask of you,' he said. 'One promise. Do not marry him until he is an American citizen. For if you do, in three years you will be married to the enemy, and I will not be able to protect you – once you lose this,' and Churchill waved the passport in the air.

'It was still only 1936', Sarah later recalled, 'but my father's conviction held me spell-bound. I did not doubt his prophetic instinct, and I gave my word to wait. "I promise you", I said, and left the room.'

Sarah sailed for New York on board a German transatlantic liner, the *Bremen*. Although correct, the crew's attitude to British passengers was, even then, far from friendly. On gala nights the German sailors, immaculately dressed, sang the new patriotic songs. 'I wondered', Sarah later recalled, 'whether my father's warning had made me more sensitive to this very definitely chilling spectacle. But I found that other British and American people on board had the same impression.'

Sarah reached the United States, and as soon as it was clear that Vic Oliver was indeed free to marry, she married him, after first ensuring that there was no barrier to his becoming an American citizen. But the persistent Press publicity had caused Churchill much distress, as his friends realized. 'I do want you to know', wrote Baldwin, when the hue and cry subsided, 'that I felt with you from my heart when I read in the papers of certain domestic anxieties that must have caused you pain. I know you well enough to realize how closely these things touch you.'

While Baldwin himself was resting in the country on doctor's orders, his Cabinet discussed its policy towards Germany, and towards British rearmament. At a decisive Cabinet meeting on 7 November 1936, the pattern for British foreign policy was set. But it did not emerge without disagreement. Opening the discussion, Sir Thomas Inskip told his colleagues that as the policy of collective security had, as he phrased it, 'disappeared', it was necessary to replace it with something new. He suggested that 'the appeasement of Germany's economic conditions' might be a hopeful policy, but he warned that if the Cabinet decided instead to stick to its plans to have the country prepared for war by 1937 there was no longer any alternative to announcing emergency powers and placing the country practically on a 'war footing.' Anthony Eden and Duff Cooper were in favour of adopting the latter course but Sir Samuel Hoare still argued that such measures would cause an 'immense upheaval' and would weaken Britain in the future. He preferred the course of adopting a much quieter foreign policy. One Cabinet Minister, the Secretary of State for Dominion Affairs, said that there was a strong current of opinion in the country against friendship with France as it was preventing Britain 'getting on terms with the dictator powers'.

It was Neville Chamberlain who produced the final, and decisive argument in favour of accelerating the search for appeasement, rather than pushing even faster ahead with defence preparations. Speaking with all the authority of Chancellor of the Exchequer, and as Baldwin's obvious successor as Prime Minister, Chamberlain told his colleagues that although the question of 'national safety' was a difficult one for him to oppose, he was 'getting concerned at the mounting cost' of the defence programmes. The cost of these programmes, he added, 'was mounting at a giddy rate'. The original estimate of £400 million had been exceeded, and the programmes were 'constantly increasing'. Soon people would be talking about an unbalanced budget, and Britain might find that her financial credit 'was not so good as it was a few years ago'.

In stressing the financial argument against the sort of defence increases which were being suggested, Chamberlain added that, while he recognized that national safety 'must come first', Britain's resources were 'not unlimited', and that the Government was in danger of putting financial burdens 'on future generations'.

A clear policy was about to emerge: the search for some form of direct agreement with Germany, in order to preserve Britain's financial resources.

For his part, Churchill sought to fight the emerging policy, and warned of the dangers of pursuing appeasement from a position of weakness. Unless there was 'a Front' against potential aggression, he told the House of Commons on 8 November 1936, not just Britain, but all the nations of Europe, 'will just be driven helter-skelter across the diplomatic chessboard until the limits of retreat are exhausted, and then out of desperation, perhaps in some most unlikely quarter, the explosion of war will take place, probably under conditions not very favourable to those who have been engaged in this long retreat'.

Churchill's arguments were gaining increasing support each time he spoke. Anthony Eden, now himself in opposition within the Cabinet, wrote, on this occasion, to thank him for his speech, and to report on its good effect in Europe.

Three days later there was another major defence debate in which Churchill made, as Harold Nicolson noted, a 'sledgehammer' attack on the Government's defence achievements so far. During this speech, Churchill warned that both the Territorial and the Regular Army lacked weapons, and were training with flags and discs. He then went on to speak at length about the sad decline of Britain's Tank Corps. He had spoken secretly two weeks earlier to the Inspector of the Royal Tank Corps at Morpeth Mansions and used the intelligence he had thus gained to warn of the lack of new equipment. 'Nothing has been done', he said, 'in the years that the locusts have eaten' to equip the Tank Corps with new machines. Both in numbers and quality of Tank Britain was now behind her main competitors.

During this debate of 11 November 1936 Churchill again called for a Ministry of Supply and interference with trade. He referred to the First Lord's statement that the Government were 'always reviewing the situation', saying that he well believed that was indeed the case: 'Anyone can see what the position is,' he said, 'the Government simply cannot make up their mind, or they cannot get the Prime Minister to make up his mind,' and he continued, in a fierce peroration: 'so they go on in strange paradox, decided only to be undecided, resolved to be irresolute, adamant for drift, solid for fluidity, all powerful to be impotent.' So Britain went on, he ended, preparing 'more months and years – precious, perhaps vital to the greatness of Britain – for the locusts to eat.'

Earlier in the debate Inskip had admitted that the Government could muster only 960 first-line aeroplanes, as against at least 1,500 German planes. Churchill responded to this admission: 'I have been staggered by the failure of the House of Commons to react effectively against these dangers.' He had never expected such a failure, and would never have believed 'that we should have been allowed to go on getting into this plight, month by month and year by year'. Even the Government's 'own confessions of error' he noted, 'had not produced a concentration of Parliamentary opinion and force capable of lifting our efforts to the level of emergency.'

Unless the House of Commons decided even at this late hour to find out the truth for itself, Churchill warned, 'it will have committed an act of abdication of duty without parallel in its long history.'

Replying specifically to Churchill's charges of the neglect of defence preparations when Churchill first had urged them, Baldwin spoke, as he had to the Defence Deputation, of the electoral difficulties in pushing for rearmament between the Fulham by-election of 1933 and the General Election of 1935. 'I have stated', he said, 'that democracy is always two years behind the dictator', and, he continued: 'I put before the whole House my own views with an appalling frankness.'

Baldwin then explained that he had been unable to act at that time because of pacifist feeling, and he went on to ask the House: 'Supposing I had gone to the country and said that Germany was rearming and that we must rearm, does anybody think that this pacific democracy would have rallied to that cry at that moment?' He could not think of anything, Baldwin added 'that would have made the loss of the election from my point of view more certain'.

It was this admission that led the indexer of Churchill's war memoirs to write, in 1948: 'Baldwin . . . confesses putting party before country.'

During his speech, Baldwin also repeated that Churchill's figures were exaggerated, and continued to argue that there was no need for a Ministry of Supply or any non-voluntary procedure, as such a Ministry would upset 'the whole trade of the country' and might also 'react on finance'. Thus finance replaced pacifism as the Government's reason for rejecting the defence measures being urged.

As for Baldwin's pleas that he would have lost the General Election had he urged rearmament between 1933 and 1935, Churchill's answer was simple and uncompromising: the Government's responsibility for the national safety was 'absolute', and required no mandate from the electorate. Furthermore, the Prime Minister had commanded 'enormous majorities' in both Houses of Parliament throughout that period. These majorities had been ready to vote for 'any necessary measures of defence'. In addition, Churchill stressed, whenever, throughout British history, the 'true facts' had been put before the country, the electorate had never yet failed to do its 'duty'.

In the absence of a clear lead from the Government, Churchill continued to work to educate the public to the gathering dangers. At a second meeting of the organizers of the Anti-Nazi Council, it was agreed to set up a new movement, the 'Defence of Freedom and Peace', based on an agreed formula of the need for all threatened nations to work in unison to withstand aggression. The 'vast mass' of public opinion was ready, in Churchill's view, to defend democracy and the movement would have the means of being its 'spear-point'. It was not to be a new society, he explained, but 'a welding together' of existing organizations, aimed at 'galvanising them into effective use'.

One of the first successes of the Defence of Freedom and Peace was the support it received from leading figures in the Labour Party. Churchill told

Austen Chamberlain, that he was surprised by the 'resolution' and awareness of 'approaching danger' which he now found among Labour people.

Further encouragement came directly from the leader of the Labour Party himself, for, a mutual friend reported to Churchill at the end of November 1936, that Clement Attlee was ready to support Churchill 'on any rearmament programme', and that he 'admires and likes you'.

It was now planned to launch the Defence of Freedom and Peace movement at a mass rally in the Albert Hall on 3 December 1936. Working both at Chartwell and Morpeth Mansions, Churchill spent many hours drafting, reading, rehearsing, and rewriting his speech, determined to make his appeal to all sections of society. 'All the left wing intelligentsia are coming to look to me for protection', he explained to Randolph, 'and I will give it whole heartedly in return for their aid in the rearmament of Britain.'

Ten days before his Albert Hall speech, Churchill was present at the second Parliamentary Defence Deputation to Baldwin. The Prime Minister was accompanied by Neville Chamberlain, Lord Halifax and Sir Thomas Inskip. In setting out the relative strengths of the British, French and German air force, Churchill drew, though he did not say so, on information that had been sent to him in confidence by the new French Prime Minister, Léon Blum. He also again stressed that whereas the French counted twelve aeroplanes in each German squadron, the British insisted on counting only nine. Yet the three 'missing' planes per squadron added up, over the total agreed German strength of 120 or 130 squadrons, to nearly 400 aeroplanes. These planes existed, no one denied that. The question was, should they be counted in the first line. Both the French Government and Churchill continued to argue that they should: that they constituted an additional effective strength, consisting of the best pilots, the best machines, with all the necessary back-up facilities, 'every bit as good as the 9 which you count', and with German industry ready, as British industry was not, to replace them in war.

Of course, Churchill said, the Air Ministry could rule them out and say '"We do not count them"': but Churchill warned 'they are there all the same, from every point of view'.

Basing himself on further secret material provided by Torr Anderson, Churchill also stressed the lack of readiness of many of the 80 British squadrons officially listed as part of the front line. The fact was, Churchill insisted, that there would be nothing approaching '80 effective Metropolitan squadrons' in the next year. Inskip replied that if 'the emphasis' was on '"effective"', he agreed with Churchill.

The Albert Hall meeting took place, as planned, on the evening of 3 December 1936. In his speech, as in his Paris speech of just over three months before, Churchill again called on democracy to defend itself from extremism under the banner of the League of Nations. If the democracies failed in this, the world would be exposed to a series of 'calamities', and it would be impossible to foretell the outcome of such a potential disaster: 'horrors', as Churchill expressed it, 'the end of which no man can foresee'.

Churchill's audience listened with appreciation and widening agreement to all he said. As in Paris, his comprehensive defence of democracy, and his clear exposition of the dangers, struck deep chords of agreement and concern. But even as they listened on that December evening, there were other thoughts and other concerns in the mind of every person present which blunted the impact of Churchill's appeal. For on the previous evening King Edward VIII had told Baldwin that he intended to marry Mrs Simpson, and Baldwin had replied that such a marriage would be unacceptable to the Government.

Churchill had known the King since his investiture at Caernarvon Castle as Prince of Wales more than a quarter of a century before. They had become friends, playing polo together, and enjoying each others company. Both before and after Edward became King, Churchill had helped him to draft several important public and ceremonial speeches. He had also met Mrs Simpson, and witnessed the King's fascination for her. 'He delighted in her company', he later wrote, 'and found in her qualities as necessary to his happiness as the air he breathed.'

Churchill also noted that all those who knew Edward well had noticed that when he was with Mrs Simpson 'many little tricks and fidgetings of nervousness fell away from him'. He was, Churchill wrote, a 'completed being instead of a sick and harassed soul'. The King's involvement was made even more 'precious and compulsive' for him because it had happened later in life than for most people. Although their relationship had been branded as 'guilty love', in Churchill's view it was 'psychical rather than sexual' and appeared to be a most 'natural' companionship, completely free 'from impropriety or grossness'.

Unknown to Churchill, or to Parliament, Baldwin had decided, and the Cabinet had agreed – with only Duff Cooper dissenting – that if the King insisted on marrying Mrs Simpson, then he must abdicate, and do so at once. The King seemed intent on marriage, however. As the abdication crisis developed, Churchill's own position was a clear one. He did not approve of the King marrying a divorced woman, although he saw no reason why they should not continue to see each other outside marriage. At the same time he saw no reason for a hasty decision either way, and wanted the King to be given more time, two or three months perhaps, in which to agree to give up the idea of marriage.

Churchill also joined those close to the King who were trying to persuade Mrs Simpson, who was then in the south of France, to help towards this solution, by withdrawing her petition for divorce. It would then be impossible for the King to marry her, and the crisis would be over. But although Churchill did not realize it, the King was determined to marry, and Mrs Simpson had decided not to put any obstacle in his way.

On 4 December 1936, as the crisis intensified, the King invited Churchill to see him, with Baldwin's permission, at Fort Belvedere, his home near Windsor

Castle. Driving there at once, Churchill found the King exhausted 'to a most painful degree'; so much so that when he asked Churchill if he could be given 'a fortnight to weigh the whole matter', possibly going to Switzerland to think out his decisions 'without undue pressure', Churchill at once assured him that Baldwin would indeed give him this period of grace. It seemed the obvious thing to be done: a little more time for reflection, in an atmosphere of calm. At the same time, Churchill strongly urged the King not to leave Britain during this 'period of grace', as everyone would say he had gone to meet Mrs Simpson.

On the following morning, December 5, Churchill sent Baldwin a full account of this conversation. The King, he reported, 'twice in my presence completely lost the thread of what he was saying, and appeared to me driven to the last extremity of endurance'. And on December 6 the Press published an appeal by Churchill to give the King a little longer to make up his mind.

With time, Churchill believed, the King would be willing to give up the idea of marriage. But pressure for a quick decision, Churchill was convinced, could only harden his present intention. Churchill pleaded 'for time and patience' for the King. The Cabinet, however, had become impatient, and on the morning of Sunday December 6, Baldwin and Neville Chamberlain both stressed that the business had to be finished before Christmas. Chamberlain was particularly emphatic on giving the King no more than eighteen days in which to make up his mind, as the continuing uncertainty was, in his view as Chancellor of the Exchequer, 'hurting the Christmas trade'.

Churchill now suggested to the King that in return for more time in which to make up his mind, the King should agree to a formula whereby he would promise 'not to enter into any contract of marriage contrary to the advice of his Ministers'.

Churchill was convinced that once the King had accepted this formula, the urgency for a decision would disappear, and with Mrs Simpson's divorce not becoming absolute for another four months, the King would then have time to reconcile himself to the need to give up all idea of marrying her. 'The only possibility of your Majesty remaining on the Throne', Churchill wrote, 'is if you could subscribe to some such Declaration.'

The King had no intention, however, of agreeing to any formula whereby the Cabinet could prevent him from marrying Mrs Simpson. But Churchill did not know this when he arrived late at the House of Commons for Prime Minister's Question Time. He had been the guest speaker at the Anglo–French luncheon club and was both tired and flustered when he reached the House of Commons. As he explained to Bob Boothby four days later, when he had risen to speak he had been unaware how far Baldwin had gone to meet his view that the King should be given more time. He therefore once again asked Baldwin to give an assurance that 'no irrevocable step' would be taken before the House received a full statement. Churchill then began to defend his Press appeal in favour of 'time and patience'.

The House of Commons, wrongly sensing a sustained political attack on Baldwin, now turned savagely on Churchill with cries of 'Drop it', and 'Twister' forcing him to stop in mid-argument.

Churchill was stunned by this unexpected hostility, and stormed out of the Chamber. A few moments later, glancing at the ticker-tapes in the Lobby, he told a fellow Conservative MP that he thought his political career was 'finished'.

Churchill's plea for time on the afternoon of December 7 was widely seen as an attempt to embarrass, if not to overthrow, Baldwin. But it was based entirely upon his belief, perhaps naïve, that, if given time, the King would agree to give up Mrs Simpson, at least as his future wife. The nation appeared, however, to be in no mood to delay the King's decision for more than a matter of days, and although Mrs Simpson herself agreed, privately, on the morning of December 9, to withdraw her petition for divorce, the King himself now insisted that nothing would shake his intention to marry her. Twenty-four hours later, on the morning of December 10, he therefore signed the Deed of Abdication.

The House of Commons met that same afternoon to hear Baldwin announce that the Deed was signed. Churchill himself described Baldwin's speech as a masterpiece of Parliamentary skill. So also was his own, and it helped to re-establish his reputation and authority in the Commons, as dramatically as they had been shattered only three days earlier.

Churchill began his speech of December 10 by saying that there had never been a sovereign who had so 'faithfully' carried out his duties in the 'spirit' of the constitution. Had the King been forced to make the decision a week earlier, Churchill believed, it would not have been possible to argue that he had reached his decision in an 'unhurried' manner. As it was, Churchill himself accepted that the King had indeed decided to abdicate 'freely, voluntarily, spontaneously' and in his own time. Speaking of his long friendship with the King, Churchill said that he would have been 'ashamed' if he had not, in his 'independent and unofficial position', endeavoured to find any lawful way to keep the King on the throne, to which he had so recently succeeded 'amid the hopes and prayers of all'.

The anger of the House which had so staggered Churchill three days before seemed totally to have disappeared now that the abdication was a fact. When Churchill spoke of the King's 'courage, simplicity, sympathy and sincerity', qualities which Churchill believed might have made 'his reign glorious in the annals of this ancient Monarchy', the House cheered him. It was tragic, he added, that these very qualities in the King had themselves led to this 'bitter conclusion'.

Churchill's final words were about the need for national unity in the face of the European situation. His remarks were listened to with attention and loudly cheered. 'Danger gathers on our path,' he said. 'We cannot afford – we have no right – to look back. We must look forward; we must obey the exhortation of the Prime Minister to look forward. The stronger the advocate of monarchical

171

principle a man may be, the more zealously must he now endeavour to fortify the Throne.'

That evening Churchill worked at Morpeth Mansions with Torr Anderson, discussing pilot training and other air force problems. But his mind was still on the events of the past few days, and he spoke of the King as a 'Poor little lamb' who had, he said, been treated 'worse than any air mechanic'.

On December 11 Churchill drove to Fort Belvedere to lunch with Edward, and to help him with his abdication speech. *The Times* was abusive about Churchill's support for the King, ascribing to it, as many MPs had done, all sorts of unworthy motives. But when Geoffrey Dawson, the editor, wrote to apologize, Churchill replied: 'Nothing that was written about me caused pain, because I have had forty years of such buffetings.' It was the paper's 'sledgehammer blows' against the King, he said, that had made him angry. And to his American friend, Bernard Baruch, Churchill wrote that he did not believe his own political position had been much affected 'by the line I took'. Even had it been, he would not, he told Baruch, have acted differently for 'in politics', he explained, 'I always prefer to accept the guidance of my heart to calculations of public feeling'.

Churchill spent Christmas with his family at Chartwell. Then, as Clementine and Mary set off for a skiing holiday in the Austrian Alps, he went for New Year's Day to Sir Philip Sassoon's house at Trent Park. On the following day, 2 January 1937, while he was still at Trent Park, he telephoned to Sir Robert Vansittart at the Foreign Office, to discuss an article he was writing. To his intense distress, Vansittart told him that Ralph Wigram had died three days before.

Churchill's correspondence reveals the impact that Wigram's death made on him. 'I was deeply shocked and grieved', he wrote to Clementine, 'to learn from Vansittart by chance on the telephone that poor Ralph Wigram died suddenly on New Year's Eve in his wife's arms. I thought him a grand fellow. A bright steady flame burning in a broken lamp, which guided us towards safety and honour. Brendan and I are going on Monday to the Funeral which is at Cuckfield, near Haywards Heath. Afterwards I shall bring him and Van back to luncheon at Chartwell. I am taking a wreath from us both. Poor little Ava is all adrift now. She cherished him and kept him alive. He was her contact with great affairs.'

That same day, 2 January 1937, Ava Wigram wrote to Churchill: 'Van says you rang to ask about Ralph's funeral. If you'd like to come I'd be very glad – as it's only for people Ralph specially cared for – & the memorial service is for the less close – I don't know what to do at all – I'm feeling so stunned. I can't believe that in five minutes our whole wonderful life together was shattered for always – It can't be true, can it. Private. I wanted to ask you to write a little thing in the papers, but I thought it was a bother. He adored you so – & always said you were the greatest Englishman alive. Please come on Monday.'

Churchill had already decided to go to Wigram's funeral, and as soon as Ava

Wigram learned of this she wrote again: 'I'm grateful you are coming to the funeral – It is 11 o'clock Cuckfield Parish Church – Haywards Heath. Would you be there in good time so I can have you by me – to be helped by you – none of his relations are coming – NOT his father or mother – or anybody so I need you very much.'

From Austria, Clementine Churchill wrote to her husband as soon as she heard the news: 'I am horrified and astonished to read in last Saturday's Times an "appreciation" of your friend Ralph Wigram by Vansittart. Did you know he was ill? I did not see any announcement of his death in Friday's Times, the day I left; & I think you must have missed it or you would have mentioned it to me – I am so very sorry – He was a true friend of yours & in his eyes you could see the spark which showed an inner light was burning – His poor little wife will be overwhelmed with grief – In these troubled times one is astonished to be standing up – with head "bloody but unbowed" –.'

As soon as Wigram's funeral was over, Churchill sent an account of it to Clementine. 'I went to Cuckfield (Sussex)', he wrote, 'for the funeral of poor Wigram. The widow was ravaged with grief, and it was a harrowing experience. Vansittart and his wife have taken her in for ten days at Denham – a good act. There appears to be no pension or anything for Foreign Office widows: but she says she can manage on her own resources. Her future seems blank and restricted. A sombre world!'

After the funeral, Churchill had given a luncheon at Chartwell for the mourners, including Vansittart, Brendan Bracken and Paul Maze. 'I felt Mr Wigram's death would make you unhappy,' Clementine Churchill wrote, 'I'm afraid you will miss him very much.' To Ava Wigram Churchill wrote, in a letter that she was to keep at her bedside until her own death nearly forty years later: 'I admired always so much his courage, integrity of purpose, high comprehending vision.' And Churchill added: 'He was one of those – how few – who guard the life of Britain. Now he is gone – and on the eve of this fateful year. Indeed it is a blow to England and to all the best that England means. It is only a week or so that he rang me up to speak about the late King. I can hear his voice in my memory. And you? What must be your loss? But you still will have a right to dwell on all that you did for him. You shielded that bright steady flame that burned in the broken lamp. But for you it would long ago have been extinguished, and its light would not have guided us thus far upon our journey.'

The death of Wigram came at a time when Churchill had seen in him the epitome of courage and farsightedness. Writing about Wigram after the war, in his memoirs, Churchill recalled the Rhineland crisis nine months before Wigram's death, and reflected: 'My friend never seemed to recover from this shock. He took it too much to heart.'

Wigram's 'profound comprehension', Churchill noted, 'reacted on his sensitive nature unduly. His untimely death was an irreparable loss to the Foreign Office, and played its part in the miserable decline of our fortunes.'

Chapter Seven

Munich:
'The sacrifice of honour'

Following the emotional upheaval of the King's abdication, the exertions of his Paris and Albert Hall speeches, and the sorrow of Ralph Wigram's death, Churchill spent most of January 1937 at Chartwell, with a brief excursion to Blenheim. He was sixty-two, and the strain of events had brought on a nervous stomach complaint that made it difficult for him to stand up, whether to make speeches or to paint. A special diet was devised by Dr Thomas Hunt, a leading expert, who advised a strict avoidance of highly seasoned food, strong coffee, raw apples, rich pastries and new bread. After dinner, one glass of port or brandy was the maximum. Cigars were to be smoked in a holder and their number reduced. All these instructions Churchill obeyed. But the indigestion was still frequent, and painful.

At the beginning of the year Sarah Churchill visited her father, bringing her husband Vic Oliver. 'There is now nothing for us', Churchill wrote to a friend, 'but to make the best of things and hope they will be happy.' A week later Sarah returned to Chartwell for lunch. 'She was very sweet and loving', Churchill reported to his wife, who was still skiing in Austria, 'and we had a nice talk.' Vic Oliver was working in provincial music halls, earning good money. 'They get special terms at the hotel', Churchill commented. 'But what a life – hand to mouth, no home, no baby!'

Churchill had found his daughter 'serious and gentle'. Like the ill-starred Duke of Windsor, he wrote, 'she has done what she liked, and has now to like what she has done'. It was for her parents, Churchill added – for himself and Clementine – 'to take special care, and make excuses for her'.

Churchill was busy now on his fourth, and final, Marlborough volume. Helped by Bill Deakin, he worked every day to try to master the complex problems of the early eighteenth century. He found it hard to keep all the complicated arguments in his head as he wrote, there were so many distractions and problems with which to contend. Throughout the early months of 1937 many people who were concerned about deficiencies in the defence programmes continued to approach Churchill for help and advice. They included officers from both the air force and the navy, businessmen in the defence industry, and industrial experts. After the disappointment of the previous year's speaking marathons Churchill was unwilling, however, to allow himself to be distracted by another campaign. He explained to a friend that 'non-official' people did not command influence at the present time. It was possible, he wrote, for 'one poor wretch' to 'exhaust himself without his even making a ripple upon the current of opinion'.

Churchill did believe that he might make some progress if he could get access to the BBC. But all that, he wrote to a friend in the United States, 'is very carefully sewn up over here', and indeed, unknown to Churchill, six months earlier a special Cabinet Committee had agreed that the BBC should be asked not to arrange any more 'independent expressions of views' on the European situation. The only Minister to speak out against this decision had been Alfred Duff Cooper.

The Government was still determined not to follow Churchill's repeated appeals to interfere with normal production in the interests of a coordinated defence programme. 'You say it is the Government policy not to interfere with normal trade,' Churchill wrote to Inskip in mid-January 1937. 'It may be Government policy, and yet not be right.' He was worried, he told Inskip, that the armament programme was falling further behind 'all the Government requires'.

But the Government's concept of what it required, particularly in the Air, was increasingly different to Churchill's. On 27 January 1937 the Cabinet met to discuss Lord Swinton's new programme, Scheme H, for increasing British front-line strength to 1,632 aircraft by 1939. This was to be achieved by including in this figure the reserves and overseas squadrons. These reserves would then have to be made up in 1940 and 1941.

Chamberlain said that as we were 'a long way behind Germany' in the number of aeroplanes Britain possessed it was important to get rid of the concept of 'counting machines' as being the basis of parity. He also warned that there was a danger that the defence programmes might be increased to such an extent that the country would not be able to afford them. He asked if the completion date of 1939 had to be adhered to rigidly. The scheme was rejected and returned to the Air Ministry to be recast in a cheaper form. During the discussion Baldwin said that MPs should be warned not to refer 'directly' to Germany, 'at a time when we were trying to get on terms with that country'.

Churchill feared that a sense of weariness would spread over the nation, particularly when, on 16 February 1937, the Government announced its new defence programme, involving the expenditure of £1,500 million between 1937 and 1942. The real effect of this announcement, he believed, would be to 'paralyse criticism at home'. The Tory Party, he explained to Lord Rothermere, feared that everything necessary was being done and that the country was being made perfectly safe', since the Government had announced its intended expenditure over the five year period. Such announcements could not, he warned, affect the 'realities' of the situation in which Britain would find herself in 1937, 1938 and 1939.

Having raised certain specific areas where he believed insufficient progress had been made, such as the provision of anti-aircraft guns, the training of their crews, and the re-equipment of the territorials, Churchill pointed to the situation on the continent where 'mighty nations' were 'arming feverishly', giving up all comforts to do so, where millions of men and weapons were being prepared for war, and where 'the finances of the proudest dictators are in the most desperate condition'. With such a situation in Europe, Churchill asked, how could the Government be certain that their programmes, adopted so late, would be ready on time?

Churchill was convinced that the only way to meet the challenge was for the whole nation to 'pull together'. But there was a growing body of opinion which believed that Hitler did not want war, and that it was wrong to stress the military side of German policy. While Churchill continued to argue, in newspaper articles and in Parliament, that countries like Czechoslovakia were now 'in fear of invasion', and that out of Germany 'the hate culture continues', the editor of *The Times*, Geoffrey Dawson, was taking another view. 'I should like to get going with the Germans,' he wrote in a private letter to a friend on 23 May 1937, and he added: 'I simply cannot understand why they should apparently be so much annoyed with *The Times* at this moment. I spend my nights in taking out anything which I think will hurt their susceptibilities, and in dropping in little things which are intended to soothe them.'

Churchill continued to fight such attitudes of appeasement and published articles drawing attention to the Nazi terror. He had also returned to Oxford, on 22 May 1937, as the guest of the Ralegh Club, telling the assembled students: 'when I came to Oxford to make a speech five years ago, I said you must rearm. I was laughed at. I said we must make ourselves safe in our island home, and then laughter arose. I hope you have learned wisdom now.' The President of the Club, James Brown, now Judge Brown QC, later recalled, in a letter to the author, Churchill's remarks both at dinner and during his speech. 'The legacy of Baldwinism', he told Brown, 'is incompetence, because of his sentimental all-men-are-brothers-so-don't-let-us-wrangle attitude.'

During the speech itself, as Brown noted, Churchill emphasized the need to 'keep in step with the League of Nations', giving a great kick at the word *step*. His theme was equally emphatic: 'We must rearm. We must have a defensive alliance with France. We must have cooperation with America as far as she is willing. We must support the League. Whenever war threatens or breaks out, we are at the side of the victim and against the aggressor and in each case we shall do what we can, through the League, to aid the victim.'

Churchill ended his speech at Oxford with a defence of democracy and the middle way. 'It is sometimes said that Communism and Fascism are poles apart,' he said. 'Perhaps they are. But what difference is there between life at the North Pole and life at the South Pole. Perhaps as one crawls out of one's igloo there may be a few more penguins at the one or polar bears at the other. At both, life is miserable. For my part I propose to remain in the Temperate Zone.'

On the following day, also in a speech to the Ralegh Club, Leo Amery attacked the League of Nations and collective security with the same energy that Churchill had defended them. But, as James Brown later recalled, 'none of us was convinced. Churchill had us in thrall.'

During his visit to Oxford Churchill said nothing of the problem that still weighed heavily on his mind: Britain's own defence programme and its deficiencies. The continuing shortage of spare parts, machine-guns and bomb sights was brought to Churchill's attention by another air force officer, Lachlan MacLean, who had been introduced to him by Torr Anderson. Like Anderson, MacLean had been wounded in the First World War, and had then joined the Royal Flying Corps.

In 1937 Lachlan MacLean was the senior Air Staff Officer at the headquarters of Bomber Group. 'Accompanying Anderson,' he later recalled, 'I was intro-duced to Winston in his flat in Westminster and he congratulated me on the paper and we discussed the air rearmament.' Thereafter, MacLean recalled, he would often write a paper for Churchill to refer to for a speech or for a letter to the Prime Minister. Sometimes they would discuss the problems at Morpeth Mansions.

After his conversation with MacLean, Churchill wrote to Inskip to advise him to get the Air Ministry to prepare a detailed list of everything a squadron required and then to pay a surprise visit to an Air Squadron. In this way, Churchill advised, Inskip might begin to learn the true state of the air force. Churchill told Inskip that he was not raising these matters in public for fear of still further exposing British weakness abroad.

Both Anderson and MacLean understood the risks they were taking in bringing Churchill so much classified material, much of it giving the lie to Government claims of a high state of efficiency and preparedness. Yet both accepted the risks, knowing that Churchill had the means, often by direct correspondence with Ministers, to try to get matters put right.

For his part, Churchill understood the dilemma facing these two officers. One day, while lying in bed working, he noticed that Anderson appeared somewhat nervous. Churchill tried to reassure Anderson that he was doing his duty. 'You must realize that loyalty to the State *must* come before loyalty to the Service.'

Churchill was scrupulously careful that none of the secret information which reached him was divulged to those outside the highest echelons of Govern-ment. And for their part, Ministers seemed to accept this arrangement. On reading MacLean's notes about spare-part deficiencies, Inskip returned them to Churchill, writing that he would not keep them among his papers as Churchill had said they should be treated 'as very confidential'.

During the spring of 1937 Churchill became aware of anxiety within the Royal Navy concerning the existing dispersal of control over the various craft concerned in the defence of trade: particularly flying boats and specialized shore-based aircraft. The Admiralty was anxious to place all these craft under a single authority, the Fleet Air Arm, and within the Naval Air Division at the Admiralty it was decided that Churchill was the man whose help would be of the greatest value in presenting the case for unity. His reputation, in the navy at least, remained high: and his advocacy was considered worthwhile.

The approach from the Naval Air Division came from a 37-year-old member of the Division, Lord Louis Mountbatten, who sent Churchill eleven pages of notes, arguing that the Admiralty should control the Fleet Air Arm.

Churchill showed Mountbatten's notes to Desmond Morton, who wrote a memorandum based on them and expressed his astonishment at Churchill's detailed knowledge of Defence matters in all areas. Churchill then spoke in Parliament as Mountbatten and his colleagues had wished.

Again and again throughout 1937 Churchill wrote and spoke of the need for greater rearmament, collective security and vigilance. In May 1937 he warned a friend not to suppose that Britain's dangers were over. 'On the contrary,' he argued, '1937 and 1938 are years of our maximum weakness.'

Neither the strain of events, nor of his daily work on Marlborough, was able to break Churchill's will to persevere. At Chartwell work seldom finished before two or three in the morning, with dictation continuing to the last moment. Bill Deakin was now a regular and welcome participant in these late night sessions. Forty years later he remembered, 'the ruthless partition of the day, the planning of things all to time. There was never a wasted moment. He had intense control.'

The typists also recalled the Chartwell scene. 'He worked so hard himself', one of them, Grace Hamblin, later recalled, 'and was so absolutely dedicated to the task in hand that he expected the same from others.' As time passed, Miss Hamblin added, 'we who worked for him realized that in full return for the stress and strain, we had the rare privilege of getting to know the beauty of his dynamic, but gentle character'.

Not only those who worked for Churchill, but those who were his political opponents, saw his qualities. When Philip Snowden, the former Labour Chancellor of the Exchequer and one of Churchill's fiercest critics, died in the early summer of 1937, Snowden's widow wrote to Churchill: 'Your generosity to a political opponent marks you for ever in my eyes the "great gentleman" I have always thought you. Had I been in trouble which I could not control myself, there is none to whom I should have felt I could come with more confidence that I should be gently treated.'

Another voice of encouragement from the Left came from the young Oxford historian, A. L. Rowse, a Labour candidate and convinced radical. 'I have often been tempted', Rowse told Churchill, 'to write to say that, although on the other side of politics, I am strongly in agreement with your views on the organization of peace in Europe, and menace of German armaments and the necessity of our own rearmament.'

Thus the scattered and hitherto belittled forces which Churchill had come to lead gathered their strength and courage, against all the rigorous forces of Government majorities, the power of the Whips, the censure of *The Times*, and the accumulated innuendoes of more than five years.

On 26 May 1937 Neville Chamberlain succeeded Stanley Baldwin as Prime Minister. In the resulting Cabinet reshuffle, no post was offered to Churchill. Among senior Ministers, Inskip remained as 'coordinator' of Defence and Hoare went to the Home Office. Alfred Duff Cooper became First Lord of the Admiralty.

One young Liberal National MP who entered the Government was the 35-year-old Robert Bernays, who, as a backbencher, had sat next to Churchill below the gangway. 'I have only one regret,' Bernays wrote, 'and that is that I am now removed too far to hear your whispered and trenchant comments on the passing Parliamentary scene.' These had always been so 'exhilarating', Bernays said. He and every other young man in the House would always be grateful for the way in which Churchill continually demonstrated 'to what heights the arts of Parliamentary debate can be made to attain'.

Churchill had now been in Parliament for more than thirty-five years. Whenever he spoke, and whatever the debate, MPs flocked in to hear him. Even when they disagreed with his arguments they did not fail to be affected by his deep sense of concern and his powers of expression. His seniority expressed itself in other ways: in his friendship and magnanimity to young MPs, and in his thirty-year membership of the Privy Council. After Austen Chamberlain's death in March 1936, Churchill was indeed the senior Conservative Privy Councillor in the House of Commons, and as such was expected to second the resolution nominating Neville Chamberlain as party leader.

Churchill agreed to do so. In his speech of nomination he stressed the fact that the leadership of the Conservative party had never been interpreted 'in a dictatorial or despotic sense', and he appealed for the continued recognition of the rights of those who disagreed with Party policy: 'The House of Commons', he said, 'still survives as the arena of free debate. We feel sure that the leader we are about to choose will, as a distinguished Parliamentarian and a House of Commons man, not resent honest differences of opinion arising between those who mean the same thing, and that party opinion will not be denied its subordinate but still rightful place in his mind.'

It was an able speech, wrote one observer, 'not untouched by bitterness'.

Neville Chamberlain's succession to the Premiership seemed to bar Churchill from any chance of entering the Cabinet. The gulf between the two men, stretching back for more than a decade, was too deep. Nor was Chamberlain's Parliamentary position threatened. He had a clear Conservative majority of nearly 250 seats, and had no need to hold a General Election until the autumn of 1940.

Churchill's friends and supporters were distressed at his continuing political isolation. 'You are indeed a *very* great man', wrote one industrialist, a former Liberal Minister of Health, 'and God knows why you are not in the Cabinet.' But when another friend from Churchill's Liberal days wrote to him to stress the extent of the public view in Manchester that 'there is no great enterprising power existing in Parliament today equal to yourself', Churchill replied that he was not keen to become a member of the Government unless there were a specific task for him. The Government, he commented, 'are very pleased with themselves at present'.

Churchill remained for most of the summer at Chartwell. The work of the Government went on without his being asked to participate in any way, even for his general advice. Every day that Churchill was out of office, Lloyd George told a friend, made his return more difficult. Lloyd George also declared that no Cabinet Minister would want Churchill in the Government 'because of his dominating intellectual force and experience'.

However happy amid his paints and books, his lakes and gardens, his family and friends, Churchill found this isolation galling in the extreme, and told one young man who visited him of his sadness that Chamberlain, like Baldwin, had not given him a job. Furthermore, in foreign affairs and defence, Churchill told his guest, 'there's no plan of any kind for anything. It is no good. They walk in a fog. Everything is very black, very black.'

Churchill's work at Chartwell during the summer and autumn of 1937 centred on two projects: editing a collection of his former magazine articles for publication in book form, with the title *Great Contemporaries*, and trying to complete the final volume of his Marlborough biography. For this latter task, Bill Deakin was his constant supporter, travelling to many archives in search of previously unpublished letters. 'A young gentleman of high attainments and agreeable manners' was how Churchill described Deakin in a letter to one archive-owner.

Even as Churchill and Deakin delved into the past, a stream of visitors continued to descend upon Chartwell, to seek Churchill's advice on the international situation, and to give him information. One such visitor was the Rumanian Foreign Minister, Nicolae Titulescu, who sought reassurance that Britain would really be prepared to defend the threatened States of Europe against German aggression. Although Churchill had no Government position, it seemed to the Rumanian leader important to ascertain his view.

Other visitors to Chartwell in the summer of 1937 included the former German Prime Minister, Dr Brüning and one of Brüning's Cabinet Ministers, Dr Treviranus, who had narrowly escaped execution at Nazi hands by fleeing from Germany. Also at Chartwell that summer was the British Ambassador to Belgrade, who approved Churchill's plan to visit Yugoslavia, not only on holiday to see the sights and to paint, but also to speak there, as he had done in Paris, about the need for a European alliance against the German menace. Both Eden and Sir Robert Vansittart gave their approval to the visit. But Churchill cancelled it in the end, afraid that it would cause him to be out of England during several important Parliamentary debates.

Yet another visitor to Chartwell that summer was the new French Air Minister, Pierre Cot, who, after his return to Paris, sent Churchill the latest French Intelligence estimates of German air strength. In his reply Churchill stated his unease 'about the relative Anglo–French air strength compared to

Germany in 1938'. It was still 'the war potential of production' that was the main cause for concern as he studied Cot's figures.

Further cause for concern for the future reached Churchill late in May 1937 in the form of a comprehensive and recent survey of British air preparedness. The author of the survey was again Lachlan MacLean, who had compiled it on the basis of the most secret reports reaching him in his capacity as Senior Air Staff Officer at Bomber Group headquarters. MacLean's conclusion was that Germany would be ready in 1938 and Britain would 'be at the peak' of chaos, with no logical plan of war.

After studying MacLean's report carefully and discussing it with Lindemann, Churchill forwarded it, deleting MacLean's name, to both Chamberlain and Inskip. When Inskip relied that 'things had improved' since the memorandum was written, Churchill asked MacLean to prepare another one.

The second MacLean report was as alarming as the first. At least 100 squadrons out of 124 were, he explained on 22 June 1937, 'equipped with obsolete aircraft'. Some squadrons were even being formed with 'training type aircraft' only, and would be quite unsuitable for combat. Unknown to Churchill, the Cabinet itself received, only six days later, an official and highly secret report which also revealed the deficiencies which MacLean had indicated. According to this official report, the Air Ministry had admitted that there was an enormous discrepancy between the aircraft supplies being manufactured and what would be required in time of war. On the basis of this secret information, the Cabinet were told that on existing policies it would be impossible for the necessary air supply preparations to be completed by November 1939.

Unaware of this particular report, but all too well aware of the situation which it described, Churchill told a private meeting of the Anti-Nazi Council that lack of Government interference in the supply situation could only encourage the Germans – the 'Nazi gangsters', 'those savages', as he called them – to acts of aggression and violence 'of every kind'.

Once more Churchill prepared to publish his views of Hitler and Nazism. First, he sent his article to Sir Robert Vansittart, for Foreign Office comment. Vansittart was away, but his Private Secretary feared that too violent an attack on Hitler and Nazi Germany might do harm, 'in the present rather delicate state of our relations with that country'. Unwilling to create extra difficulties for British Foreign policy, when the defence situation was so weak, Churchill agreed to delete certain passages, 'to take the sting out of the article'. Even so, as published in the *Evening Standard* on 17 September 1937, the article was outspoken.

'I find myself pilloried by Dr Goebbels's Press as an enemy of Germany,' Churchill wrote. 'That description is quite untrue.' All his life he had worked to allow Germany her true place in the world, to avoid a vindictive peace in 1919, to prevent punitive reparations, and to encourage German democracy. His duty, however, lay to his own country, and in warning of the scale and dangers of German rearmament. 'I can quite understand', he added, 'that this action of mine would not be popular in Germany. Indeed, it was not popular any-where.'

In his article Churchill went on to tell the German Government: 'We cannot say we admire your treatment of the Jews or of the Protestants and Catholics of Germany.' Nevertheless, these matters 'as long as they are confined inside Germany, are not our business'. It was also possible, he wrote, to 'dislike Hitler's system and yet admire his patriotic achievement', and he added that if Britain were defeated he hoped she would find such an 'indomitable' champion to restore her to her former position.

Churchill now made a plea for a change in Nazi policy, asking, as he had done several times before, that 'the Fuhrer of Germany' should become 'the Hitler of peace'. 'Success', he said, 'should bring a mellow, genial air' and, changing the mood to fit the new circumstances, 'preserve and consolidate in tolerance and goodwill what has been gained by conflict'.

Churchill had, in private, no illusions about the likelihood of Hitler becoming more 'mellow'. He told his friend Lord Linlithgow, who had recently succeeded Willingdon as Viceroy of India, that he did not think there would be war in 1937 'because the French Army is at present as large as that of Germany and far more mature'. Next year and the year after, he warned might 'carry these Dictator-ridden countries to the climax of their armament and of their domestic embarrassments'.

In the privacy of his letter to Linlithgow, Churchill expressed his deepest fears for the immediate future: 'it would seem that 1938 will see Germany relatively stronger to the British Air Force and the French Army than now'.

On 12 October 1937, at a banquet in London, Churchill privately expressed his dismay at the lack of air readiness. Sir Maurice Hankey, who was present at the banquet, wrote at once to Inskip that, from Churchill's remarks, he judged that Churchill had a 'pretty shrewd knowledge of the situation'.

Further precise knowledge of Britain's air weakness was about to reach Churchill, within forty-eight hours of his remarks at the banquet. It concerned the visit to Britain of a high-level official German Air Mission, headed by General Milch, which planned to visit England for a week, beginning in five days time.

Among those whose job it was to plan for General Milch's visit was Lachlan MacLean, who had been told by the head of Bomber Command that to 'get up any sort of show' it would be necessary to search out planes from all over the country. In a letter written that same day, 12 October 1937, MacLean reported to Anderson, who at once passed on the information to Churchill, that the Air Ministry had decided to allow the German Air Mission to inspect, on the ground, one example of each modern type. These types were not yet fully equipped, with the result that they had not yet even been used for training. The Air Ministry was therefore in difficulties, first having to get the planes ready, and then having to train the pilots in order to lay on a fly-past for the German Air Mission.

In his covering note Lachlan MacLean warned that General Milch headed a group in Germany 'which suspects the real state of affairs, and that the mission is out to find confirmation of their suspicions'. Once the weakness of Britain's air readiness was revealed, MacLean added, It 'must inevitably influence German policy with regard to us, and foreign policy generally'. At present, he commented, 'we are bluffing with the sky as the limit, without holding a single card, and we have then invited our opponents to come round and see what cards we hold, trusting to sleight of hand to put across a second bluff'.

Churchill was much alarmed by MacLean's report. But he could not decide what to do with it. At the banquet on October 12 he had already told Hankey that he could not even use his information in Parliament, because of what he described to Hankey as 'the present dangerous world situation'. Recalling this conversation, and in view of Hankey's own position of authority both as Secretary to the Cabinet and Secretary to the Committee of Imperial Defence, Churchill now decided to put MacLean's report of the German Air Mission to Hankey himself.

Churchill wrote to Hankey on 16 October 1937, sending him, as he explained, 'one small instalment' of the 'alarming' reports he had received about the RAF. It was, he said, for Hankey's 'personal information', and he added: 'I trust to our friendship and your honour that its origin is not probed. But look at the facts!'

Churchill then set out the gist of MacLean's report, without naming his source. Drawing on MacLean's detailed notes and enclosures, Churchill pointed out that a power-driven turret was to be shown to the German Air Mission, 'as if it was the kind of thing we are doing in the regular way'. 'Ought it to be shown at all?' he asked. One of the only men who knew how the turret worked had been specially called upon to give a demonstration. Churchill asked Hankey to look at the statement of the Air Officer Commander-in-Chief, Bomber Command, Ludlow-Hewitt, that he was being 'forced to address himself to the task of making a show', as well as the effort needed to put a hundred bombers in the air, most of which, as the Mission would readily see, 'can barely reach the coast of Germany with a bomb load'.

Appealing to Hankey for his help, Churchill recalled the 'essential part' Hankey had played in the First World War, as Secretary to the Cabinet, 'in saving the country over the convoy system', how, when young officers had gone to Hankey 'and told you the truth, against Service rules, you saw that the seed did not fall on stony ground'.

To Churchill's amazement Hankey responded not with appreciation or suggestions, but with a stern rebuke. While agreeing in this particular instance 'not to probe the origin of the information' which Churchill had sent, he went on to castigate Churchill in outspoken terms. 'It shocks me not a little', he wrote, that officers of high rank in the Forces should be in 'direct communication' with a 'leading Statesman' who, though notorious for his patriotism, was 'a critic of the Departments under whom these officers serve'.

Hankey went on to point out to Churchill that those officers who gave him information 'jeopardize their official careers, for a slip might prove disastrous to them'.

Having told Churchill that he felt 'in his bones' that the giving of information to Churchill was 'wrong', 'infectious', and 'subversive to discipline', Hankey went on to speak about the position 'of the recipient of such illicit information'. It could, he said, be 'embarrassing'. Indeed, Hankey added, had he approached Churchill with such material before the Great War, when Churchill was First Lord, he felt sure that 'you would have turned on me pretty hard', and might well have demanded an Inquiry.

Churchill was staggered by Hankey's rebuke. Ten years later, in a private letter to Eden, he was to describe Hankey's friendship in the later years as 'the caress of a worm'. Now Churchill wrote tersely to Hankey in reply: 'My dear Maurice, I certainly did not expect to receive from you a lengthy lecture when I went out of my way to give you, in strict confidence, information in the public interest. I thank you for sending me the papers back, and you may be sure I shall not trouble you again in such matters.'

Even while Churchill was being rebuffed by Hankey, the Cabinet was learning, from the Secretary of State for Air, Lord Swinton, that by December 1939 Britain's front-line air strength of 1,736 as against Germany's 3,240 first-line aircraft, would even so be only a 'facade', as the British figure did not include reserves.

Swinton's conclusion, the gist of which was only to reach Churchill, through Anderson, some months later, was a stark one. At the present time, Swinton wrote, the Royal Air Force was in a 'position of grave inferiority' to Germany 'in effective air strength'. When the existing British expansion programme was completed it would not 'provide an adequate remedy'. In conclusion, Swinton noted that Baldwin's pledge of parity would not even be made good by 1939.

There was one further sequel to the visit of the German Air Mission. On 20 October 1937 Churchill himself dined privately with the Mission at a London Club. Lord Swinton was among those present. A month later a member of the British Embassy in Berlin sent the Foreign Office an account of the Mission's reaction to the dinner. 'Lord Swinton's charm delighted them,' the diplomat reported. Although Churchill had obviously impressed them as a personality, the Mission 'had not taken to him' as he had appeared to be 'an implacable enemy of German aspirations'.

Throughout 1937, Churchill had tried to combat the pro-German feeling that was gaining in strength. He was encouraged to do so by Paul Maze, the painter whom he had first befriended on the western front in 1915, and who now wrote to urge him to write as often as he could in the papers because the 'German propaganda spread about is most harmful, especially in Mayfair society!'

Churchill had an uphill struggle. The confusion in attitudes towards Germany had intensified since the Rhineland crisis of the previous year. 'We have

Randolph Churchill: a photograph taken during one of his three unsuccessful attempts to enter Parliament in the 1930s.

Winston S. Churchill

DUTY

"Let us, therefore, addr
ourselves to our duty and
bear ourselves that, if t
British Commonwealth a
Empire lasts for a thousa
years, men will say : 'T
was their finest hour.'"

WINSTON CHURCHIL
IN PARLIAMENT,
JUNE 18, 1940.

Our artist thinks he knows how Mr. Winston Churchill secures his information regarding Germany's rearmaments.

LEFT Churchill and Ralph Wigram walking in the grounds of Chartwell. The photograph was taken by Ava Wigram with her box camera: Churchill signed it, and Ava Wigram added to it a press cutting of Churchill's speech of 18 June 1940. This photograph stood, framed, at her bedside, until her death in 1974.

ABOVE A cartoon published in the *Daily Record and Mail* on 23 July 1936, speculating on the source of Churchill's information about German rearmament during the 1930s.

RIGHT Wing Commander Torr Anderson, DFC, Director of the Royal Air Force Training School, who gave Churchill secret information about air force deficiencies.

ABOVE Churchill at the unveiling of a memorial plaque to Lawrence of Arabia at the City of Oxford High School, 14 October 1936.

RIGHT Pierre Etienne Flandin, Prime Minister of France from November 1934 to June 1935, and Foreign Minister from January to June 1936, who agreed to send Churchill the French Government's secret intelligence estimates of German air strength.

LEFT ABOVE Randolph Churchill (with a fur collar) among the crowd outside Buckingham Palace on 18 February 1936, watching the arrivals for King Edward VIII's first investiture.
LEFT BELOW King Edward VIII and Mrs Simpson on a cruise in the Adriatic in the summer of 1936, before their romance became widely known.
ABOVE Sir Thomas Inskip, Minister for the Coordination of Defence: a photograph taken in December 1936, during the Abdication crisis.

ABOVE Stanley Baldwin, the outgoing Prime Minister, receiving a gift from his successor, Neville Chamberlain, May 1937.
BELOW Neville Chamberlain, Sir Kingsley Wood and Sir Samuel Hoare, photographed in London during Chamberlain's premiership.

ABOVE Churchill and Sir Samuel Hoare, on 31 May 1937, not long after Churchill had learned that he had not received a place in the new administration: Hoare, who had resigned as Foreign Secretary at the end of 1935, was now Home Secretary.
BELOW The Foreign Secretary, Anthony Eden (left) and Sir Robert Vansittart, his Permanent Under Secretary, leaving the Foreign Office, September 1937.

ABOVE Churchill signing autographs during the Conservative Party Conference at Scarborough on 7 October 1937.

BELOW Churchill in his constituency, at the opening of a fifty-acre recreation area, 14 October 1937. His medals include those for the campaign of 1897 on the northwest frontier of India, the battle of Omdurman in 1898, and the Boer War, 1899 to 1901, when he had been taken prisoner.

RIGHT Churchill with Consuelo Balsan, formerly the wife of his cousin 'Sunny' Marlborough, and the wife of Colonel Jacques Balsan. This snapshot was taken by a fellow guest and painter, Paul Maze.

LEFT Churchill painting in the south of France.
ABOVE Violet Pearman, Churchill's principal secretary from 1929 to 1938, photographed at the Château de l'Horizon, Maxine Elliot's villa near Cannes.
BELOW The window display in Harrods, Knightsbridge, on the publication of Churchill's *Great Contemporaries* in January 1938.

LEFT Churchill and his son Randolph, photographed on 2 March 1938 at the time of Anthony Eden's resignation from the Cabinet, 'a good week', as Churchill had called it, 'for Dictators'.

ABOVE Lord Hailsham, the Lord Chancellor, photographed outside 10 Downing Street with Sir Kingsley Wood, the Secretary of State for Air from May 1938 to April 1940.

BELOW 'Going thro' the Files', a cartoon published in the *Yorkshire Observer* on 21 May 1938, commenting on Churchill's call for the setting up a Ministry of Supply. He had first suggested this in 1936 in a letter to Sir Thomas Inskip (left). But it was still under consideration when Sir Kingsley Wood (right) became Secretary of State for Air in 1938, and was not in fact created until late in 1939.

ABOVE Joachim von Ribbentrop, the German Foreign Minister, talking to his British counterpart, Lord Halifax, at a farewell party at the German Embassy on 10 March 1938.
BELOW Neville Chamberlain arriving at Heston airport after his first visit to Hitler in Germany, 16 September 1938.
RIGHT Neville Chamberlain on his arrival at Cologne on 22 September 1938 during the Czech crisis. Ribbentrop (left) shakes hands with Sir Horace Wilson, while Chamberlain looks on.

Hitler at Bad Godesberg, 22 September 1938, flanked by his interpreter and Neville Chamberlain.

ABOVE LEFT 'Four's Company', a cartoon by Bernard Partridge published in *Punch* after the Munich Agreement, showing the four participants, Mussolini, Daladier, Chamberlain and Hitler, drinking to their agreement. The President of Czechoslovakia, whose country had been partitioned, but who had not been invited to the conference, looks on dolefully from the portrait frame above.

ABOVE RIGHT Alfred Duff Cooper in Downing Street, on his way to resign from the Cabinet after the Munich Agreement, 3 October 1938. Churchill wept when he heard that Duff Cooper had resigned.

BELOW 'Now boys . . .', a cartoon published in *Tribune* on 21 October 1938, showing Churchill, Anthony Eden (centre) and Alfred Duff Cooper (right) being rebuked by Neville Chamberlain (as the schoolmaster) for their speeches after Munich warning of the continuing Nazi menace.

ABOVE Churchill in his study at Chartwell, photographed on 25 February 1939.

LEFT Bill Deakin, Churchill's research assistant from 1936 to 1939, first on the biography of Marlborough, then on the *History of the English-speaking Peoples*, and again from 1946 to 1949 on the Second World War memoirs. During the war Deakin parachuted into Nazi-occupied Yugoslavia as the first British liaison officer with Tito and his partisans.

RIGHT Churchill and Brendan Bracken setting off from Bracken's house for the House of Commons for the debate on the Italian invasion of Albania, 13 April 1939.

ABOVE Churchill with Anthony Eden and the Rumanian Foreign Minister, Grigore Gafencu (right), after a luncheon given at the Foreign Office on 24 April 1939.
BELOW A poster which appeared in the Strand, London, in the last week of July 1939. On 25 July 1939 the *Daily Mirror* asked: 'The writing on the wall? This giant poster is causing considerable comment.'
RIGHT Churchill at Consuelo Balsan's château, photographed by Paul Maze on 21 August 1939, before Churchill's return to England, and the crisis leading to the outbreak of war.

Churchill arrives at the Admiralty on 4 September 1939, to begin work as First Lord of the Admiralty, a post which he had held from 1911 to 1915. On 10 May 1940 he left the Admiralty again, to become Prime Minister.

abundant evidence', the former Cabinet Deputy Secretary, Tom Jones, wrote to a friend, 'of the desire of all sorts of Germans to be on friendly terms with us.' Jones added: 'I keep on and on preaching against the policy of ostracising Germany, however incalculable Hitler and his crew may be, and the duty of resisting Vansittart's pro-French bias.'

In seeking to combat views of this sort, Churchill wrote more than a hundred articles in 1937 alone, including a monthly article syndicated throughout the United States in *Collier's*, a fortnightly article in the *Evening Standard*, and a weekly article in the *News of the World*. This last, with a readership of over four million, represented, as Churchill wrote to its owner, 'the stable, sagacious, good-humoured, kind-hearted mass of the British nation'. In addition, as a result of the strenuous efforts of Emery Reves, a young Hungarian refugee who had fled from Berlin and was then living in Paris, Churchill's articles were now appearing in more than a dozen European newspapers, and almost as many foreign languages. The theme of his articles was clear: Nazi tyranny was evil, Nazi ambitions were dangerous, and unless the threatened States of Europe were to combine in a common effort of defence, each would succumb in its turn, unaided, to the Nazi will.

Several of Churchill's closest friends, particularly those who lived in the very Mayfair society of which Paul Maze had written, disagreed with his interpretation of Nazi intentions, and of Nazi tyranny. Even Lord Londonderry, who three years earlier had warned the Cabinet of the dangers of Germany's air rearmament, now argued publicly that Anglo–German friendship was still possible, despite the nature of Nazism. Lady Londonderry, who had visited Hitler in Berlin in February 1937, had been strongly impressed by his 'great desire' for friendship with England. Surely, she wrote in the *Anglo–German Review* on her return to England, 'this offer of friendship merits acceptance in the spirit in which it has been made, instead of the rather suspicious view with which our Foreign Office with its Gallic bias, appears to take it'.

In a letter to Lord Londonderry on 23 October 1937, Churchill told his cousin: 'you cannot expect English people to be attracted by the brutal intolerances of Nazidom even though these may fade with time'. Nor could Englishmen be expected to welcome friendship with Germany if it meant giving the Germans a free hand in Central and Southern Europe. Such an attitude, Churchill believed, 'means that they would devour Austria and Czechoslovakia as a preliminary to making a gigantic middle-Europe block'.

Churchill went on to tell Londonderry that it was his deep conviction that it would be 'wrong and cynical in the last degree to buy immunity for ourselves at the expense of the smaller countries of Central Europe'. It would also go against opinion in the United States and Britain to allow Nazi tyranny to dominate countries which now enjoyed 'a considerable measure' of democracy. British goodwill for Germany could easily be achieved, however, Churchill concluded, if Germany ceased to 'commit crimes'.

Inside Germany it was believed that the British Government would never bring itself to challenge Germany's actions, at home or abroad. Even the German army, Desmond Morton reported to Churchill in October 1937, were said to favour 'a military parade against Czechoslovakia', once it had become certain 'that neither France nor England will intervene on the Czechs' behalf'. A month later Churchill wrote to his friend Lord Linlithgow of the 'increasingly grim' situation in Europe. Peace, he warned, 'dwells under the shield of the French army'. But in a few years' time the German army would not only be 'much larger' than the French army, but 'increasingly its equal in maturity'.

The 'deadly years' of British policy, Churchill told Linlithgow, were 1932 to 1935 – '"the years that the locusts have eaten"'. 'I expect', Churchill added, 'we shall experience the consequences of these years in the near future.'

Churchill had no intention, however, of giving up his faith in the eventual re-emergence of Britain's will to resist. The British people, he told Linlithgow, were 'united and healthy', the British spirit was 'reviving', and the working people were ready 'to defend the cause of liberty with their lives'. The United States, Churchill noted, 'signals encouragement to us, for what that is worth'.

The American 'signal' was, in fact, an attempt by Roosevelt to try to involve the United States more directly in European affairs. Churchill supported Roosevelt's initiative, as did Anthony Eden. But Neville Chamberlain opposed it, and was strengthened in his opposition by a confidant whose influence was growing daily, Sir Horace Wilson. Eden resented Wilson's influence – inside the Foreign Office he was known as 'Creeping Jesus' – and was angered by Chamberlain's somewhat aloof attitude to the United States, an attitude that Wilson encouraged.

Horace Wilson had entered the civil service at the time of the Boer War, and by dint of hard work and diligence had risen to be the Chief Industrial Adviser to the Government. In this capacity, he had become an indispensable aide to Neville Chamberlain during Chamberlain's six years as Chancellor of the Exchequer. When Chamberlain moved to 10 Downing Street he wanted Wilson to move with him, and later he was to appoint Wilson to be both Head of the Civil Service and Head of the Treasury, a position of considerable power.

From the outset of Chamberlain's premiership, Wilson had a room adjacent to the Cabinet room. Often, after Chamberlain had been in dispute with Eden over foreign policy, and as Eden left the room, Chamberlain would ask Wilson to see him, and would look to Wilson to put his mind at ease. Wilson quickly became indispensable: helping to remove, as he himself later recalled, the 'poison' of Eden's or Vansittart's views, and encouraging Chamberlain to persevere in his new course, of reconciliation with Germany and Italy, and suspicion of the American initiative.

Wilson was also an advocate of direct Anglo–German talks, with the French excluded. He therefore supported Lord Halifax's visit to Germany at the end of 1937. Ostensibly, the visit was a social one; Halifax was to join Goering on a hunting expedition on one of Goering's estates. But during the visit Halifax had long talks with all the leading Nazi personalities, as well as with Hitler.

On his return from Germany Halifax gave the Cabinet a detailed account of his visit. His aim, he said, had been to obtain an 'impression of the German outlook and the possibilities of a settlement'. He had been 'warmly received by the German crowds' and had generally encountered 'friendliness'. There was a desire for 'good relations between Germany and the United Kingdom'. Hitler did not consider the world to be in a dangerous state and Goering had said that 'not one drop of German blood would be spilt in Europe unless it was forced on them'.

Halifax said that he expected the Germans to continue to work to achieve their aims in Central Europe in such a way that other countries would not need to become involved. He believed that 'the basis of an understanding might not be too difficult as regards Central and Eastern Europe'.

Hitler had asked Halifax if Britain was prepared to reach an understanding about colonies. He had also talked of the possibility of disarmament, beginning with 'the possible abolition of bombing aeroplanes'. According to the official record, the Cabinet expressed itself 'interested' in this, for although it entailed the risk of 'enabling the German army to dominate Europe' it also removed 'the risk of a knock-out blow at the outset of a war'.

Chamberlain believed that any agreement on colonies should be 'a quid pro quo' for agreements on Central Europe 'and on armaments', to which, he said, 'he attached special importance as they threatened to crush all the nations'. He hoped for some kind of limitation in the size and power of weapons rather than in their numbers. As to the League of Nations, Chamberlain told his colleagues, 'he took the same view as Herr Hitler. At present it was largely a sham, owing more particularly to the idea that it could impose its views by force.'

On 21 December 1937 the House of Commons, against Chamberlain's wishes, debated Halifax's visit to Hitler. Chamberlain was afraid that the debate might endanger the Government's search for a rapprochement with Germany. In this fear he was not entirely mistaken, for Churchill, in a powerful speech, denounced Nazi tyranny and the persecution of the Jews. It was horrible, he said, that attempts should be made to blot out a race from the society 'in which they have been born', or that, from their earliest years, 'little children should be segregated, and that they should be exposed to scorn and odium. It is very painful.'

Lord Halifax's visit, Churchill declared, had caused 'widespread commotion', because the idea was growing that Britain might be 'making terms' for herself at the expense both of 'small nations' and of 'large conceptions' which many millions of people held dear.

Knowing full well that Neville Chamberlain despised the League of Nations, even if he did not know that 'he took the same view as Herr Hitler', Churchill took the opportunity of his speech on Halifax's meeting with Hitler to stress once more the importance of the League of Nations, not only as a necessary centre of any coordinated military effort against aggression, but as the focal point of morality in international affairs. Churchill explained that the arms he had been urging the Government to make for five years would not protect Britain if the 'moral forces involved in the public opinion of the world' were ignored. In a phrase which he had first heard used by Ralph Wigram, Churchill told the House of Commons that it would be wrong for any nation to give up 'one scrap of territory just to keep the Nazi kettle boiling'. After the debate Ava Wigram wrote to tell Churchill 'how necessary' his speech had been and how much she wished 'Ralph could have known about it.'

Churchill returned to Chartwell for the Christmas holiday and for the ever pressing work on his final Marlborough volume, of which he had now completed 200,000 words. Clementine Churchill had gone to Austria to recover from one of those periods of fatigue, of which her daughter Mary has written sympathetically: these 'bouts of mental and physical exhaustion were as much "illnesses" as influenza or measles'. Clementine's exhaustion, while often brought on by relatively trivial causes, needed long spells of recuperation, and above all absence from the tensions and exhilarations of life at Chartwell, and the financial problems of organizing so large a household, and so much entertaining of both political colleagues and friends.

Each time Clementine was away on her frequent and at times prolonged recuperations, Churchill, in long and tender letters, sought to calm and comfort her, and to make her feel that she was missed by all those at Chartwell, and by no one more than himself. Without her, Churchill was lonely, and felt he had no ally with whom to share his deepest worries and concerns.

Churchill and his son spent the Christmas of 1937 at Blenheim and the New Year of 1938 at Chartwell. Sarah was back in America, on tour with Vic Oliver. Clementine, Mary and Diana were in Austria. 'On Christmas night we all went to a dance at one of the big hotels', Clementine reported to her husband, 'and I provided Champagne for dinner!' Churchill's own holidays were proving somewhat overcast. 'I had a horrible cold', he wrote to a friend, 'which has kept me indoors for the best part of a fortnight. I have turned on all the electric heaters, and sealed down the windows.' But on 2 January 1938 he set off for the brilliant sunshine of the Riviera, for two weeks at the Château de l'Horizon: he was looking 'very tired', Mrs Pearman wrote to a friend.

'I am coming quite alone, with no servant,' Churchill wrote to his hostess Maxine Elliot, 'but Mrs Pearman, whom you know will overtake me with mails etc and the usual consignment of book proofs a few days later.' As Churchill travelled from London to Paris, Clementine wrote to him from Austria: 'I like to think of you today speeding towards the South, and, I hope sunshine'; and she added: 'Do not work too hard there.'

Before going to Cannes, Churchill stayed for two days at the British Embassy in Paris, where the news of the hour was Sir Robert Vansittart's removal from his position as Permanent Under Secretary of State at the Foreign Office, to a new and entirely nominal post of Diplomatic Adviser to the Government. Churchill was emphatic that Vansittart's displacement 'was a very dangerous thing', the British Ambassador in Paris wrote to Sir Maurice Hankey. Vansittart's dismissal, Churchill argued, would be represented everywhere 'as a victory for the pro-Germans in England'. In addition, Churchill feared that the French Government would rightly interpret the change as detrimental to the close Anglo–French cooperation which Vansittart had championed.

While he was still at the British Embassy in Paris, Churchill had a long talk with Léon Blum, who had been Prime Minister from mid-1936 to mid-1937, and was to be Prime Minister again from March to April 1938. Blum began, as Churchill reported to his wife, 'by admitting the bad state of French aviation, and that I had warned him about it 18 months ago!' It was difficult, Churchill reflected, 'to persuade people of facts till too late'. Blum also confirmed certain ominous news which bore out other of Churchill's fears about British air preparedness. When the French Prime Minister, Camille Chautemps, and the Foreign Minister, Edouard Daladier, had seen Chamberlain in London, so Blum reported, 'Neville told them that we were making 350 machines a month. They were deeply impressed.' But now it appeared that Chamberlain 'was wrongly informed, the true figure being only $\frac{1}{2}$'. As a result, Churchill added, there was 'a certain reproaching' going on between Chamberlain and the Air Ministry.

Churchill had already learned from Desmond Morton that 'what happened', as he told Clementine, 'was that poor Neville believed the lie that the Air Ministry circulated for public purposes' and did not know the true figures. 'This gives you some idea', Churchill reflected, 'of the looseness with which we are governed in these vital matters.'

As for the outcome of this episode, 'it ought', Churchill wrote, 'to make Neville think. He does not know the truth: perhaps he does not want to.'

From Paris Churchill travelled south to the Château de l'Horizon, for a month's relaxation, painting and writing. But even there he could not escape the burden of a heavy mail bag – often ten and even twenty letters a day – dominated by news of Nazi plans and exercises. On 4 January 1938 a young British journalist, Ian Colvin, wrote to him from Berlin of a planned German occupation of strategically important Czech towns, probably in March. Four days later a German professor wrote to Churchill, to accuse him of wishing to stir up quarrels between Britain and Germany. Churchill replied at once: 'As long as Germany does not embark upon a policy of aggression there can be no possible quarrel between our two countries,' though of course, he added, 'it is painful to every country to see the cruel persecution of the Jews, Protestants and Catholics, and the general suppression of Parliamentary life.'

After a week in the south of France, but cheated within a few days of his arrival of the sunshine he had hoped for, Churchill was back in his old routine of writing. Mrs Pearman wrote to tell Professor Lindemann that Churchill was working 'very, very hard' and that she herself was glad he was not at Chartwell where he would have 'tired himself out'. In England Bill Deakin worked on correcting the Marlborough footnotes and references, and passing on to the printer extra passages which Churchill continued to send him. From England Torr Anderson continued to send Churchill details of setbacks and gaps in the pilot training and aircraft production programmes.

While in the south of France Churchill dined with the former French Prime Minister, Pierre Étienne Flandin, who gave a 'most pessimistic' account of French morale. The Duke of Windsor, Eden and Lloyd George were also dinner guests at the Château. 'There is much talk about the bad state of the Air Force', Churchill wrote to his wife, 'upon which a great deal of information has been sent to me through sources of which you are aware.' He did not, however, intend to speak publicly about these deficiencies. 'The Ministers', he explained, 'are at last realizing all these facts which I explained and predicted in detail two or three years ago.'

Not only were Ministers realizing how far behind they were, they were now also working towards their new policy, replacing 'parity' by the search for improved relations with Germany.

In December 1937 and January 1938 the Government was also in consternation over the mounting cost of the defence programmes, after a panel of Treasury experts, led by Inskip, and including Sir Horace Wilson, had reported on their findings. On 15 December 1937 Inskip had written to the Cabinet that 'economic stability' was 'the fourth arm in defence'. If any country detected any strain in Britain's economic situation, he warned, there would no longer be any deterrent to war. It was, therefore, necessary, he concluded, to reduce Britain's defence commitments, including a continental army to defend Belgium and France, as well as reducing the Air Ministry's suggested future expansion programme.

There was a fierce dispute in the Cabinet on 22 December 1937 when Lord Swinton argued that the Air Ministry's new plan was 'carefully worked out' and could not be reduced without completely reversing Baldwin's publicly declared policy of parity. To this Neville Chamberlain replied: 'No pledge can last for ever', and insisted that the scheme be reduced. Lord Halifax pointed out in consequence, that it was therefore even more important to improve 'relations with Germany'.

As a result of this discussion, the three Defence Departments were asked to reduce their estimates.

On 21 January 1938 the Air Staff warned the Cabinet in a 'most secret' report that the scale of air reserves contemplated in the revised air programme was 'inadequate'. Commenting on the new restrictions on defence spending, the Secretary of State for India – Lord Zetland – wrote to the Viceroy to explain that the Government had given up trying to achieve an 'ideal' standard of defence because the cost of the programmes was proving too great.

Neville Chamberlain was not alarmed by this sombre conclusion. He believed that the new policy was preferable as it was based upon getting away from the belief that war was inevitable, and seeking avenues of contact and reconciliation with Germany.

On 27 January 1938 Chamberlain outlined the first phase of the new policy to his inner Cabinet. His plan was to enable Germany to become once more one of the 'African colonial powers', by giving her certain territories to administer.

Four days later Chamberlain's adviser, Sir Horace Wilson, explained the new policy in a letter to a friend. He hoped it would alleviate the general mood of depression by encouraging the idea that the outlook was 'less dangerous'.

Churchill returned to Chartwell in the first week of February. One of his first visitors was the former British Air Attaché in Berlin, Frank Don, who, although still a serving officer, came privately to report to Churchill about the marked German superiority in machines, men, reserves and supplies. In March another source of information was the young diplomat, and Wigram's colleague of 1935, Michael Creswell. Just back after two and a half years in Berlin, Creswell was to give Churchill up to date information on the growing weakness of the French army vis-à-vis the German army, a situation about which Churchill had warned repeatedly.

On 17 February 1938, during a meeting of the Foreign Affairs Committee of the House of Commons, it became apparent that Eden was becoming isolated in his efforts to get a stronger policy with regard to Italy. Churchill supported Eden during the Committee meeting, saying that Britain should 'not throw sops or slops about', and not keep giving way to Italy. On the following day, however, Eden attended a meeting between Chamberlain and the Italian Ambassador during which Chamberlain made it clear he wanted to open conversations with the Italian Government.

After this meeting, Eden told Chamberlain that he felt that direct conversations were not the right way to deal with the Italian Government, which was not honouring promises it had already made.

Chamberlain agreed to put the matter before the Cabinet, and did so on 19 February 1938, when he explained that he was trying to get on better terms with Italy and Germany because of the burden of rearmament, and that it was possible to make 'an adjustment in our relations with Italy'. Furthermore, Chamberlain believed that the Italian desire for conversations was an opportunity not to be missed, and he wanted to tell the Italian Ambassador that Britain was now prepared to open diplomatic conversations in Rome. Eden replied that he did not think Mussolini's attitude had changed. He also believed that the Italians were giving the Germans a free hand in Austria, and that diplomatic conversations with Britain would increase Mussolini's prestige, giving him greater value for Hitler.

The majority of the Cabinet supported Chamberlain. Eden then told them that he could not carry such a policy in the House of Commons. On 20 February 1938, after talking to the Prime Minister, Eden announced his resignation from the Cabinet. Thus Chamberlain's main critic in the Cabinet was out-manoeuvred, and defeated.

That night, after he had heard the news of Eden's resignation, Churchill was unable to sleep. 'From midnight to dawn', he recalled ten years later, 'I lay in my bed consumed by emotions of sorrow and fear.' There had seemed 'one strong young figure standing up against long, dismal drawling tides of drift and surrender, of wrong measurements and feeble impulses'. Now he was gone. 'I watched the daylight slowly creep in through the windows, and saw before me in mental gaze the vision of Death.'

On 21 February 1938 Eden prepared to make his resignation speech in the House of Commons. Churchill was worried that when the moment to speak came Eden might hesitate to reveal the full extent of his disagreement with the Government. He therefore urged Eden that morning not to allow his 'personal feelings of friendship' towards his ex-colleagues to prevent him from making his case as fully as possible, or saying anything that might inhibit him in any future criticisms.

Churchill urged Eden to speak not only on his own behalf, but on behalf of his cause, which was also 'the cause of England'. In his speech, Eden rose to the occasion, insisting that the moment had come for Britain 'to stand firm'. But Chamberlain replied that Britain should lose no opportunity of beginning talks with both Italy and Germany, in the cause of peace.

Eden's resignation was a relief to those who wished to pursue negotiations with Italy and Germany. With Eden gone, Sir Maurice Hankey wrote to a friend, 'I felt there was just a possibility of peace', while Sir Thomas Inskip told Hankey that as a result of Eden's resignation he could at last sleep at night.

Neville Chamberlain was likewise relieved by the departure of so critical a colleague, telling the House of Commons that direct negotiations with the dictators were essential, because the League of Nations could no longer protect anyone. Churchill again spoke forcefully in defence of the League. Small countries in Europe, he warned, would now see that the dictators represented determination and strength whereas the democracies were weak and 'confused'. In these circumstances they would no longer look to the democratic powers for protection but would start to try to come to terms with their enemies.

Since Eden's resignation, Churchill said, 'all over the world, in every land, under every sky, and every system of government, wherever they may be, the friends of England are dismayed, and the foes of England are exuberant'. It will be universally believed, he said, 'that it is Signor Mussolini's superior power which has procured the overthrow of the British Foreign Secretary'.

Churchill feared that Eden's resignation marked the end of the 'old policy' of trying to maintain the rule of law in Europe and establishing sufficient deterrents against the aggressor. In its place he feared a new policy of 'submission' in order to preserve peace.

Churchill ended his speech with a prophetic warning. With Austria and Czechoslovakia already threatened, he believed that a time would come when retreat would no longer be possible: 'I predict', he said, 'that the day will come when, at some point or other, on some issue or other, you will have to make a stand, and I pray to God that, when that day comes, we may not find through an unwise policy, that we have to make that stand alone.'

With Eden's resignation, the change in direction of British policy had become widely known, accentuating the divisions in public opinion. Commenting on the Eden resignation debate, Lord Beaverbrook's *Daily Express* accused Churchill of supporting a 'violent, foolish and dangerous' campaign to drive Britain into war. But the *Yorkshire Post*, the most influential Conservative newspaper outside London, said that Churchill had voiced many people's 'anxiety'.

This anxiety increased considerably as Nazi pressure mounted on the Austrian Government, and Hitler spoke publicly and violently against the forthcoming plebiscite, in which Austrians were to be asked to vote for or against independence. On 12 March 1938, a few days before the plebiscite was to be held, German forces massed on the Austrian border. At that moment Churchill was lunching at 10 Downing Street, as one of Chamberlain's guests, to say farewell to the German Ambassador, von Ribbentrop, who was about to return to Berlin to become Foreign Minister. During the luncheon Chamberlain received a message reporting that according to the German Government the German troops massing at the Austrian frontier were merely 'training'. Churchill recalled the uneasy atmosphere as he and the other guests said goodbye to the guests of honour. Ribbentrop and his wife, however, were completely unruffled and Churchill recalled how 'they tarried for nearly half-an-hour engaging their host and hostess in voluble conversation'. As the guests were about to depart, Churchill exchanged some words with Frau Ribbentrop: 'in a valedictory vein, I said, "I hope England and Germany will preserve their friendship." "Be careful you don't spoil it," was her graceful rejoinder.'

That same evening German troops crossed into Austria. Clementine Churchill's cousin, Unity Mitford, an admirer of Hitler, was convinced that every Austrian would rejoice at the Nazi success. Churchill was outraged, telling Unity Mitford that Hitler's 'dastardly outrage' against Austria was the result of the Dictator's knowledge that a 'fair plebiscite' would have gone against the Nazis.

On 14 March 1938 Churchill explained to the House of Commons what he believed to be the results and implications of Hitler's occupation of Austria. It was essential, he said, for Britain to make its position clear. 'Delay' he believed 'would be harmful' and he asked: 'Why should we assume that time is on our side? I know of nothing to convince me that if the evil forces now at work are suffered to feed upon their successes and upon their victims our task will be easier when finally we are all united.'

The 'gravity' of Hitler's occupation of Austria, Churchill said, could not be exaggerated. Hitler was confronting Europe with a carefully worked out 'programme of aggression' and as this programme unfolded the only choice was either to 'submit' as Austria had done, or to take effective measures to make resistance possible. Churchill warned that resistance would be hard, but he continued: 'I am persuaded – and the Prime Minister's speech confirms me –

that it is to this conclusion of resistance to overweening encroachment that His Majesty's Government will come, and the House of Commons will certainly sustain them in playing a great part in the effort to preserve the peace of Europe, and, if it cannot be preserved, to preserve the freedom of the nations of Europe.' If Britain delayed, Churchill warned, the situation would become even more difficult. 'How many friends would be alienated,' he asked, 'how many potential allies should we see go, one by one, down the grisly gulf, how many times would bluff succeed, until behind bluff ever-gathering forces had accumulated reality?'

Churchill went on to warn the House of Commons that in two years time the German army would be stronger than that of the French and 'all the small nations will have fled from the League of Nations to try to come to terms with the Nazis'. People were concerned about the tragedy of Austria and the persecution of its people but, Churchill warned, the *Anschluss* has even wider ramifications. Vienna was the centre of Eastern European communications and, together with the Danube, gave Nazi Germany military and economic control of all Eastern Europe. The Little Entente – Rumania with its oil, Yugoslavia with its minerals and Czechoslovakia with its munitions – together with their combined armies had hitherto been a formidable power. Now, however, Czechoslovakia was isolated, and a 'wedge' had been driven into the heart of the Little Entente. For this reason, Churchill warned: 'We cannot say "the past is the past" without surrendering the future.'

Churchill went on to urge the Government to make good its declaration on defence. 'We shall', he said, 'have to lay aside our easy habit and methods.' He also urged 'a renewed, revivified, unflinching adherence to the Covenant of the League of Nations'. The first step should be to make 'common cause' with France, and then with all the other threatened States. War could only be avoided by a 'Grand alliance', together with 'Staff arrangements', all grouped under the Covenant of the League of Nations, but this could only be effective if it were done immediately.

Churchill concluded that such a plan would unite the country, even though he admitted that it contained an element of risk. But he urged those who dismissed it as impracticable, and wished to reject it, 'to ponder well and earnestly upon what will happen to us if, when all else has been thrown to the wolves, we are left to face our fate alone'.

Members of Parliament applauded Churchill's speech: 'the speech of his life', Harold Nicolson called it, but Chamberlain's Cabinet had no intention even of trying Churchill's plan, and four days later, at the Cabinet's special Foreign Policy Committee, the discussion turned on the question of dismembering Czechoslovakia. Inskip wondered whether the Germans would be satisfied by the taking over of the Sudeten German region of Czechoslovakia. Chamberlain in reply said he believed that 'the seizure of the whole of Czechoslovakia would not be in accordance with Herr Hitler's policy which was to include all Germans in the Reich but not to include other nationalities'. He rather thought that Hitler would wish to reduce Czechoslovakia to a condition of 'dependent neutrality'.

Inskip felt that 'Czechoslovakia's present political position was not permanently tenable', and that she was, in fact, 'an unstable unit in Central Europe'. Furthermore he saw no reason to try to help such a 'unit' to survive. Hankey, however, reminded the inner Cabinet that 'the frontier of Czechoslovakia was an old one which had endured for 200 years. The Germans in the Sudeten areas represented migration into those districts from across the frontier.'

Unlike Churchill, both Chamberlain and Halifax were anxious not to take any united action in conjunction with France and Czechoslovakia. Instead they wished to come to some arrangement about Czechoslovakia which would be acceptable to Hitler.

The whole inner Cabinet were agreed that if France were attacked by Germany Britain 'would always come to her aid' as Britain could not in its own interests 'afford to see France overrun'. That made it even more essential that there should be no 'formal commitment' to France, such as Churchill had urged. Without such a formal commitment, Halifax felt, both France and Germany would be kept 'guessing', and would be less inclined to take action. To take on such a commitment, however, 'might involve us in war in the very near future when Britain was very unprepared'. Halifax concluded that the choice was between 'mobilising our friends and resources and going full out against Germany' or telling France that she 'could not count on military assistance from us if she got embroiled with Germany over Czechoslovakia'. In the latter case France should be told that she would be 'well advised to exert her influence at Prague in favour of an accommodation being reached with Germany'.

Chamberlain favoured the second course, telling his colleagues that Britain was 'in no position from the armament point of view' to go to war with Germany. Although he believed that France's army was, as Churchill had pointed out in the House of Commons, still strong, in all other respects he said – 'finance, air, the domestic situation' – France was 'in a hopeless position'. Chamberlain concluded that 'if Germany could obtain her *desiderata* by peaceable methods there was no reason to suppose that she would reject such a procedure in favour of one based on violence'.

Inside the Foreign Office, Halifax also discussed Churchill's idea of a Grand Alliance, telling his advisers that 'the long and difficult negotiations' needed to conclude it would themselves appear 'both a provocation and an opportunity to Germany to dispose of Czechoslovakia' before the Grand Alliance could be organized.

On 22 March 1938 the Cabinet finalized its decision. Britain's defence weaknesses were such that it would be impossible to prevent Germany invading and overrunning the whole of Czechoslovakia. To prevent this it would be necessary for Britain to take the initiative in the search for an arrangement which would prove, as Chamberlain had called it, 'more acceptable to

Germany'. It was finally agreed that it would be 'a mistake to plunge into a certain catastrophe in order to avoid a future danger that might never materialize'. Halifax described the planned diplomatic pressure on the Czech Government to give in to Sudeten demands as 'a disagreeable business' which should be done 'as pleasantly as possible'.

Knowing nothing of the British Government's decision to put pressure on Czechoslovakia, Churchill continued to warn of the dangers of German pressure. He told the House of Commons on 24 March 1938, only two days after the Cabinet's secret decision, that Czechoslovakia would be forced to make concessions which were not based on justice until her independence, her very sovereignty, had been destroyed.

In this speech Churchill appealed once more for a Ministry of Supply and a Ministry of Defence, and for a greater awareness of the Nazi danger. A few weeks before the German annexation of Austria, Chamberlain had said that the tension in Europe was greatly relaxed. He would surely say so again, Churchill believed. But presently, Churchill warned, 'another stroke' would come, while all the time, all the 'rigours of Nazi domination' were being imposed on Austria.

'For five years', Churchill told the House of Commons, 'I have talked to the House on these matters – not with very great success. I have watched this famous island descending incontinently, fecklessly, the stairway which leads to a dark gulf. It is a fine broad stairway at the beginning, but after a bit the carpet ends. A little further on there are only flagstones, and a little further on still these break beneath your feet.'

Historians, Churchill added, would never be able to understand it, if 'mortal catastrophe' were to overtake Britain. They would never understand how a victorious nation, 'with everything in hand, suffered themselves to be brought low, and to cast away all that they had gained by measureless sacrifice and absolute victory – gone with the wind!'

'What I dread', Churchill went on, 'is that the impulse now given to active effort may pass away.' In fact, unknown to Churchill, the Cabinet had continued for two and a half months to discuss the conflict between the need to economize and the need to increase the defence programme. They had failed to reach any conclusion, however. During the Cabinet discussions, Inskip had gone so far as to tell his colleagues, on 8 February 1938, that the 'burden in peacetime' of taking the necessary and advised steps to defend the country was too great for Britain to contemplate.

Throughout February and March 1938 Lord Swinton had continued to fight for Cabinet approval for the Air Ministry's minimum requirements. These had been set out in a new proposal, Scheme L. This new programme, Swinton told the Cabinet on 1 April 1938, was 'essential to meet the German menace'. Without it air parity would be impossible for another three years, until March 1941. Yet even Scheme L, Swinton warned Chamberlain six days later, was not sufficient to provide 'a safe air defence'.

Swinton also told Chamberlain that the Air Staff had made its recommendations on the scale of reserves with regard to the financial restrictions imposed
on them and that as a result the scale was well below what they regarded as 'a
proper insurance'. Without 'control and National Service', Swinton added,
there could be no adequate air programme. But Sir John Simon, the Chancellor
of the Exchequer, reiterated Chamberlain's view, and that of the majority of the
Cabinet, when he said that no further funds could be made available. Instead,
Simon told the Cabinet of 6 April 1938, it was better to 'preserve the financial
strength of the country'. Thus defence spending had to remain below what the
Air Staff considered its absolute minimum; even though, five days earlier,
Simon himself had announced a Budget surplus of £28 million.

Churchill was informed of Scheme L by Torr Anderson, who also continued
to send him details of delays and set-backs in the implementation of existing
programmes. Churchill, meanwhile, was casting about for some means of
rallying support for Czechoslovakia. The *Evening Standard* did not approve of
his arguments, with the result that his fortnightly articles were abruptly
cancelled.

Angered, but undeterred, Churchill transferred his articles to the *Daily
Telegraph*, and throughout April 1938 he tried to focus attention on the need for
closer cooperation with France. After a two-day visit to Paris during which he
spoke to several leading French politicians, he had a long talk with Halifax,
arguing that Britain and France should form the 'nucleus' around which the
smaller States of Europe could rally. Halifax later reported to the Cabinet that
he had pointed out to Churchill 'some of the obvious difficulties in the way of
this'. He had also instructed the British Ambassador in Paris to tell the French
not to take seriously 'Winston's exuberant interpretations' of the Government's policy. On the question of Staff talks with the French, which Churchill
had also urged, Halifax told him, not quite truthfully, that the Government
now thought this to be a good idea. In fact, the Cabinet were opposed to any
such talks.

On 14 April 1938 Churchill published an article in the *Daily Telegraph* in
which he warned the French people that their constant changes of Government were encouraging pro-German opinion in England: 'All the Heil Hitler
brigade in London society', he wrote, 'exploit and gloat over what they are
pleased to call "the Parliamentary impotence of the French democracy".'
Churchill also warned that what was to the French an 'amusing game' was
being 'turned in deadly fashion to their detriment – and to our common
danger'.

On 16 April 1938 Neville Chamberlain announced that an Anglo–Italian
agreement had been signed. Churchill immediately recognized the agreement
as 'a first step' in an attempt to 'patch up something even more specious with
Germany', as he wrote to Eden on April 18. Indeed, Chamberlain himself, at a
private meeting, told a number of senior Conservatives – but not Churchill –
that 'he had not abandoned hopes of similar arrangements with Germany'.

A more personal worry pressed on Churchill during April 1938, highlighted at the beginning of the month when *The Times* announced that Chartwell was for sale, and the *Daily Express* distressed him with the headline: 'Winston puts his mansion up for sale.' It was indeed a fine house, with five reception rooms, nineteen bed and dressing rooms, eight bathrooms, and three cottages, all set in eighty acres, with its own heated and floodlit swimming pool.

Churchill was running out of funds. Although he was not a minister and did not have a minister's salary he was devoting an enormous amount of time to his Parliamentary speeches and public duties. As a result, he could not spend as much time as he needed on the writing and journalism from which he derived a great proportion of his income. The cost of a team of secretaries, of preparing his books and articles, of the flat in London, the continual lunches and dinners with political colleagues, and the 'open house' at Chartwell, had all drained his finances to danger point. Normally, he would have been able to sell his American stocks, built up so carefully after the Crash. But his faith in the recovery of the American market had been premature, and when the stock-market fell again, he found himself heavily in debt on his share account.

Churchill explained his problems to Brendan Bracken, and Bracken, who had once been referred to as Churchill's 'faithful cheela' – or disciple – set about finding a solution. The main area of hope was Churchill's contract for the new, four-volume history of the *English-speaking Peoples*. If he could finish this in eighteen months, he would receive £15,000 from the publishers. But his debt with his stockbroker stood at £18,000.

Bracken explained the situation to Sir Henry Strakosch, the industrialist who had been supplying Churchill with the figures of German arms expenditure, and Strakosch agreed to take over Churchill's share portfolio, to pay the debt, and to be responsible for the shares for three years, 'on the undertaking' that Churchill 'incur no further liability'.

Churchill's relief and gratitude were considerable. Chartwell was at once withdrawn from the market, and with the fourth Marlborough volume now virtually finished, the new book was embarked upon at once. Bill Deakin was delighted to help organize the setting up of a research team, although before doing so he was sent by Churchill to Prague to find out from the Czech President himself whether the Czech Government approved of Churchill's plan of a Grand Alliance, and of its central European aspect, a block of Danubian States linked first for economic and then for military coordination.

On 13 May 1938 Churchill gave lunch at Morpeth Mansions to the leader of the Sudeten German nationalists, Conrad Henlein. Also present were the Liberal leader, Archie Sinclair, and 'Prof' Lindemann, who took notes of the discussion. Henlein was on a brief visit to London to urge all those he met to support full autonomy for the Sudeten Germans. It was Vansittart who had asked Churchill to see him.

Churchill questioned Henlein closely about his real intentions: did the Sudeten Germans want to be a part of Germany, or to remain within Czechoslovakia? Henlein insisted that autonomy *within* Czechoslovakia was his maximum and final demand. The Czech frontiers would remain, he said, where they were, and would continue to be manned by Czech troops. The Sudeten Germans would control their own local and municipal affairs, but Prague would remain in charge of foreign policy, defence and communications.

These assurances, which Churchill sent on at once to Chamberlain and Halifax, provided a basis for combining satisfaction for the Sudeten Germans and the preservation of Czech territorial integrity. There was no reason, Churchill told an audience at Bristol three days later, why the Sudeten Germans should not become 'trusted and honoured partners' of the Czech State which was, he said, 'the most progressive and democratic of the new States of Europe'.

Henlein was reported to have been impressed by the reception of his autonomy scheme, and to have accepted that it was the maximum for which he could expect support in Britain. According to one observer, writing to Churchill after the visit, Henlein had taken away from this meeting 'the firm impression' that Churchill incorporated and represented the *real* strength of the British', and of a British determination 'to tolerate no aggression' against Czechoslovakia.

Although Henlein had been impressed by Churchill, and had in his turn impressed Churchill by his acceptance of autonomy, Hitler was less pleased. Ten days later, on May 28, Sir Robert Vansittart reported to Lord Halifax that Henlein was 'in very bad odour' in Berlin, because he wanted to negotiate with the Czechs 'on his London line'.

Once Hitler learned of Henlein's willingness to accept Czech sovereignty, he began, from Berlin, to increase the scale and style of anti-Czech propaganda. Churchill saw clearly where this new extremism would lead, and in an article in the *Daily Telegraph* on 23 June 1938 he urged the Sudeten Germans to realize that they would be more secure within a 'tolerant' Czechoslovakia than under German rule, 'reduced to shapeless pulp by those close-grinding mandibles of the Gestapo'.

Throughout the summer of 1938 Churchill remained convinced that the integrity of Czechoslovakia could be preserved by means of a firm British policy, in conjunction with France, Czechslovakia, and any other State threatened by Germany. But he also feared that Chamberlain would continue his search for a general agreement with Germany and that this would blunt the edge of defence preparations.

In May Lord Swinton resigned, having fought in vain for a clear decision on the Air Ministry's expansion Scheme L, and having been attacked in the House of Commons for delays in air expansion. Churchill defended Swinton in a public speech: 'in my opinion', he said, Swinton was 'one of the least blameworthy among those responsible.' Swinton's 'contribution to rearmament', Churchill declared, had been 'far greater than that of some others who now hold high office of State'.

Lord Swinton was succeeded at the Air Ministry by Sir Kingsley Wood, the former Minister of Health, and Chamberlain's Parliamentary Private Secretary from 1924 to 1929. No place was found for Churchill, nor was a Ministry of Supply set up, as he had urged.

Churchill at once opened up a correspondence with Kingsley Wood. As with his letters to Swinton, one of his themes was the need for greater scientific research into air warfare and air defence. 'When I think of what might have been done in this period', he wrote to Kingsley Wood, 'to make us all safe, I find it difficult to express my grief.' But he would be glad to continue to send his ideas to the new Air Minister, being sure, as he wrote, that 'you will not turn and ask me, under penalty, where I got my information from!'

Press speculation about Churchill's possible return to the Government had followed every development in Cabinet policy. So too had sympathetic articles about Churchill's position. On 15 May 1938 an article in the *Sunday Referee* by Leo S. Condon, entitled 'Why Winston is out of it', described Churchill as 'the most dynamic statesman in our generation'. The article continued: 'in the House of Commons his voice is listened to more closely than any other man's – and that includes the Prime Minister. The mere hint that Mr Churchill may speak in a debate sends members trooping into the chamber, and causes the Cabinet Minister who must deal with Mr Churchill to study his notes with care. When Mr Churchill is in the House of Commons you may usually find him in the smoking room, the centre of a Conservative group, speaking rapidly, listening attentively, breaking matchsticks into little pieces and throwing them about him on the floor, standing up to emphasise a point, then bouncing firmly back in his seat. His words are echoed and repeated in the lobbies. He has been called "the Prime Minister of the Smoking Room". He has more influence than any MP outside the Cabinet. Why then, is he not in the Cabinet? That is a question that everyone is asking. He has brains – brilliance many would call it. He has experience. He has held every possible Cabinet post a man could hold, except one – the Premiership.'

Churchill did not expect, however, to be asked into the Cabinet. 'The Government have a solid majority', he wrote to a friend, 'and Chamberlain will certainly not wish to work with me.' And yet there were several members of Chamberlain's Cabinet who like the Press and the public believed that he ought to be in the Government. These Ministers encouraged him to send them his ideas, and sought his advice. One of them was the new Secretary of State for War, Leslie Hore-Belisha. Another was Duff Cooper.

At Sir Thomas Inskip's invitation, Churchill visited the Austin 'shadow' factory at Birmingham, which, in the event of war, would be ready to come into production at once. At Duff Cooper's invitation, he visited the Fleet, writing to the First Sea Lord on his return to London: 'I keenly enjoyed our expedition, and think it a great compliment that you should have conducted me personally upon it. A visit to the Fleet is a tonic in every sense.'

The purpose of Churchill's visit to the Fleet was to see, as part of his work on the Air Defence Research Committee, a new submarine interception system,

'Asdic'. Although impressed by 'Asdic', Churchill was still dissatisfied with the pace and scale of research. He was also increasingly worried about the lack of anti-aircraft defences for cities and vulnerable points. 'We have not got a dozen modern anti-aircraft guns in the country,' he wrote in protest to the deputy editor of the *News of the World*, after an article in the paper assuring its readers that all was well. Even the guns on order, Churchill added, were on a scale 'hopelessly below our requirements'.

In June 1938 Churchill published his collected speeches of the past decade. The volume, edited and introduced by Randolph, was called *Arms and the Covenant*. 'It is a memory to me of years of struggle,' wrote Desmond Morton, 'and not a little bitterness, as it must be to you.' Now both Morton and Churchill believed that it might be too late to obtain the military and air strength needed to make diplomacy effective.

Replying to Morton, Churchill wrote that although he would have been glad 'to help in the work of rearmament' in late 1935 or in 1936, 'now the whole scene has changed'. Much had been done, he added 'and much can never be done', while his own 'particular knowledge' of those days was no longer essential.

Each of Hitler's actions confirmed all that Churchill had forecast and feared: Nazi propaganda continued to abuse the Czechs, and all the evils of Nazi practice were being imposed on Austria with increasing severity. 'It is easy', Churchill wrote in the *Daily Telegraph* on 6 July 1938, 'to ruin and persecute Jews, to steal their private property; to drive them out of every profession and employment; to fling a Rothschild into a prison or a sponging-house; to compel Jewish ladies to scrub the pavements; and to maroon clusters of helpless refugees on islands in the Danube; and these sports continue to give satisfaction.'

Inside Czechoslovakia, Conrad Henlein had demanded not only autonomy for the Sudeten Germans, but also their right to profess what he called 'German philosophy'. For the Czechs it was an unacceptable request to allow Nazi activities and overt racism, both against Jews and Slavs. As the conflict between Berlin and Prague intensified, Chamberlain sent a leading Liberal peer, Lord Runciman, to try to effect a compromise. Churchill continued to approve the principle of any compromise based on Sudeten German autonomy. But in the *Daily Telegraph* on 18 August 1938 he warned that any German attempt to crush Czechoslovakia would ultimately involve 'all the greatest nations of the earth'.

Churchill repeated this warning to Major Ewalt von Kleist, an emissary of the German General Staff, who visited him at Chartwell on the following day. Von Kleist – who was hanged by the Nazis after the bomb plot against Hitler less than six years later – asked Churchill for a letter to enlighten the German General Staff as to where Britain stood: 'The spectacle of an armed attack by Germany upon a small neighbour', Churchill wrote in his letter, 'and the bloody fighting that will follow will rouse the whole British Empire and compel the gravest decisions.'

Once war began, Churchill warned von Kleist, it would be fought 'to the bitter end'. Germany had now to consider 'not what might happen in the first few months, but where we should all be at the end of the third or fourth year'. It would be 'a grave mistake', Churchill added, for the German Government to imagine 'that the slaughter of the civil population following upon air-raids would prevent the British Empire from developing its full war power'. The submarine, Churchill wrote, was 'practically mastered by scientific methods', and Britain would have 'the freedom of the seas and the support of the greater parts of the world'. Churchill's final warning to von Kleist was: 'The worse the air-slaughter at the beginning, the more inexpiable would be the war.'

Churchill was convinced that Britain would fight if Czechoslovakia were invaded. This was the basis of his letter to von Kleist. In Germany, however, Hermann Goering told the French Ambassador that he had received definite assurances from London that in the event of a war between Germany and Czechoslovakia, 'Britain would not lift a finger.'

Would British policy be that outlined by Churchill, or that forecast by Goering? At a Cabinet meeting on 30 August 1938, Lord Halifax reported that Churchill had urged a joint note to Berlin from a number of powers. But Halifax himself, as he told his colleagues, felt that it would be embarrassing to ask other countries to join in, as they might then ask what we intended to do if the Germans invaded Czechoslovakia.

During this Cabinet meeting three Ministers wanted to send a warning to Germany not to invade Czechoslovakia. One of the three, Duff Cooper, wanted to send the Fleet to Scapa Flow, as a sign of naval preparedness. But the majority decided to issue no threats.

As the Cabinet's deliberations continued, Churchill still tried to influence its decision, writing to Halifax to urge the Government to issue a joint note together with France and Russia, warning Hitler not to attack Czechoslovakia, and proposing that President Roosevelt should be asked to approach Hitler direct, in order to emphasize 'the gravity of the situation'. Churchill also suggested certain British naval movements, in order to cause 'a stir' in the ports, as he himself had done in 1914, when First Lord of the Admiralty.

Churchill believed that these activities might have an effect on Hitler, as there were rumours of 'grave technical hitches in the German mobilization'. He also hoped that the 'peaceful elements' in Germany might be encouraged to make a stand, if Britain and France were to act firmly.

On 2 September 1938 the Soviet Ambassador, Ivan Maisky, asked to see Churchill, and told him that the Soviet Government wanted to consult with Britain and France to discuss means of defending Czechoslovakia. That same day, the Czech Government formally offered autonomy to the Sudeten Germans. Lord Runciman urged Henlein to accept autonomy. But after being summoned to see Hitler, Henlein rejected the terms which, less than four months before, he had told Churchill he was willing to accept.

On 7 September 1938 *The Times*, in a leading article which many believed must reflect the British Government's policy, suggested that, as Henlein had now rejected the autonomy proposals, Czechoslovakia should cede the Sudetenland to Germany.

Although, officially, the Foreign Office dissociated the Government from the article in *The Times*, Churchill wrote to a correspondent that the proposal was widely interpreted as Government policy. Furthermore, he believed that the mountain defence line of the Sudetenland was a vital safeguard to the national existence of the Czechoslovak State.

Hitler now demanded in strident terms that the Sudetenland be transferred to Germany. Far from sending a warning to Hitler, Chamberlain and Sir John Simon, meeting as a special 'Situation in Czechoslovakia Committee' of the Cabinet, decided to enter into negotiations with him, and without the Czechs being invited to participate.

On 10 September 1938, at a second meeting of this Czechoslovakia Committee, Chamberlain, Halifax, Simon and Hoare were read a telegram from the British Minister in Berlin, advising against any warning to Hitler. While these four Ministers were meeting, Churchill reached Downing Street, and waited for the meeting to end. 'We found Churchill waiting in the hall', Sir Samuel Hoare later recalled. 'He had come to demand an immediate ultimatum to Hitler. He was convinced it was our last chance of stopping a landslide, and according to his information, which was directly contrary to our own, both the French and the Russians were ready for an offensive against Germany.'

The following morning, 11 September 1938, Churchill went to the Foreign Office, and advised Halifax to warn Hitler that any violation of Czech territory meant immediate war. But Halifax had decided that the only way to prevent war was to agree to the separation of the Sudetenland from Czechoslovakia. This was precisely what *The Times* had suggested four days before.

During 11 September 1938 the British Government agreed that a Four-Power Conference should be summoned, at which Britain, France, Germany and Italy, would arrange the details of the transfer. Czechoslovakia was not to be a member of this Conference. Hitler, meanwhile, was demanding a plebiscite in the Sudetenland, to determine the will of its inhabitants.

Churchill confined his personal forbodings to a friend. 'Owing to the neglect of our defences', he wrote that same day, 'and the mishandling of the German problem in the last five years, we seem to be very near the bleak choice between War and Shame. My feeling is that we shall choose Shame, and then have War thrown in a little later on even more adverse terms than the present.'

These feelings were shared by several younger MPs, who felt that the situation could only be retrieved, and Czechoslovakia defended, if Churchill were brought into the Government. In his diary Leo Amery noted how he had found some of the young MPs 'particularly Harold Macmillan, very wild, clamouring for an immediate pogrom to get rid of Neville and make Winston

Prime Minister'. But, Amery added, 'I poured cold water on that sort of talk.'

On the 13 September there was a meeting of the Czechoslovakia Committee of the Cabinet. Those present included Chamberlain, Simon, Hoare, Halifax and Sir Horace Wilson. The Committee discussed means of arranging the plebiscite in the Sudeten area, which Hitler was demanding. The Committee was worried that a plebiscite might be considered a 'maximum triumph for Herr Hitler' and that the Czechs might consider it a 'disintegration of their State'. It was generally agreed, however, that the Cabinet Ministers would have great reluctance in involving Britain in a war if 'the alternative was a plebiscite, provided a plebiscite on fair and reasonable terms could be provided'.

On 14 September 1938 Chamberlain told the Cabinet that he was now determined to persuade the Czechs to surrender the Sudetenland, and, if Hitler insisted on it, to agree to a plebiscite. No democracy, Chamberlain told his colleagues, could refuse a plebiscite. 'The root factor of the present situation', he told his Cabinet, was that Britain and France together were not in a position to fight Germany, as 'a result of our failure to take adequate steps to rearm'.

On 15 September 1938 Chamberlain flew to see Hitler, at Berchtesgaden, and to discuss the plebiscite with him face to face. It was a dramatic gesture, Chamberlain's first flight in an aeroplane, and a means of seeking a solution without the Czechs themselves being involved.

When Randolph Churchill heard that Chamberlain was actually going to meet Hitler he wrote to warn his father that in future he should 'emulate my deepest distrust' of Chamberlain, his policies and his colleagues. Randolph added: 'There is no infamy of which they are not capable', and he went on to explain to his father that when Cabinet ministers talked to Churchill himself they spoke in 'honourable terms', but Randolph got a different picture from his own contacts who were the 'underlings' and were thus less 'discreet'.

At his meeting with Chamberlain, Hitler assured the British Prime Minister that 'he did not wish to include the Czechs inside the German Reich'. For his part, Chamberlain said he was not opposed to the separation of the Sudetenland from Czechoslovakia, telling Hitler that 'he did not object to the principle of self-determination', or, indeed, attach very much importance to it. What he wanted was a fair and peaceful settlement.

As a result of Chamberlain's remarks to Hitler, all that was now needed was to negotiate the details of the transfer and gain final Cabinet approval for the agreement. Returning to London, Chamberlain told his Cabinet colleagues that he was against a debate in Parliament, as any discussion there might ruin the 'very delicate negotiations'. 'In effect', Chamberlain told his Cabinet colleagues, 'Parliament would be informed of the decision of His Majesty's Government after it had been taken.'

On 18 September 1938 Chamberlain told the French Prime Minister, who had come to London, that as the Czechs and Sudetens could not agree, there would have to be a plebiscite. After some resistance the French agreed to a joint Anglo-French plan, whereby the German-speaking areas would be transferred to Germany.

At the Czechoslovakia Committee of the Cabinet late that same afternoon, Halifax said that when the Czechs realized what the results of the plebiscite were bound to be they 'might then agree to dispense with the formality of a plebiscite'. Furthermore, the Ministers decided that 'it should be stated pretty bluntly' to the Czech President, Edouard Beneš that if he 'did not leave himself in our hands that we should wash our hands of him'.

Britain and France now pressed Beneš to agree to the transfer of Czech sovereign territory to Nazi Germany. Were Czechoslovakia to refuse to give up the Sudetenland, Beneš was informed, then Britain and France would take no responsibility for the consequences. The Czechs were also instructed not to mobilize their army.

Sensing the increasing pressure on the Czechs, both from Britain and France, Churchill flew to Paris on the morning of 20 September 1938 to see whether the French Government might agree to abandon its pressure, and to support Czechoslovakia if it were invaded. Talking to two of his friends in the French Cabinet, Paul Reynaud and Georges Mandel, Churchill urged them to oppose the transfer of the Sudetenland to Germany. But Reynaud and Mandel told Churchill that, like Duff Cooper and Hore-Belisha in the British Cabinet, they too were in a minority.

Reynaud and Mandel spoke 'gloomily of resignation'. Churchill persuaded them not to do so. That afternoon, as he flew back to London, he was tempted, as he later recalled, to send a telegram to President Beneš to stand firm. The telegram would have been short, and clear: 'Fire your cannon, and all will be well.' But in the end Churchill decided not to send it, feeling, as he later recalled, that he would be grasping responsibilities 'which I had no right to seek, and no power to bear'.

Churchill opposed the Anglo–French plan. 'The partition of Czechoslovakia', he told the Press on 21 September 1938, 'under pressure from England and France amounts to the complete surrender of the Western Democracies to the Nazi threat of force.' Furthermore it would bring peace 'neither to England nor to France'. The two countries would, on the contrary, be in an even weaker position, for the 'neutralisation of Czechoslovakia' would liberate twenty-five German divisions for the western Front, and give the Nazis 'the road to the Black Sea'.

It was not only Czechoslovakia that was threatened, Churchill argued, but also 'the freedom and democracy of all nations'. The belief 'that security can be obtained by throwing a small State to the wolves is a fatal delusion'.

Chamberlain was convinced that he could finalize the details of a peaceful cession of the Sudetenland, and on 22 September 1938 he flew back to Germany, to see Hitler at Bad Godesberg, on the Rhine. Sir Horace Wilson went with him.

While Chamberlain was on his way to meet Hitler, Churchill went to 10 Downing Street, where he was told that Chamberlain would be taking a 'firm stand', based on the transfer of the Sudeten territories 'gradually, under an international commission', rather than immediate German occupation, and a guarantee for 'what remains of the Czechs' after the transfer. Furthermore, Polish and Hungarian claims to Czech territory, which were being pushed by Hitler, would also be resisted. Returning to his flat at Morpeth Mansions, Churchill passed on this news to a group of Peers and MPs who had gathered there, including Lord Cecil of Chelwood, Lord Lloyd, Lord Horne, Archie Sinclair, Brendan Bracken and Harold Nicolson. Going up in the lift, Churchill said to Nicolson: 'It is the end of the British Empire.'

The group at Morpeth Mansions was agreed that Hitler was unlikely to agree to Chamberlain's terms, and was convinced that if he refused to accept them there would be war. If Chamberlain came back with 'peace with honour' or broke off the negotiations, the group would support him. But if he came back with 'peace with dishonour' they would oppose him. When someone commented that if war did break out it would be 'inconvenient having our Prime Minister in German territory', Churchill replied in a flash: 'even the Germans would not be so stupid as to deprive us of our beloved Prime Minister.'

During the meeting, Nicolson spoke of his fears of what Downing Street had called the possibility of 'a general agreement'. What can that mean? he asked. Everyone agreed, as Nicolson wrote in his diary that night, 'that this is a terrifying prospect'. It might mean giving way on more than the Czech issue in return for such 'valueless concessions as "a fifty years peace" and "no bombing of open towns"'.

The Godesberg meeting was stormy. Hitler said it would take too long to carry out the Anglo–French plan, whereupon Chamberlain agreed to Hitler's demand that there should be no plebiscite in areas where more than half the population was German-speaking, but an immediate German occupation instead. Chamberlain also agreed that all Czech fortifications and war materials in the transferred areas should be handed over to Germany intact. At a private meeting between Wilson and Hitler, when Hitler asked what would happen if the Czechs refused these terms, Wilson told him: 'I will make those Czechos sensible.' Chamberlain likewise assured Hitler that he would persuade the Czech Government to accept the plan.

During the afternoon of 23 September 1938, while Chamberlain, Hitler and Horace Wilson were in conference at Bad Godesberg the Czechoslovakia Committee of the Cabinet, presided over by Lord Halifax, and with Vansittart in attendance, asked the Prime Minister by telegram to withdraw the British advice given to the Czechs not to mobilize. The Cabinet Committee or inner Cabinet had been informed that the Soviet Union would come to the aid of Czechoslovakia if it were attacked by Germany. The Committee also discussed the problems of mobilization in Britain itself, and decided to send a telegram to Chamberlain to see if he would authorize such mobilization in his absence.

Halifax's telegram withdrawing British opposition to Czech mobilization was eventually sent without Chamberlain's authorization, and against Sir Horace Wilson's advice.

But later that evening, Sir Horace Wilson telegraphed to the inner Cabinet, in answer to their request for measures of mobilization in Britain itself, that the decision could wait until his and Chamberlain's return on the following day.

On 24 September 1938 Chamberlain returned from Germany, and that same afternoon he explained the Godesberg conclusions to his inner Cabinet. 'The most difficult part', he told them, 'was the immediate occupation by German troops, which was very difficult to deal with politically; but having once agreed to cession the sooner the transfer took place, the better.' Chamberlain told his colleagues that he was 'satisfied that Hitler was speaking the truth' when he said this was a 'racial question' and that he had no intention of taking over the rest of Czechoslovakia. Chamberlain did not think Hitler would make any more concessions. If he resorted to hostilities, Czechoslovakia would be 'over-run' in any case.

At this inner Cabinet meeting, Chamberlain also told Halifax, Simon and Hoare that he thought he had established 'some degree of personal influence over Herr Hitler'. According to the official, and secret, Cabinet records, Hitler had told Chamberlain 'that if we got this question out of the way without conflict', it would be 'a turning point in Anglo–German relations'. That, Chamberlain told his colleagues, was 'the big thing of the present issue'. He was also satisfied 'that Herr Hitler would not go back on his word once he had given it to him'.

The full Cabinet met on the following day, September 25, when Chamberlain urged his colleagues to agree to the immediate transfer of the Sudetenland to Germany. But many Ministers, who were not members of the inner Cabinet, and knew nothing of its discussions, expressed doubts at the wisdom of forcing Czechoslovakia to give in. Four Ministers, Halifax, Hailsham, Duff Cooper and Hore-Belisha, expressed their unease. Four Ministers, Sir Thomas Inskip, Sir Kingsley Wood, Malcolm MacDonald and Lord Stanhope, the President of the Board of Education, advised acceptance of Hitler's terms.

As the meeting broke up, Churchill again went to Downing Street to urge Chamberlain to issue a joint declaration with Russia, warning Germany not to try to resolve the crisis by force. He was told that a message being taken personally by Sir Horace Wilson to Hitler 'is in no way a retreat'.

Churchill returned to Morpeth Mansions and passed on this assurance to his friends, telling them that the younger members of the Cabinet had 'revolted', and were insisting on standing firm. Churchill had himself suggested to Chamberlain that the Fleet should be mobilized, as an earnest of British firmness, and Duff Cooper had strongly pressed this course, to which Chamberlain acceded.

That evening, Rex Leeper drafted, and Lord Halifax issued, a communiqué from the Foreign Office, stating that if Germany invaded Czechoslovakia, 'the immediate result must be that France will be bound to come to her assistance, and Great Britain and Russia will certainly stand by France'. Halifax later told Churchill that Chamberlain had been 'much put out' when he read the communiqué and had 'reproached' Halifax for not showing it to him first. But on the following day, 27 September 1938, unknown to Churchill and indeed to most members of the Cabinet, the British Government informed both Berlin and Prague of a new British plan to ensure that the Czechs would withdraw from the main Sudetenland border towns within four days, from all German-speaking majority areas within two weeks, and from all other areas within a month. Once these withdrawals were completed, the British Government announced, negotiations would begin between Britain, France and Germany to guarantee Czechoslovakia's reduced frontier.

It was this British plan which finally convinced the Czech Government that their original borders of 1918 could no longer be preserved. And Chamberlain reinforced this conclusion when he declared, that same day, in a radio broadcast, that it seemed to him impossible 'that a quarrel which has already been settled in principle should be the subject of war'. It was also a quarrel, he said, 'in a faraway country between people of whom we know nothing'. This phrase caused offence to people like Churchill, who knew a great deal about Czechoslovakia, and who regarded the Czechs as almost the last remaining democratic people in central Europe; a people moreover whose re-emergence as a sovereign State in 1918 had been one of the features of British policy and British enthusiasm.

But Chamberlain did not share this sense of common interest or common feeling, and on the morning of 28 September 1938 he telegraphed to Hitler to ask for one further meeting, at which the two leaders could settle the final details of the transfer of the Sudetenland to Germany. Once more, the Czechs were not to be present at the negotiating table.

While waiting for Hitler's reply, Chamberlain went to the House of Commons to give an account of the crisis so far. While he was speaking, a message was brought in, and passed along the front bench to him. It was Hitler's reply, agreeing to Chamberlain's request for a further meeting, and inviting him to Munich.

Chamberlain at once broke off his speech to read the message. To an excited and appreciative audience Chamberlain announced that he would fly to Hitler's four-power meeting to which the French and Italians had also been invited. Most MPs rose to their feet. Churchill, Eden, Amery and Harold Nicolson sat still. MPs near them angrily demanded that they should get up. Then, as Chamberlain left the Chamber, Churchill went over to shake his hand, wishing him 'God Speed'. But in a Press statement issued a few hours later, Churchill warned: 'This new triumph of the Nazi regime, and the great accessions of military strength which it brings them, weights the balance heavily against democracy and freedom in Europe.'

As Chamberlain prepared to fly to Munich, the British Government sought to carry out his earlier assurance to Hitler, that the Czechs would be urged to accept the transfer. At eight o'clock that night Lord Halifax telegraphed to the British Minister in Prague that the Czechs should immediately make known their acceptance of the British plan and timetable.

President Beneš bowed to this pressure, and within three hours accepted the British plan. On the following morning Chamberlain flew from London to Munich, to inform Hitler that the Sudetenland was now German. During the Munich Conference, as the British, French, German and Italian delegates worked out how Czech territory was to be transferred to Germany, the Czech representatives were kept waiting in another room. Indeed, it was only after the Munich Agreement had been signed, and the Sudetenland formally transferred to Germany, that the Czech representatives were informed of their nation's fate.

During these final hours of the Munich Conference, Churchill was at the Savoy Hotel, at a meeting of his Freedom and Peace movement. He had decided, together with several Liberal and Labour politicians, to ask Eden and Attlee to join them in a telegram to Chamberlain, to the effect that if Chamberlain were to impose 'further onerous terms' on the Czechs, 'we shall fight him in the House'.

Both Eden and Attlee refused to sign. Harold Nicolson, who was among those at the Savoy meeting, noted in his diary that Eden would not sign because it would look like a vendetta against Chamberlain, and Attlee because he had not got the approval of his Party.

In deepest gloom, the Savoy gathering began to realize that they could do nothing, and they were almost in despair. Even Churchill, Nicolson noted, seemed to have 'lost his fighting spirit.' All sensed their helplessness, and as the meeting broke up one of those present noticed that 'there were tears in Winston Churchill's eyes'.

That same night, after the Freedom and Peace group had broken up, Churchill himself remained at the Savoy, where he dined with his friends of the Other Club: the all-Party, non-political gathering which he and F. E. Smith had founded nearly thirty years before. On that 'Munich' night, those present included Lloyd George, 'Prof' Lindemann, Bob Boothby, Brendan Bracken, Archie Sinclair, and the editor of the *Observer*, J. L. Garvin. Two members of Chamberlain's Cabinet were also present, Duff Cooper, the First Lord of the Admiralty, and Walter Elliot, the new Minister of Health, both personal friends.

One of the youngest guests present, Colin Coote, later recorded how, during the dinner, Churchill was in 'a towering rage and a deepening gloom'. The failure to persuade Eden or Attlee to sign the telegram to Chamberlain had much upset him. Coote also recalled how Churchill 'turned savagely upon the two ministers present, Duff Cooper and Walter Elliot'. An 'echoing timbre' to his usual voice betrayed his deep emotion. That night, Coote noted, 'it was not an echo, but a supersonic boom'. How, Churchill asked the two Ministers, 'could honourable men with wide experience and fine records in the Great War condone a policy so cowardly? It was sordid, squalid, sub-human, and suicidal.'

Duff Cooper was unable to defend a policy with which he was so out of sympathy. The atmosphere of the dinner was electric. In his diary Duff Cooper wrote of how 'I insulted Prof Lindemann, Bob Boothy *and* I insulted Garvin, so that he left in a rage. Then everybody insulted everybody else and Winston ended by saying that at the next General Election he would speak on every Socialist platform in the country against the Government.'

'The sequel to the sacrifice of honour', Churchill warned his friends, 'would be the sacrifice of lives, our people's lives.'

While the Other Club dinner proceeded in deepening gloom, the Munich Agreement was being signed in Germany. In London, several late editions of the evening newspapers announced the terms. Areas of the Sudetenland with a majority of German-speaking inhabitants would be transferred by 10 October 1938; areas where the balance of population was uncertain were to be worked out by an International Commission and a plebiscite then held in them. Within a month the Sudetenland would become sovereign German territory.

Hearing newsboys in the Strand calling out that agreement had been signed, Colin Coote ran out to buy a newspaper. When he returned to the group, Duff Cooper seized the paper and in fury and disgust read aloud the terms of the Munich Agreement. He was greeted with appalled silence, and then he himself, in silence, walked out of the room.

As Churchill left the hotel, he passed an open door leading into one of the hotel's restaurants. From inside the crowded room the sound of merriment and laughter assailed him. Churchill stopped in the doorway, silent and impassive. Then, as he turned away, he muttered, as if to himself: 'Those poor people! They little know what they will have to face.'

The following afternoon Chamberlain flew back from Munich to London, the hero of the hour. Watching the cheering crowd in Downing Street from a Foreign Office window, one of Ralph Wigram's colleagues of 1936, Orme Sargent, commented to those beside him: 'One would have thought we were celebrating victory over a great enemy, rather than the betrayal of a minor ally.' Clementine Churchill was equally distressed, and 'solemnly discussed' the idea of marching to Downing Street and 'hurling a brick through the window of Number Ten'.

On the following day Duff Cooper resigned from Chamberlain's Cabinet. Duff Cooper's wife telephoned Churchill to tell him the news. Later she recalled how, as she spoke, 'His voice was broken with emotion. I could hear him cry.'

Chapter Eight

The coming of war

Following Chamberlain's return from Munich, Churchill was at Chartwell, alone. During the morning he had only a single visitor, a young BBC producer, Guy Burgess. Churchill showed Burgess a message he had just received from President Beneš, in Prague, asking for advice. 'But what advice can I give?' Churchill asked Burgess. 'Here I am, an old man, without power and without party. What advice can I give, what assistance can I proffer?' When Burgess suggested that Churchill could still use his 'eloquence', Churchill replied, almost with a 'wink at himself', that Beneš could indeed depend on his eloquence – 'some would say in over-bounding measure'.

As Burgess left Chartwell, Churchill gave him a copy of his new book of speeches, *Arms and the Covenant*. That night, Burgess thanked Churchill for listening to him 'so sympathetically'. He added: 'you alone have the force and the authority to galvanize the potential allies into action'.

Churchill now settled down to prepare his speech for the Munich debate, knowing that, in the euphoria of the hour, it would not be easy to warn once more of dangers; dangers even greater than those of the past. In Cabinet on the morning of the first day of the Munich debate, Chamberlain expressed his personal conviction that, as a result of his negotiations with Hitler, 'we were now in a more hopeful position'. The contracts he had made with the dictators 'opened up the possibility that we might be able to reach some agreement with them which would stop the armaments race'.

Until Britain was convinced that other countries would act in the same way, Chamberlain added, it would be 'madness' to stop rearming. But that was not the same thing, he pointed out, 'as to say that as a thank offering for the present detente' that we were immediately announcing a 'great increase in our armaments programme'. Ever since he had been Chancellor of the Exchequer, Chamberlain told his colleagues, he had been 'oppressed with the sense that the burden of armaments might break our backs'. That is why he had come to the conclusion that he had to try to remove the problems that lay behind the armaments race.

The Cabinet decided that the House of Commons should be told that at Munich Chamberlain had improved on Hitler's earlier terms. He had successfully negotiated a delay in Czech evacuation of the ceded territories from 1 October to 10 October. The boundaries of the other areas to be occupied by Germany on October 10 and areas where a plebiscite would be held were to be fixed by an International Commission. Although it was not known precisely what this Commission would decide, the map which was to be revealed to the

235

House of Commons would not show the areas likely to be given to the Germans.

The Munich debate began on 3 October 1938, and continued for three days. Chamberlain told the House of Commons that the 'triumph' of the Munich Agreement was the fact that it showed that the Great Powers could resolve their differences without resorting to war. In so doing they had 'averted a catastrophe' which would have destroyed civilization.

Chamberlain also explained that ever since he had become Prime Minister he had made it his main concern to pacify European tensions and to remove the suspicions and hatreds which had 'poisoned the air'. Although the 'path which leads to appeasement' was long and difficult he hoped that now the problem of Czechoslovakia was out of the way there might be 'further progress along the road to sanity'.

Chamberlain then outlined his aim for the months and years ahead: to devote himself to 'the gradual removal of hostility between nations, until they feel they can safely discard their weapons, one by one'. Chamberlain also explained that the guarantee to the new Czechoslovakia would give her 'greater security than she has ever enjoyed in the past'.

Halifax, in the House of Lords, explained that the Anglo–French guarantee was more serious than the already broken French commitments to aid Czechoslovakia because the country no longer contained 'restless and dissatisfied minorities'. As Chamberlain had told the Commons, Halifax told the House of Lords that he had hopes for the future because Germany and Britain had now agreed to resolve their differences 'through consultation'.

Many of the speakers who followed Chamberlain in the House of Commons could not share the Government's optimism. Clement Attlee on behalf of the Labour Party, Sir Archibald Sinclair for the Liberals, and Anthony Eden all spoke against Chamberlain's policy.

As the Munich debate continued in the House of Commons and in the country, the Government became aware of an enormous undercurrent of doubt and criticism. On 5 October 1938 Sir Samuel Hoare warned Chamberlain that, in order to meet the growing discontent, a reconstruction of the Government was 'urgent'. But, Hoare went on, 'I do not believe that there is any basis of a working agreement between Winston and ourselves.' As to Eden, he added, 'I would get him back if and when you can.'

The extent of the gap between Churchill and the Government became clear that same day, when Churchill rose to make his Munich speech. If he did not begin, he said, by paying the usual tribute to the Prime Minister for his handling of the Munich crisis, it was not because of any lack of 'personal regard' or because he was not sympathetic to the strains the Prime Minister had been going through, but because he believed that it was 'much better to say what we think about public affairs' rather than to try 'to court political popularity'.

Churchill then went on to explain why in his view the Munich Agreement was a 'total and unmitigated defeat': the Government's assertion that Hitler had been 'made to retract' for the first time at Munich was not true. 'We really must not waste time', he said, 'after all this long Debate upon the difference between the position reached at Berchtesgaden, at Godesberg and at Munich. They can be very simply epitomised, if the House will permit me to vary the metaphor. £1 was demanded at the pistol's point. When it was given, £2 were demanded at the pistol's point. Finally, the dictator consented to take £1 17s 6d and the rest in promises of goodwill for the future.'

Churchill could not understand why there had ever been any fear of war 'if all along France and Britain had been prepared to sacrifice Czechoslovakia'. There had been no need for a crisis: 'The terms which the Prime Minister brought back with him could easily have been agreed, I believe, through the ordinary diplomatic channels at any time during the summer.' Indeed, Churchill believed that the Czechs might have made better terms with Hitler if they had been left to themselves.

Had Britain, France and Russia guaranteed the security of Czechoslovakia in March 1938, immediately after Hitler's annexation of Austria, Churchill argued, neither submission nor war, but justice might have prevailed. A firm front against territorial change might even have stimulated opposition to Hitler by those soldiers and civilians, inside Germany, who 'dreaded war', as moderate opinion always did. Now, however, all was over: 'Silent, mournful, abandoned, broken, Czechoslovakia recedes into darkness. She has', Churchill said, 'suffered in every respect from her association with the western democracies.' She had suffered from the willingness of Britain and France to accept Hitler's demand for 'self-determination' for the Sudeten Germans.

People in Britain and other liberal democracies, Churchill said, had the right to talk about 'self-determination'. But such talk 'comes ill out of the mouths of those in totalitarian states' who did not permit even 'the smallest element of toleration to every section and creed within their bounds'. It was a gross misuse of the expression 'self-determination', Churchill believed, because it was clear that 'this mass of human beings to be handed over, has never expressed the desire to go into the Nazi rule'. Even now, Churchill thought, if given a fair chance to express their opinion they would not want to become part of Germany.

Churchill went on to describe Czechosolovakia's position: 'Not only are they politically mutilated, but, economically and financially, they are in complete confusion. Their banking, their railway arrangements, are severed and broken, their industries are curtailed, and the movement of their population is most cruel. The Sudeten miners, who are all Czechs and whose families have lived in that area for centuries, must now flee into an area where there are hardly any mines left for them to work. It is a tragedy which has occurred.' Furthermore, he said, that might well not be the end of 'the misfortunes which have overcome the Czechoslovakian Republic'.

'At any moment', Churchill warned, 'there may be an order for Herr Goebbels to start again his propaganda of calumny and lies; at any moment an incident may be provoked, and now that the fortress line is turned what is there to stop the will of the conqueror? Obviously, we are not in a position to give them the slightest help at the present time, except what everyone is glad to know has been done, the financial aid which the Government have promptly produced.'

Churchill declared: 'I venture to think that in future the Czechoslovak State cannot be maintained as an independent entity. I think you will find that in a period of time which may be measured by years, but may be measured only by months, Czechoslovakia will be engulfed in the Nazi regime. Perhaps they may join it in despair or in revenge. At any rate, that story is over and told.'

What had happened to Czechoslovakia at Munich had only been possible, Churchill believed, as a result of what Britain had 'left undone' in the previous five years, 'five years of futile good intention, five years of eager search for the line of least resistance, five years of uninterrupted retreat of British power, five years of neglect of our air defences'. These, Churchill said, were all the features of past policy 'which mark an improvident stewardship for which Great Britain and France have dearly to pay'.

Churchill continued: 'We have been reduced in those five years from a position of security so overwhelming and so unchallengeable that we never cared to think about it. We have been reduced from a position where the very word "war" was considered one which could be used only by persons qualifying for a lunatic asylum.'

'When I think of the fair hopes of a long peace which still lay before Europe at the beginning of 1933 when Herr Hitler first obtained power, and of all the opportunities of arresting the growth of the Nazi power which have been thrown away, when I think of the immense combinations and resources which have been neglected or squandered, I cannot believe that a parallel exists in the whole course of history.'

Churchill turned fiercely on the Government which, he said, had neither prevented Germany from rearming nor rearmed Britain, which had quarrelled with Italy without saving Abyssinia, and which had abandoned the League of Nations without making 'alliances and combinations' that might have provided security.

Churchill went on to reject Chamberlain's assertion that the Munich Agreement would lead to a reduction of European tension. It had, he said, pointed the way to each of the States of central and eastern Europe, to make the best terms they could 'with the triumphant Nazi power', and opened for Germany the road down the Danube valley to the Black Sea, with all its resources 'of corn and oil'.

Churchill also spoke of the Czech army. 'If the Nazi dictator', he said, 'should choose to look westward, as he may, bitterly will France and England regret the loss of that fine army of ancient Bohemia which was estimated last week to require not fewer than 30 German divisions for its destruction.' Germany, he pointed out, had gained twelve divisions when she had taken over Austria. Meanwhile Britain was preparing just one division in the next four years. It was not just the interests of Czechoslovakia, he warned, that were being abandoned. The very independence of France and Britain were now at risk.

It was not only the loss of military power that had to be considered, Churchill went on. It was also 'the character of the Nazi movement' and the nature of Nazi rule. Chamberlain had spoken of his wish to see 'cordial relations' between Britain and Germany. But this, Churchill believed, could never be. Diplomatic relations were possible, and so were 'correct' relations. But there could never be real friendship 'between the British democracy and the Nazi Power, that Power which spurns Christian ethics, which cheers its onward course by a barbarous paganism, which vaunts the spirit of aggression and conquest, which derives strength and perverted pleasure from persecution, and uses, as we have seen, with pitiless brutality the threat of murderous force.' That Power, Churchill declared, 'cannot ever be the friend of British democracy'.

Churchill then set out his deepest fears of the consequences of the Munich Agreement. 'What I find unendurable', he said, 'is the sense of our country falling into the power, into the orbit and influence of Nazi Germany, and of our existence becoming dependent upon their goodwill or pleasure.' It was to prevent that, he went on, that he had tried his best 'to urge the maintenance of every bulwark of defence – first the timely creation of an Air Force superior to anything within striking distance of our shores; secondly the gathering together of the collective strength of many nations; and thirdly, the making of alliances and military conventions, all within the Covenant, in order to gather together forces at any rate to restrain the onward movement of Nazi Power'. But his efforts had all been in vain. 'Every position has been successively undermined and abandoned on specious and plausible excuses.'

The House of Commons listened intently to Churchill's slow and sombre delivery. Even those who supported the Munich Agreement were stunned by the strength of his conviction and the power of his presentation. One MP later recalled how, as he sat listening, he was suddenly aware of a strange sensation: there was sweat on his palms. Churchill had managed to express all the pent-up doubts and fears of many of those present.

At the end of his speech Churchill referred to the public enthusiasm at the moment of Chamberlain's return from Munich, telling the House of Commons, in five forceful sentences: 'I do not grudge our loyal, brave people, who were ready to do their duty no matter what the cost, who never flinched under the strain of last week – I do not grudge them the natural, spontaneous outburst of joy and relief when they learned that the hard ordeal would no longer be required of them at the moment; but they should know the truth. They should know that there has been gross neglect and deficiency in our defences; they should know that we have sustained a defeat without a war, the consequences of which will travel far with us along our road; they should know that we have passed an awful milestone in our history, when the whole

239

equilibrium of Europe has been deranged, and that the terrible words have for the time being been pronounced against the Western democracies: "Thou art weighed in the balance and found wanting." And do not suppose that this is the end. This is only the beginning of the reckoning. This is only the first sip, the first foretaste of a bitter cup which will be proffered to us year by year unless by a supreme recovery of moral health and martial vigour, we arise again and take our stand for freedom as in the olden time.'

That night the House of Commons voted on what had become the most divisive and emotional issue in inter-war politics. Thirty Conservative MPs refused to vote for their Party or their Prime Minister. Among these implacable enemies of the Munich Agreement were Churchill himself, Eden, Duff Cooper, Brendan Bracken, Harold Macmillan and Bob Boothby.

Churchill saw no future now, in Europe, except a war, based on the moment of Hitler's choosing, against the victim of Hitler's choice. Bitterly he wrote to the French Minister of Justice, Paul Reynaud, of how, as a result of Munich, no nation would 'risk its future upon the guarantee of France'. Nor did he blame France alone. 'You have been infected by our weakness', he wrote, 'without being fortified by our strength. The politicians have broken the spirit of both countries successively.' The 'magnitude of the disaster', he wrote, left him 'groping in the dark'. For thirty years he had worked consistently with France. 'I make no defence of my own country,' he told Reynaud, 'but I do not know on what to rest today.'

Churchill returned to Chartwell in a mood of deep despondency. In many letters he referred to his deep distress and in one he explained why he felt he was 'groping in the dark'. Until Munich the 'peace loving powers' had 'been definitely stronger than the Dictators', but in 1939 'we must expect a different balance'. It was this new situation, he wrote, which 'staggered' him and momentarily caused him to despair. But, in his characteristic way he immediately struggled to grasp the 'larger hope' and turned to the possibility of greater United States involvement in Europe. But he understood the strength of American isolation, and in a broadcast to the United States two weeks after Munich, he asked whether with all their sympathy for the democracies, the American people would 'wait until British freedom and independence' had succumbed, before they took up the cause. For by then the cause would be 'three-quarters ruined', and the Americans themselves would be alone.

It was not only the Munich Agreement but the evolution of Government policy, that continued to distress Churchill. Chamberlain's decision to adjourn the House of Commons for four weeks was one point of dispute. Churchill urged Chamberlain to recall Parliament on 18 October, but his appeal was mocked at by Chamberlain's supporters, who burst into derisive laughter. Churchill's sense of a national emergency was shared however, by one other Conservative, Harold Macmillan, who objected to the House of Commons being treated like a 'kind of Reichstag', being called together only to approve what the Government had already done.

Chamberlain was not deterred in his course by this sort of criticism. 'All the world seemed to be full of my praises except the House of Commons', he wrote to his sister after Munich, and he had no intention, he told her, of being influenced by Churchill's 'poison gas'. One area of dispute remained: Churchill's continuing advocacy of a Ministry of Supply. But as Chamberlain told Sir Horace Wilson, he had 'already warned' the editor of the *Sunday Times* against supporting it, and he would shortly speak to the editor of *The Times*.

Chamberlain's belief that he could improve relations with Germany seemed to be confirmed when a young friend, Bill Astor, reported after a visit to Berlin 'that Hitler definitely liked me and thought he could do business with me'. Furthermore, a policy of trying to improve relations with Germany continued to be a substitute for the stupendous efforts of rearmament which Churchill had called for during the Munich debate. In late October 1938, Kingsley Wood pointed out to the Cabinet that the British air force had 1,606 front-line planes with 412 in reserve, as against the German equivalent of 3,200 with 2,400 in reserve, and asked in the light of these figures for a substantial increase in the scale as well as the pace of Britain's air construction. Chamberlain rebuked him: 'A good deal of false emphasis had been placed on rearmament,' he told the Cabinet, 'as though one result of the Munich Agreement had been that it would be necessary for us to add to our rearmament programmes.' He had no intention of starting a 'new arms race' by approving new, larger scale programmes, although it might be possible to accelerate 'existing programmes.'

In a private letter, Sir Horace Wilson explained the Prime Minister's thinking to Kingsley Wood. According to Wilson, the Air Ministry's proposal to try and meet German productive capacity was unacceptable to the Prime Minister because Germany might see it as a decision to 'sabotage the Munich Agreement'. Sir John Simon argued in Cabinet that it was not even necessary to plan for a British army to be sent to the continent, as Germany was 'extremely unlikely to violate the neutrality of Belgium'.

Inside the Cabinet, the joint pressure from Kingsley Wood to increase the air programme, and from Hore-Belisha to increase the army programme, was considerable. But Simon echoed the same arguments that Chamberlain had used as Chancellor of the Exchequer between 1934 and 1937, that the increases which the Air Ministry and War Office considered essential would injure Britain's financial strength. Chamberlain also pointed out, in the Cabinet of 7 November 1938, that in foreign policy 'we were doing our best to drive two horses abreast, conciliation and rearmament', and that it was 'by no means certain that we could beat Germany in an arms race'.

Ten days after this Cabinet, the Liberal Party proposed the immediate creation of a Ministry of Supply, to coordinate the complex problems of arms manufacture. Churchill supported the Liberal proposal, telling the House of Commons, and Chamberlain personally: 'I have used all the arguments of urgency and I have endeavoured to explain many of the processes of detail, three years ago, two years ago, and, finally, only six months ago. I have pleaded this cause in good time; I have pleaded it when it was already too late; and perhaps my right hon. Friend may remember I have even adjured him not to be deterred from doing right because it was impressed on him by the devil.'

Churchill was now forced to admit that 'neither reason nor persuasion nor coaxing has had the slightest effect against the massive obstinacy of the powers that be, the powers that have led us to where we are now'.

Churchill went on to rebuke the Conservative majority in the House of Commons, those 'pledged, loyal, faithful supporters on all occasions of His Majesty's Government'. It was not right for them to blame the Cabinet. Much power lay with the MPs themselves. 'One healthy growl from those benches three years ago', Churchill declared, 'and how different today would be the whole lay-out of our armaments production!'

What was now needed, said Churchill, was for fifty Conservative back-benchers to vote for the Liberal proposal. Such a vote, he argued, 'would not affect the life of the Government, but it would make them act'. It would make 'a forward movement of real energy'. Churchill then set out in detail what he believed were the continuing deficiencies in Britain's defences and planning, and he went on to warn that now was the time for everyone to hear the 'deep repeated strokes' of the alarm bell, and hear it as a 'call to action' before it became 'the knell of our race and fame'.

Churchill's appeal for fifty Conservatives to support the call for a Ministry of Supply was a failure. Only two Conservatives, his faithful friends Brendan Bracken and Harold Macmillan, joined him in the protest. In Berlin the Nazi Press was exultant. One German headline read: 'Great Defeat of Churchill.'

The German headlines reflected Churchill's own thoughts, and in a letter to Duff Cooper he expressed the extent of his misgivings. 'Chamberlain has now got away with everything,' he wrote. 'Munich is dead, the unpreparedness is forgotten, and there is to be no real, earnest, new effort to arm the nation.' Even the Munich 'breathing space', bought, Churchill wrote, 'at hideous cost', was now to be wasted.

Churchill was, at that very moment, in danger of losing even his own Parliamentary seat, for inside his local Conservative constituency, pressure had been growing to replace him by someone who would support Chamberlain. Even one of Churchill's oldest constituency stalwarts was disturbed by Churchill's speech during the Munich debate, complaining that it was believed to have broken up 'the harmony of the House'. On 4 December 1938 Churchill was forced to defend himself when Colin Thornton-Kemsley, hitherto one of Churchill's staunchest constituency supporters attacked him, and strongly defended Chamberlain's policy of seeking friendship with Germany.

Churchill beat off his constituency critics, and a motion regretting that the Government had not heeded Churchill's warnings over the past five years was carried by 100 votes to 44. But later in the month he was again obliged to defend himself. In his speech he criticized the 'mood of intolerance' growing in the Conservative Party and warned that it could damage the quality of the House of Commons. And early in the new year, in a third attempt to have him unseated, the Conservatives of the Chigwell branch passed a resolution condemning his attitude during the Munich crisis, and electing Thornton-Kemsley as Chairman of their local Committee. The other branches, however, gave Churchill their support, and the danger passed.

Churchill's friends sought to encourage him in what was becoming an increasingly lonely and desperate struggle. Sir Terence O'Connor, now Neville Chamberlain's Solicitor General, wrote to Churchill that there had been nothing since the days of Charles James Fox 'to compare with the frequency and mastery of your parliamentary performance'. O'Connor added: 'You seem to have made unerring contacts with the currents of feeling that are vital to our country at this moment. And you have done so much to align and validate the temper of England.'

There were many indications of the extent to which Churchill's political isolation did not reflect his support in the country at large. From the week of Munich, more and more individuals had turned to him for guidance, or urged his inclusion in the Government. A young Oxford economist, Roy Harrod, encouraged Churchill to renew contact with Attlee, and to seek an electoral pact between Labour, the Liberals and discontented Conservatives. A leading Liberal organizer and historian, Ramsay Muir, appealed to Churchill 'to do what you alone *can* do: take the lead in a movement of national regeneration, and start what I may call a "National Opposition"'. Were he to do so, Muir added, 'I think I can promise you the whole-hearted support of the Liberal Party, which is by no means so negligible as it looks.'

Despite the obvious growth in Churchill's public support, and perhaps because of that growing support, Neville Chamberlain went so far as to criticize Churchill's judgment in a public speech. In reply, Churchill defended his record. 'The Prime Minister', Churchill told his constituents on 9 December 1938, 'said in the House of Commons the other day that where I failed, for all my brilliant gifts, was in the faculty of judging. I will gadly submit my judgement about foreign affairs and national defence during the last five years, in comparison with his own.'

Churchill then set out the facts as he saw them: 'In February the Prime Minister said that tension in Europe had greatly relaxed. A few weeks later Nazi Germany seized Austria. I predicted that he would repeat this statement as soon as the shock of the rape of Austria passed away. He did so in the very same words at the end of July. By the middle of August Germany was mobilising for those bogus manoeuvres which, after bringing us all to the verge of a world war, ended in the complete destruction and absorption of the Republic of Czecho-Slovakia. At the Lord Mayor's banquet in November at the Guildhall, he told us that Europe was settling down to a more peaceful state. The words were hardly out of his mouth before the Nazi atrocities on the Jewish population resounded throughout the civilised world. When, earlier in the year, the Prime Minister made a heart-to-heart settlement with Mr de Valera and gave up to him those fortified ports on the South Coast of Ireland, which are vital to our food supply in time of war, he led us to believe that henceforward Mr de Valera and the country now called Eire, were reconciled to us in friendship. But I warned him, with my defective judgement, that if we got into any great danger, Mr de Valera would demand the surrender of Ulster as a price for any friendship or aid. This fell out exactly for Mr de Valera has recently declared that he cannot give us any help of friendship while any British troops remain to guard the Protestants of Northern Ireland.'

Churchill then turned his attention to Chamberlain's predecessor: 'In 1934', he said, 'I warned Mr Baldwin that the Germans had a secret Air Force and were rapidly overhauling ours. I gave definite figures and forecasts. Of course, it was all denied with all the weight of official authority. I was depicted a scaremonger. Less than six months after Mr Baldwin had to come down to the House and admit he was wrong and he said, "We are all to blame" and everybody said, "How very honest of him to admit his mistake." He got more applause for making this mistake, which may prove fatal to the British Empire and to British freedom, than ordinary people would do after they rendered some great service which added to its security and power. Well, Mr Chamberlain was, next to Mr Baldwin, the most powerful Member of that Government. He was Chancellor of the Exchequer. He knew all the facts. His judgement failed just like that of Mr Baldwin and we are suffering from the consequences of it to-day.'

Churchill then referred to the Liberal leader, Lord Samuel, telling his constituents: 'Four years ago when I asked that the Air Force should be doubled and redoubled – more than that was being done now – Lord Samuel thought my judgement so defective that he likened me to a Malay running amok. It would have been well for him and his persecuted race if my advice had been taken. They would not be where they are now.'

'It is on the background of these proved errors of judgement in the past,' Churchill ended, 'that I draw your attention to some of the judgements which have been passed upon the future, the results of which have not yet been proved.'

Churchill received an increasing number of invitations to write and speak on foreign affairs. One such invitation came from Oxford, from a young man who described himself as 'an excellent rebel Tory'. His name was Edward Heath. Thirty-one years later he was to become Prime Minister. Other Conservatives wrote to Churchill urging him to form a breakaway party. If there really were a reasonable alternative to the existing Government, Churchill wrote to one such correspondent, 'they would be chased out of power by the country'. But the difficulties of forming and organizing a new party 'have often proved insuperable'.

What Churchill was able to do was to respond to two requests for major interviews, one with *Picture Post* and the other with the *New Statesman and Nation*. Both editors wanted to use the interviews as clarion calls to their readers for a more vigilant defence of democracy both at home and abroad. The editor of *Picture Post*, Stefan Lorant, had been imprisoned for six months by the Gestapo in 1933, but had managed, as a Hungarian by birth, to obtain his release. He asked if he could do a series on Churchill's life, 'not as a stunt, but because in the past years you have been consistently right in matters of foreign policy'.

The editor of the *New Statesman and Nation*, Kingsley Martin, was likewise eager to publish a substantial interview with Churchill in order, as he explained at the beginning of December 1938, 'to set people's minds thinking about the degree of compulsion which may be necessary, and about the best ways in which we can preserve our liberties'.

As 1938 came to an end, Churchill was more isolated politically than at any time since his wilderness years had begun nine years before. Even the groups of dissident Conservative MPs who were gathering around Anthony Eden, Duff Cooper and Leo Amery did not wish to be associated too closely with him. But his public support had never been so high, his articles so widely read, or his views so frequently sought. Not only were his fortnightly articles in the *Daily Telegraph* reprinted in more than twenty cities across the world, including Cairo, Jerusalem, Warsaw, Helsinki and Rio de Janeiro, but they were also being published in five Australian newspapers, four New Zealand papers, in Canada, Ceylon, India, Singapore, Kenya and Hong Kong.

Meanwhile, Churchill's literary work continued without respite. Unfortunately, the publication of the fourth and final Marlborough volume had coincided with the last weeks of the Munich crisis, and its reception had therefore been overshadowed to some extent by the political storm. Even so, it had been well received, and Churchill again found pleasure in signing and sending out more than a hundred copies as personal gifts. Anthony Eden wrote to say that he hoped, as he read it, to forget 'the haunting apprehensions of the present days'.

As soon as the Munich crisis had passed, Churchill returned to his next literary task, the four-volume *History of the English-speaking Peoples*. Once more, Chartwell reverberated with the sound of dictation long into the night, of secretaries hurrying to produce the different drafts, of research assistants – led by Bill Deakin – searching for the right reference book; all the hustle and bustle of creative writing.

To his wife, who was seeking new strength in the West Indies, Churchill wrote on 19 December 1938: 'My darling, it seems an age since you left, yet very little has happened that matters. I have been toiling double-shifts at the English Speaking Peoples.' The 'score' that night was, he told her, 180,000 words already written, or 30,000 above his target of a thousand a day. 'It is very laborious,' he added, 'and I resent it, and the pressure. But if nothing intervenes, it will be done by about July.'

Churchill then turned to a more personal matter. 'Are you better and more braced up?' he asked her. 'How is the voice? Have the rest and repose given you the means of recharging your batteries. That is what I want to know: and even more – Do you love me?'

'I feel so deeply interwoven with you', Churchill added, 'that I follow your movements in my mind at every hour and in all circumstances.' Do cable 'every few days', Churchill asked his wife, 'just to let me know all is well, and that you are happy when you think of me'. Otherwise, he admitted, 'I get depressed and anxious about you and your health'.

In a further letter ten days later Churchill commiserated with his wife on the death of the man who had courted her for two years before she had met Churchill. Much as she had enjoyed his company, and despite two secret engagements, she had not felt sufficiently in love to marry him. But Churchill remembered just how close they had been. 'Many are dying now', he wrote, 'that I knew when we were young,' and he went on to reflect: 'It is quite astonishing to reach the end of life and feel just as you did fifty years before. One must always hope for a sudden end, before faculties decay.'

Clementine Churchill was moved by her husband's letter. 'I am glad you wrote to me about it,' she replied, 'because at that moment I longed for you. I wanted to put my arms around you and cry and cry.'

During the first week of 1939 Churchill remained at Chartwell to work on his book. During the week Bill Deakin introduced him to another Oxford graduate, Alan Bullock, who undertook to help with research. As Churchill delved into the past, he became increasingly aware of the troubled but triumphant course of the evolution of British institutions. In his interview with Kingsley Martin, which was published in the *New Statesman and Nation* on 7 January 1939, Churchill said that Britain's democratic freedom had been secured by Magna Carta, Habeas Corpus and the Petition of Right. Even in war, democracy was essential as it meant that war leaders were constantly made aware of 'weak points' in their policy and actions. 'War is horrible', Churchill said, 'but slavery is worse', and the British people would rather die fighting than 'live in servitude'.

On 8 January 1939 Churchill gave a long interview to the *Daily Herald*, during which he and Hannen Swaffer discussed the First World War. The lesson to be drawn, Churchill told Swaffer was that in peace or war 'it is the good cause that really matters'. In the first war the people turned on the autocratic countries, Russia, Austria and Germany, whereas in 'haggard France' and in 'war stricken Britain', the people 'were more resolute at the end than they were at the beginning'. The same was true today, Churchill argued, telling Swaffer: 'If the Democracies are prepared to die rather than become slaves and to see the loss of all the fruits of centuries, they will remain unconquered.' If the dictators realized this, Churchill added, the matter might never be put to the proof.

In the second week of January 1939, while Clementine was still in the West Indies, Churchill took a short holiday in the south of France, flying first to Paris with 'Prof' Lindemann, lunching with Paul Reynaud, talking in the afternoon with Léon Blum. After their conversation Churchill wrote to his wife of how it had confirmed him in the belief that war could have been avoided at the time of Munich. While not minimizing Germany's 'great preponderance in the air', both he and Blum believed, that because of the apparent weakness of the German army on the French front, 'if the worst had come to the worst, we should have been far better off than we might be at some future date'.

That evening Churchill took the night train to Cannes. Once more his destination was Maxine Elliot's Château de l'Horizon. 'The journey was very comfortable', he wrote to his wife on the following day, 'and I slept blissfully.' As for his holiday plans, he wrote, 'I propose to stay here for a fortnight and work hard on the book.' He was writing more than three times his original target of a thousand words a day, 'a formidable grind', he commented, 'but if accomplished will put things on a very satisfactory basis'.

Churchill also wrote of his political isolation. He doubted very much whether 'after all I have said, they can be able to swallow me – it would have to be "horns and all". But I can truthfully say I do not mind.' It would not be 'much fun', Churchill added 'to take these burdens and neglects upon my shoulders, certainly not without powers such as they would not have dreamed of according'.

Still in France, Churchill worked to finish his book as soon as possible. The sunshine having been replaced by grey skies and cold winds, he had stayed in bed every morning, and made 'great progress' with the book.

Churchill returned to England at the end of January 1939. 'Never have I seen you in such good form', Maxine Elliot wrote to him a few days later, recalling how 'we rocked with laughter continually'. Despite the gloomy international situation, Churchill never lost his sense of fun. 'Your joie de vivre is a wonderful gift', Maxine Elliot added, 'and on a par with your other amazing gifts – in fact you are the most enormously gifted creature in the whole world and it is like the sunshine leaving when you go away'.

Following Churchill's return from France a series of articles in the British Press questioned Chamberlain's wisdom in not bringing Churchill into the Cabinet. On 25 February 1939 *Picture Post* published a long illustrated article, based on its photographer's visit to Chartwell. Churchill's 'abiding care', the magazine declared, 'is the safety of Britain, the Empire and the Commonwealth. Should some great emergency arise, it would be strange, indeed, were he to be still left "out in the cold" while lesser men fumble with vital matters which he could treat as a master. His qualities and experience might then be national assets; and the true greatness which he has often seemed to miss by a hair's breadth, might, by common consent, be his. His future, like ours, is "on the knees of the Gods".'

In January 1939 Sir Thomas Inskip had been replaced as Minister for the Coordination of Defence by the former First Sea Lord, Lord Chatfield. Although still without hope of, or wish for, a Cabinet post, Churchill began to sense a change in Government attitudes. On 6 February 1939 Chamberlain confirmed a French statement that if either Britain or France were attacked, the other country would come to its aid. This led Churchill to write to Halifax to say that he now felt the Government position and his own were drawing closer.

'I think we are approaching the show-down,' Churchill wrote to a friend, 'but there is certainly more confidence and resolution here than before.' But unknown to Churchill, that hope was being expressed somewhat more euphorically by Chamberlain than Churchill had perceived it. 'I myself', Chamberlain wrote to his sister, 'am going about with a lighter heart than I have had for many a long day.' His information led him to believe that at last Britain had 'got on top of the dictators'. The atmosphere was not yet right, but things were already moving 'in the direction I want'.

That direction, Chamberlain confided, and his own aim, was still to be able, by means of diplomacy, to 'advance towards disarmament'. If he were given three or four more years in charge, he added, 'I believe I really might retire with a quiet mind'.

Chamberlain had been particularly impressed by a recent speech by Hitler, in which he spoke of the good fortune for the world if the British and German people could cooperate 'in full confidence with one another'. These words were 'all the more impressive', Chamberlain told his sister, 'because they were spoken at the end of a year which was full of international tensions and crises, yet that year found solutions for problems which seemed almost insuperable'.

This mood of optimism led Chamberlain to tell the Press correspondents in the House of Commons, on 10 March 1939, of how Europe was now 'settling down to a period of tranquillity'. That same day Sir Samuel Hoare, on Chamberlain's recommendation, spoke of the possibility that, if Hitler, Mussolini, Franco, Chamberlain and Daladier were to work together, they might in an 'incredibly short space of time transform the whole history of the world' by freeing Europe from the nightmare of war and the burden of arms expenditure. Such a friendly collaboration between the dictators and the democrats would be the means, Hoare told his audience, of creating a new 'Golden Age'.

Four days after these remarks, Hitler ordered the German army to the borders of what remained of Czechoslovakia. Speaking that day to his constituents, Churchill said: 'The Czechoslovakian Republic is being broken up before our eyes.' There was nothing Britain could do to help the Czechs for they were completely defenceless this time. Nevertheless, he added, 'Although we can do nothing to stop it, we shall be sufferers on a very great scale.'

While Hitler increased his pressure upon the Czechs, and summoned the Czech President to Berlin, Churchill was in his constituency, once more defending an attack by Thornton-Kemsley.

Thornton-Kemsley later recalled how it was made clear to him that a 'revolt' in Churchill's constituency would be appreciated by those 'in high places'. During the meeting Thornton-Kemsley said Churchill should either leave the Conservative Party or support Chamberlain. Churchill defended himself by saying that his Munich speech prophecies were coming true and that he was certain that his work since 1933 out of office and in his independent capacity had gained him more 'goodwill' from the general public than he had ever enjoyed before.

Churchill's defence of his position won him the applause of his audience. He was simply attempting, he said, amid their applause, to ensure a foreign policy 'which will arrive at peace with honour'.

During this speech to his constituents, Churchill raised wider constitutional and philosophical questions. 'What is the use of sending members of Parliament', he asked, 'to say popular things of the moment, and saying things merely to give satisfaction to the Government whips and by cheering loudly every Ministerial platitude?' How could Parliament survive if its members stamped out 'every independent judgement?'

Even while Churchill was defending himself in his constituency, Hitler was completing the last stage of his occupation of Prague, and of the two Czech provinces of Bohemia and Moravia. By midday on 15 March 1939 German troops were in full control of the Czech capital. Hitler himself spent the night in the President's Palace. 'In Anglo–German relations', Lord Halifax told the German Ambassador, 'the clocks had been put back considerably.'

With the shock of Hitler's occupation of Prague, pressure mounted for Chamberlain to make a decisive change in British policy. Speaking at Birmingham on 17 March 1939 Chamberlain asked: 'Is this the end of an old adventure, or the beginning of a new?' Was it, he went on, 'a step in the direction to dominate the world by force?' Two days later, in the lobby of the House of Commons, Churchill urged Chamberlain to place Britain's anti-aircraft defences on full alert. Such a measure would, he wrote in a letter on the following day, take away from Hitler the temptation 'to make a surprise attack on London, or on the aircraft factories about which I am even more anxious'.

In proposing a full anti-aircraft alert, Churchill referred to his own experience in 1914, when he had persuaded Asquith to let him send the Fleet to its action stations in the North Sea '*before* the diplomatic situation became hopeless'. Churchill made no reference in his letter to a visitor he had received before raising the issue. This was Major Forbes Fraser, whom he had known as a young officer on the western front in 1916, and who was now Chief Intelligence Officer of the Air Raid Precautions department of the Home Office. Fraser had asked to see him 'to discuss certain matters'. Once more, an expert had turned to Churchill in order to confide, and to seek guidance. He and others like him were brave men, patriots, and outside politics; but even at this late stage their sense of a lack of leadership continued to lead them to Churchill.

Churchill's other informants continued to warn him of deficiencies in Britain's defences. After the German occupation of Prague, Lachlan MacLean and Anderson continued to keep him informed about the deficiencies and weaknesses in the Royal Air Force. As to the progress of Air Defence Research, Churchill was still perturbed and in a letter to Kingsley Wood, marked 'for yourself alone', he set out his continuing fears. Unless Kingsley Wood were to intervene personally, Churchill wrote, 'another year may well be lost. What we need', Churchill argued, 'is an exceptional priority,' and he added: 'We go buzzing along with a host of ideas and experiments which may produce results in '41, '42 and '43.' But, he asked, 'where will you find anything that can operate in June, July and August of 1939?' Those would be the most dangerous months, he warned, because of all the other deficiencies.

Kingsley Wood responded to Churchill's appeal, arranging for 'Prof' Lindemann to go to Farnborough to see the latest experiments with aerial mines, and authorizing Sir Hugh Dowding, the head of Fighter Command, to go down to Chartwell to discuss details of aerial interception and ground control.

Two weeks had passed since Hitler's occupation of Prague. And despite Chamberlain's Birmingham speech, the Government's actual policy remained unclear. Distress had been caused among many MPs by a 'preliminary' Anglo–German economic agreement, signed in Dusseldorf on the day of the march on Prague, whereby, in return for Anglo–German industrial cooperation, Germany would be able to increase her foreign exchange holdings. Sir Horace Wilson had been particularly keen on this economic agreement, and hoped that it would lead to even closer Anglo–German contacts. But there had been uproar in Parliament when it was learned that Britain was giving Germany the foreign currency with which she could buy arms and raw materials, at the very moment when German arms were being used to crush Czechoslovakia, a small and democratic State.

On 28 March 1939 thirty Conservative MPs, led by Eden, Duff Cooper and Churchill, proposed a motion in favour of the setting up of an all-Party Government. Among those who signed the motion was Harold Macmillan, who told his constituents two days later, that 'something must be done immediately if we are to avoid war and, worse even than war, defeat'.

Chamberlain now acted with a determination that surprised even his strongest critics, issuing on 31 March 1939 a British guarantee on behalf of Hitler's next potential victim, Poland. But hardly had the guarantee been given, when *The Times* declared, in its leading article, that the new obligation 'does not bind Great Britain to defend every inch of the present frontiers of Poland'. According to *The Times*, the 'key word' in the British guarantee was not 'integrity' – that is to say the existing frontiers of Poland – but 'independence'. Chamberlain's statement, *The Times* commented, 'involves no blind acceptance of the status quo'.

Speaking in the House of Commons on 3 April 1939, Churchill referred in unambiguous terms to the 'sinister passage' in *The Times*, similar to that of 7 September 1938 'which foreshadowed the ruin of Czechoslovakia'. But neither Britain nor France, he said, were concerned now with 'particular rights or places', but with the need to resist by force of arms any further 'acts of violence, of pressure or of intrigue'. Now was not the time for territorial negotiations. 'After the crime and treachery committed against Czechoslovakia,' Churchill declared, 'our first duty is to re-establish the authority of law and public faith in

Europe.' In addition, the Soviet Union, which had been excluded from the Munich conference, despite its Treaty with Czechoslovakia, must be brought in as a 'partner'.

Chamberlain welcomed neither Churchill's attack on *The Times* nor his advocacy of closer contacts with Russia, writing to his sister that same day, in a private letter, of how his statement on Poland 'was unprovocative in tone, but firm, clear but stressing the important point (perceived alone by *The Times*) that what we are concerned with is not the boundaries of States, but attacks on their independence. And it is we who will judge whether this independence is threatened or not.'

This interpretation of the Anglo–Polish guarantee was never made public. But it was to lead, within three weeks, to considerable British pressure on Poland to make some concessions to the German demands, as they arose during the summer for the annexation of those areas taken away from Germany in 1919, including the 'Polish Corridor', substantial parts of western Poland, and the Free City of Danzig, with its mixed German and Polish population.

Churchill's advocacy of cooperation with the Soviet Union was not at all to Chamberlain's liking. But Churchill was now convinced that the urgency of the situation might make such cooperation an essential adjunct to the preservation of peace in Europe. Immediately after the debate of 3 April 1939 he had confronted the Soviet Ambassador, Ivan Maisky, in the smoking room of the House of Commons. Lloyd George and Harold Nicolson were also present, the latter recording in his diary how Churchill had told Maisky that, although he had never liked the Communist system, 'if we are to make a success of this new policy, we require the help of Russia'. Could the Russians give assurances to the Poles and Rumanians that if Russia came to their aid she would promise not to destroy their independence?

In the event, despite prolonged Anglo–Soviet negotiations, the Russians and Poles were unable to reach agreement on the nature of Russia's military measures in support of Poland. But the pace of events was now such that within three days of this meeting the world's attention had switched elsewhere, to the Adriatic Sea, where Italian troops were massing under Mussolini's orders for the invasion of Albania.

When the news of these Italian moves reached London, Churchill was at Chartwell. At midday it was announced on the wireless that Italy had begun the invasion of Albania: Italian troops had actually landed on Albanian soil. Among the guests at Chartwell was Harold Macmillan, who later recalled how, as soon as the Italian news was heard, 'maps were brought out; secretaries were marshalled; telephones began to ring. "Where is the British Fleet?" That was the most important question.'

To answer this question, Churchill mobilized his secretaries and research assistants, all busy with work on the *English-speaking Peoples*. It turned out, Macmillan later recalled, 'that the British Fleet was scattered throughout the

Mediterranean. Some ships, as Churchill put it, were 'lolling about inside or outside widely-separated Italian ports'. Macmillan added: 'I shall always have a picture of that spring day and the sense of power and energy, the great flow of action, which came from Churchill, although he then held no public office. He alone seemed to be in command, when everyone else was dazed and hesitating.'

On the following day Churchill prepared a note for Chamberlain on where he felt the British Fleet should be, and how it should, if necessary, seize the Greek island of Corfu, in order to use the island as a base to deter any further Italian assault on Albania. The seizure of Corfu would, Churchill argued, deter Mussolini's continued advance. 'But action ought to be taken tonight.'

Churchill reinforced his letter with several telephone calls to Downing Street, and a call for the summoning of Parliament. 'I suppose', Chamberlain wrote to his sister, 'he has prepared a terrific oration which he wants to let off.'

Churchill also continued to press the Government to set up a Ministry of Supply, and in the Cabinet itself the Minister of War, Leslie Hore-Belisha, also urged this course. The two men decided to meet in London to discuss the issue. But Churchill having hurt his foot, Hore-Belisha went down to Chartwell, where Churchill urged him to persevere in Cabinet.

On the following day, 13 April 1939, the House of Commons debated the Italian invasion of Albania, and Chamberlain's three new ventures in foreign policy: a guarantee to Greece, talks with Turkey, and a guarantee to Rumania. If such a potential 'great design' were perfected, Churchill told the House of Commons, 'even now, at the eleventh hour', it would spare the world from 'the worst of its agonies'. He was still worried, he said, about the Government's reluctance even now to switch industry to a war footing, and to coordinate the needs of the three Services by means of a Ministry of Supply. Without 'compulsion', there would be no hope of equipping the armies we were trying to recruit. How could Britain possibly continue, he asked, 'with less than the full force of the nation incorporated in the governing instrument?'

There was another essential need, Churchill believed: recognition of the 'deep interest' of Soviet Russia 'against the further eastward extension of the Nazi power', and the development of the 'fullest possible cooperation' between Britain, France and Russia. 'No prejudices', he said, should be allowed to interfere with that cooperation.

Churchill now turned to a subject about which he had often spoken in private, but not yet referred to in public: his fear that somewhere at the centre of power there was a restraining, and even deceiving hand. His listeners knew that he was referring to Sir Horace Wilson. 'How was it', he asked, 'that on the eve of the Bohemian outrage Ministers were indulging in what was called "sunshine talk", and predicting the dawn of a golden age? How was it that last week's holiday routine was observed at a time when, quite clearly, something of a very exceptional character, the consequences of which could not be measured, was imminent?'

Churchill's remarks continued: 'I do not know. I know very well the patriotism and sincere desire to act in a manner of perfect rectitude which animates Ministers of the Crown, but I wonder whether there is not some hand which intervenes and filters down or withholds intelligence from Ministers. Certainly it was so in the case of the German air preparations four years ago. The facts were not allowed to reach high Ministers of the Crown until they had been so modified that they did not present an alarming impression.' It seemed to him, Churchill warned, 'that Ministers run the most tremendous risk if they allow the information collected by the Intelligence Department, and sent to them I am sure in good time, to be sifted and coloured and reduced in consequence and importance, and if they ever get themselves into a mood of attaching importance only to those pieces of information which accord with their earnest and honourable desire that the peace of the world shall remain unbroken'.

As soon as the debate was over, Churchill spoke to the Chief Whip, and, according to Chamberlain's own report to his sister, expressed a 'strong desire' to enter the Cabinet. Chamberlain did not reject this suggestion out of hand. 'It caught me', he told his sister, 'at a moment when I was certainly feeling the need of help.' But he had found in Churchill's speech 'an acid undertone which brought many cheers from Labour benches', and had 'felt depressed' when Churchill had finished. In addition, he told his sister, the question was whether Churchill, who would certainly help the Government as one of its front bench spokesmen, would 'help or hinder' in the Cabinet. Last Saturday for instance, Chamberlain confided, 'he was at the telephone all day urging that Parliament should be summoned for Sunday and that the Fleet should go and seize Corfu that night!' Would he, Chamberlain went on to ask, 'wear me out, resisting rash suggestions of this kind?'

On 15 April 1939 Chamberlain announced his intention to set up a Ministry of Supply, a step first argued by Churchill in Parliament three years earlier, in April 1936. Although the post was not to go to Churchill, his friends rejoiced in the decision itself. 'Winston has won his long fight', wrote Brendan Bracken to a friend in the United States. The policy he had advocated three years before was now being adopted. 'No public man in our time', Bracken wrote, 'has shown more foresight', and he added that Churchill's 'long, lonely struggle to expose the dangers of the dictatorships' would one day be seen as 'the best chapter in his crowded life'.

The man chosen by Chamberlain to be the new Minister of Supply, with full responsibility for assessing and coordinating the war needs of the three armed Services, was the Minister of Transport, Leslie Burgin, who had first entered Parliament, as a Liberal, in 1929, and whose only other Government post had been as Parliamentary Secretary at the Board of Trade. As soon as Burgin's appointment became known, the call for Churchill's inclusion in the Cabinet mounted, with the *Evening News* suggesting that he be made either First Lord of the Admiralty or Secretary of State for Air.

On the evening of 27 April 1939, after Hitler had announced that he no longer considered the Anglo–German Naval Agreement to be binding on Germany, Churchill spoke in the House of Commons, in favour of a Government Bill for the introduction of eventual compulsory military service. The Bill was passed with a large majority. According to a report of the debate in the *Daily Telegraph*, Churchill was in 'his most striking and effective form. To hear him, members hurried in, filling the Chamber and side galleries.' The compulsory national service register ought, he said, to have been introduced immediately after Munich. The Military Training Bill did not go far enough. 'A gesture was not sufficient, we wanted an army and might want it soon.'

If compulsory service were rejected, Churchill warned, 'the whole resistance of Europe to Nazi domination would collapse'. Great and small powers alike would make the best terms they could with Nazi Germany, and Britain would be left 'alone with our great possessions to settle up with the dictators ourselves'.

As a result of Churchill's speech, he found himself at the centre of his first Parliamentary demonstration of support for a very long time. 'Rarely has Mr Churchill been more warmly cheered after a speech,' the *Daily Telegraph* reported.

While speculation grew as to whether Churchill would be brought into the Government, the object of that speculation continued to work at Chartwell on his massive *English-speaking Peoples*. As a result of Mrs Pearman having been taken ill in the summer of 1937, he had decided to employ, for the first time, a full-time resident secretary, who could both live and work at Chartwell, in addition to two or three additional typists who lived nearby. By means of the resident secretary, dictation could proceed until two or three in the morning, without a taxi having to be summoned to take a wilting secretary home.

The woman chosen for the task, Kathleen Hill, was thirty-seven years old, and had spent ten of her working years in India. 'I had never been in a house like that before,' she later recalled. 'It was alive, restless. When *he* was away it was as still as a mouse. When he was there it was vibrating.' Sometimes, she added, Churchill could be very ruthless. 'He used to get impatient of delays. He was a disappointed man waiting for the call to save his country.'

Work on the *English-speaking Peoples* continued throughout the spring and summer of 1939. Guided by a team of researchers advising him on what he should read, and preparing summaries of books already published, Churchill found inspiration in the study of British history. As he worked, he was supported by an impressive team: the Oxford historian G. M. Young provided him with copious notes, while two former assistants from the Marlborough era, Maurice Ashley and John Wheldon, prepared draft chapters and Alan Bullock pieced together the early history of Australia and New Zealand. Based at Chartwell, Bill Deakin sought to coordinate the twin floods of material coming in for the basis of Churchill's narrative, and Churchill's own dictated chapters going out for expert scrutiny and continual revision. 'It is very hard to transport oneself into the past', Churchill had written to Maurice Ashley in

March 1939, a week after Hitler's occupation of Prague, 'when the future opens its jaws upon us.'

The impact of this hive of historical activity was considerable, and Churchill drew a contemporary lesson from his scrutiny of the past. 'In the main,' he wrote to Ashley in mid-April, 'the theme is emerging of the growth of freedom and law, of the rights of the individual, of the subordination of the State to the fundamental and moral conceptions of an ever-comprehending community.' Of these ideas, Churchill added, 'the English-speaking peoples were the authors, then the trustees, and must now become the armed champions. Thus I condemn tyranny in whatever guise and from whatever quarter it presents itself.' All this of course, Churchill reflected, 'has a current application'.

On 4 May 1939, in one of his fortnightly articles in the *Daily Telegraph*, Churchill forecast some 'new outrage or invasion' by Hitler, most probably against Poland. To avert this, he argued, the Polish Government should accept the involvement of the Soviet Union in a new alliance system, and the British Government should do its utmost to bring such an alliance about. There was no way of maintaining an eastern front against German aggression, he warned, 'without the active aid of Russia'. But Neville Chamberlain felt, as he told his sister, 'deep suspicions of Soviet aims, and profound doubts as to her military capacity even if she honestly desired and intended to help'. Even worse, Chamberlain confided, was his feeling that an alliance with Russia 'would definitely be a lining up of opposing blocs'. This would probably make any further negotiations with the dictators impossible.

After consulting with Horace Wilson, Chamberlain decided to play down the alliance aspect, and to replace it with 'a declaration of intentions'. Slowly, the impetus for an Anglo–Soviet alliance waned. For his part, Horace Wilson continued to work, with Chamberlain's approval, for closer Anglo–German economic ties. Talking privately to the left-wing Socialist Sir Stafford Cripps at Morpeth Mansions on 22 June 1939, Churchill, so Cripps recorded in his diary, 'inveighed strongly against the PM;' he said that Chamberlain would not bring him or Eden into the Cabinet because 'it would stop all possiblity of appeasement'.

Appeasement did indeed continue, with the British Embassay in Warsaw being asked to put pressure on the Poles to make concessions to Germany, not unlike the concessions which the Czechs had been forced to make at Munich. The source of much of this pressure was the British Ambassador in Berlin, Sir Nevile Henderson, who was convinced that as a first step the Free City of Danzig must revert to Germany. If Danzig were left as a 'running sore', he told Lord Halifax, the Poles would lose the Polish Corridor itself. Unless she makes concessions now, 'Poland will miss the tide'.

Chamberlain shared these views. Were Hitler asking for Danzig 'in the normal way', he told the owner of the *Daily Telegraph* on 3 July 1939, 'it might be possible to arrange things'. Chamberlain added that he himself had 'not yet given up hopes of peace', and that he could not help thinking that Hitler 'is not such a fool as some hysterical people make out'. Hitler would probably be prepared to compromise, Chamberlain believed, so long as he did not feel humiliated in the process.

Chamberlain also mentioned, in this entirely private conversation, that he had 'one or two good ideas' which he was exploring, but which were proving quite difficult to develop when there 'are so many to cry "nous sommes trahis" [we are betrayed] at any suggestion for a peaceful solution'. The Foreign Office was particularly alert to any possible 'betrayal', with one senior official commenting, as the German pressure on Poland mounted, that Sir Horace Wilson was 'working like a beaver for a second Munich'.

At Chartwell Churchill continued to work on his history. In London the Press continued to urge the Government to find him a place in its inner counsels. Day after day the headlines and the leading articles called for his return. But Churchill did not fret. He explained to Lord Rothermere that he had given his warnings and was now 'consoled for being condemned to inaction by being free from responsibility'.

In Germany Churchill's exclusion from the Government was a cause of incredulity. On 5 July 1939 Hitler's Financial Secretary, Count Schwerin von Krosigk, told two senior British soldier diplomats who had called on him in Berlin: 'Take Winston Churchill into the Cabinet. Churchill is the only Englishman Hitler is afraid of.' The mere fact of giving Churchill a Ministerial post, von Krosigk added, would convince Hitler that Britain really means 'to stand up to him'. An account of this conversation was also sent to Lord Halifax with the observation that Churchill's inclusion in the Cabinet might actually avert war as Hitler would realize Britain meant to resist further aggression.

Rumours abounded: three days after this conversation in Berlin, the *New Statesman and Nation* reported speculation that the Cabinet was divided about Churchill's return. It was said that Chamberlain feared that the return of Churchill would destroy any last-minute hopes of appeasement over Danzig.

On 4 July 1939 the *Evening Standard* reported 'an immense movement now to put Mr Churchill in the Government'. Among those supporting him in the House of Commons were Nancy Astor, Harold Macmillan and Harold Nicolson, as well as the Liberal leader, Sir Archibald Sinclair. 'The campaign is aided', the *Evening Standard* noted, by a 'terrific barrage from the newspaper artillery', including the *News Chronicle*, *Manchester Guardian*, *Yorkshire Post*, *Daily Mirror*, *Observer* and *Daily Telegraph*.

As the *New Statesman* had suggested, the *Evening Standard* agreed that Chamberlain would 'stand fast on this occasion' and not invite Churchill to join the Government. Unknown to the newspapers, the Prime Minister was, indeed, still debating whether a German–Polish war could be avoided if Poland made concessions. 'I doubt', he wrote to his sister on 15 July 1939, 'if any solution short of war is practicable at present, but if the Dictators would have a modicum of patience I can imagine that a way could be found of meeting

German claims while safeguarding Poland's independence and Economic Security.' He was also thinking, he told his sister, of proposing a twelve-month truce to Mussolini in order to let the tension relax.

While Chamberlain continued to hope that some European agreement might be possible 'to let the temperature cool down', Churchill, at a private dinner at which Joe Kennedy, the American Ambassador, had spoken in a defeatist manner, declared emphatically: 'there can never be peace in Europe while eight million Czechs are in bondage'.

Remaining at Chartwell for most of the summer, Churchill worked on his book, wrote his regular articles for the *Daily Telegraph* and the *News of the World*, and received a stream of visitors: Léon Blum, Malcolm MacDonald, 'Prof' Lindemann and General Ironside. So pleased was Churchill to have the chance of a good talk with a senior General that on the day of Ironside's visit, 24 July 1939, the two men talked after dinner until five in the morning. The content of their talk was sombre. It was now too late for any appeasement. Churchill told Ironside that the 'deed was signed', and Hitler was going to make war. Once war began, so Churchill forecast, Poland would be crippled or annihilated, Italy would join Germany 'to create diversions', Egypt would be captured 'chiefly by Italian forces', Germany would press on to the Black Sea 'via Rumania' and Hitler would make an alliance with Russia as soon as Russia saw 'how the land lies'.

A month after this conversation, the Nazi–Soviet Pact was signed. A month later, Poland had been defeated by Germany and partitioned between Hitler and Stalin.

As the night advanced, Ironside and Churchill discussed how Britain could counter the initial German victories. Churchill revived one of his First World War plans, to send British battleships into the Baltic Sea. Three days later Ironside noted in his diary how Churchill had walked up and down the room at Chartwell, 'full of patriotism and ideas for saving the Empire'. He must, Ironside added, 'be chafing at the inaction'.

Work on the *English-speaking Peoples* continued at Chartwell throughout the first two weeks of August, with Bill Deakin in almost constant attendance. But when Chamberlain announced his decision to adjourn Parliament until the beginning of October, Churchill broke off his work on the history to prepare yet another speech, warning that such an adjournment could only encourage the Germans to believe that Britain would not take decisive action when the crisis came. During the debate itself, on 2 August 1939, Churchill was supported by Attlee, Eden and Sinclair.

The situation in Europe, Churchill argued, was 'graver than it was this time last year'. All along the Polish frontier, from Danzig to Cracow, there were heavy massings of German troops, 'and every preparation is being made for a speedy advance'. Troops and supplies were moving eastward. Buildings had been cleared 'for the accommodation of the wounded'. Was this, then, the moment, when even the Royal Navy was largely mobilized, for the House of

Commons to separate for two whole months. It would be quite wrong, Churchill declared, 'for the Government to say to the House, "Begone! Run off and play. Take your masks with you. Do not worry about public affairs. Leave them to the gifted and experienced Ministers", who, after all, so far as our defences are concerned, landed us where we were landed in September last year, and who, after all – I make all allowances for the many difficulties – have brought us in foreign policy at this moment to the point where we have guaranteed Poland and Rumania, after having lost Czechoslovakia, and not having gained Russia.'

Among those Conservatives who supported Churchill's arguments in the debate were Leo Amery, Harold Macmillan, and another of the young Munich abstainers, Ronald Cartland. All were rebuked by Neville Chamberlain who, as the *Manchester Guardian* reported, 'fell back on stale party gibes, cracked the disciplinary whip, and warned his supporters to obey'. After Chamberlain's speech, Ronald Cartland reported to his sister Barbara, that when he and his friends had left the Chamber 'disconsolately', he himself had expressed the view to Churchill that there was nothing more they could do. To this Churchill had replied with vigour: 'Do no more my boy? There's a lot more we can do. This is the time to fight – to speak – to attack!'

Churchill certainly intended to follow his own advice, and in a fifteen-minute broadcast to the United States on 8 August 1939, a broadcast spiced with irony, he began: 'Holiday time, ladies and gentleman! Holiday time, my friends across the Atlantic! Holiday time, when the summer calls the toilers of all countries for an all too brief spell from the offices and mills and stiff routine of daily life and bread-winning, and sends them to seek if not rest at least change in new surroundings, to return refreshed and keep the myriad wheels of civilised society on the move.'

And how, Churchill went on, had the world spent its summer holidays twenty-five years before. 'Why, those were the very days', he said, 'when the German advance guards were breaking into Belgium and trampling down its people on their march towards Paris!', hacking their way through a country 'whose neutrality and independence they had sworn not merely to respect but to defend'.

Now, Churchill said, there was 'a hush all over Europe, nay, over all the world'. Only in China was it broken by the continuing dull thud of Japanese bombs. The Chinese, he said, were fighting 'our battle – the battle of democracy'. They were defending 'the soil, the good earth, that has been theirs since the dawn of time', and defending it 'against cruel aggression'.

Churchill went on: 'Give them a cheer across the ocean – no one knows whose turn it may be next. If this habit of military dictatorships breaking into other people's lands with bomb and shell and bullet, stealing the property and killing the proprietors, spreads too widely, we may none of us be able to think of summer holidays for quite a while.'

What sort of a hush, Churchill asked his listeners, was 'hanging over

Europe'. Alas, he answered, it was 'the hush of suspense, and in many lands it is the hush of fear'. His broadcast then continued: 'Listen! No, listen carefully; I think I hear something – yes there it was quite clear. Don't you hear it? It is the tramp of armies crunching the gravel of the parade-grounds, splashing through rain-soaked fields, the tramp of two million German soldiers and more than a million Italians – "going on manoeuvres" – yes, only on manoeuvres! Of course it's only manoeuvres – just like last year. After all, the Dictators must train their soldiers. They could scarcely do less in common prudence, when the Danes, the Dutch, the Swiss, the Albanians – and of course the Jews – may leap out upon them at any moment and rob them of their living-space . . .'

The German and Italian armies, Churchill warned, might yet have 'another work of liberation' to perform: 'It was only last year they liberated Austria from the horrors of self-government. It was only in March they freed the Czechoslovak Republic from the misery of independent existence. It is only two years ago that Signor Mussolini gave the ancient kingdom of Abyssinia its Magna Charta. It is only two months ago that little Albania got its writ of Habeas Corpus.' No wonder, Churchill said, 'that the German and Italian armies were tramping on, when there is so much liberation to be done, and no wonder there is a hush among the neighbours of Germany and Italy while they are wondering which one is going to be "liberated" next'.

The Nazis said they were being encircled, Churchill went on, but it was they who would have encircled themselves 'with a ring of neighbours who have to keep on guessing who will be struck down next'. All depended upon Hitler, a man who, 'in a single day', could release the world 'from the fear that now oppresses it, or in a single day can plunge all that we have and are into a volcano of smoke and flame'. If Hitler did not make war, Churchill ended, 'there will be no war. No one else is going to make war.'

Churchill now prepared to go, as the guest of the French army, to visit the Maginot Line, the defensive chain of fortresses along France's frontier with Germany. Before going, he went, as Kingsley Wood's guest, to watch fighter exercises at Biggin Hill, just north of Chartwell, and together with Kingsley Wood inspected the planes and talked to the pilots. Then, accompanied by a friend, Louis Spears, whom he had known since before the First World War, and who was now a Conservative MP, Churchill flew to France on the morning of 14 August 1939.

From Paris, where he was resting briefly at the Ritz, Churchill wrote to his wife of how one of the most senior of French Generals, Joseph Georges, 'who will command the Army in a war, has put all aside and will conduct me. He met the aeroplane and drove me to the restaurant in the Bois where in divine sunshine we lunched; and talked "shop" for a long time.'

According to French military opinion, nothing would happen until the snow began to fall in the Alps, to give Mussolini 'a protection for the winter'. This

259

would point to early or mid-September, 'which would still leave Hitler two months to deal with Poland before the mud season in that country'.

Louis Spears, who was present at the luncheon, also recorded, but in later years, the conversation as he recalled it. General Georges, he remembered, was as certain as he and Churchill that the Germans had 'benefited from the time gained at Munich'. Hitler's capture of the Czech armament firm of Skoda was a 'major disaster' as the French artillery could no longer maintain its 'incomparable superiority'. The Germans had also 'forged ahead' in the air and all that France and Britain could do to catch up was place orders in the United States.

Spears remembered during the lunch Churchill's persistent questions about the Maginot Line itself, not the fortress chain, but the 'shoulder' of the line, 'where it came to an end about Montmédy and was thence prolonged by field works opposite the Ardennes, and on to the sea'. Spears could not remember the General's reply but he did recall vividly 'Churchill's pursed mouth, his look centred on the fruit on the table as if he were crystal-gazing'. Spears also wrote how Churchill's face 'had ceased smiling, and the shake of his head was ominous when he observed that he hoped these field works were strong, that it would be very unwise to think the Ardennes were impassable to strong forces'. Remember, Churchill told his two companions, that Britain and France were now faced 'with a new weapon, armour in great strength, on which the Germans are no doubt concentrating', and that forests would be 'particularly tempting' to such forces, offering as they did 'concealment from the air'.

From Paris, Churchill and Spears travelled eastward to Strasbourg, and on 15 August 1939 the French military authorities took Churchill round several sections of the Maginot Line which had never been shown to any foreigner. At Neufbrisach Churchill looked across the Rhine to where, on the German side, German troops and fortifications could easily be seen. 'The trip', wrote Spears, 'tore to shreds any illusion that it was not Germany's intention to wage war and to wage it soon.' The Germans' 'grim, relentless preparations were quite clear to see'. Every French commander, Spears recalled, 'had tales to tell and they all led to the same conclusion'.

On 17 August 1939 Churchill returned to Paris, and then, after a night at the Ritz, travelled westward to Consuelo Balsan's château at Dreux. He had known Consuelo since the turn of the century when, as the young Consuelo Vanderbilt, she had married his cousin Sunny Marlborough. The marriage had broken up, but Churchill and Consuelo had remained good friends, and her château had long been a favourite haven. As he was being driven there from Paris, he dictated some notes to his secretary. Then he fell silent. Churchill, she later recalled, 'grew graver as he sat wrapped in thought, and then said slowly and sorrowfully: "Before the harvest is gathered in – we shall be at war."'

While Churchill rested at Consuelo's château, and was joined by his wife and their daughter Mary, a giant poster in one of London's main shopping streets proclaimed, in mysterious anonymity: 'What Price Churchill?' And the mail now brought to Churchill from England contained hundreds of letters from ordinary people, insisting that he ought to be in the Government, in a national effort to cause Hitler to pause before taking the final step to war.

Churchill later recalled the 'sunshine days' at the château, in the presence of 'a pleasant but deeply anxious company'. One could feel, he wrote, 'the deep apprehension brooding over all, and even the light of this lovely valley at the confluence of the Eure and the Vesgre seemed robbed of its genial ray'. Churchill added: 'I found painting hard work in this uncertainty.'

In the grounds of Consuelo's château was a small mill, another favourite subject of Churchill's canvasses of earlier visits. Staying at the mill that August was Churchill's friend, the French artist, Paul Maze. 'I worked alongside him,' Maze wrote in his diary on 20 August 1939. 'He suddenly turned to me and said: "This is the last picture we shall paint in peace for a very long time."'

As Churchill and Maze painted together, Churchill would make the occasional remark about the relative strengths of the French and German armies: 'Then his jaw would clench his large cigar, and I felt the determination of his will. "Ah," he would say, "with it all, we shall have him."'

It was impossible at Dreux to follow the day-to-day evolution of events, and Churchill was increasingly anxious to know 'what was going on'. On 22 August 1939 he left for Paris and London. As he went, Paul Maze handed him a letter, 'only to be read when you are over the Channel'. Its message was short: 'Don't worry, Winston, you *know* that you will be Prime Minister and lead us to victory.'

On his way through Paris, Churchill lunched with General Georges. 'He produced all the figures', Churchill later wrote, 'of the French and German armies, and classified the Divisions in quality. The result impressed me so much that for the first time I said: "But you are the masters."' To this, however, Georges replied: 'The Germans have a very strong army, and we shall never be allowed to strike first.'

That evening Churchill reached Chartwell. Waiting for him was W. H. Thompson, who had been his personal bodyguard in 1921 and 1922, when he was at the Colonial Office, from 1924 to 1929, when he was Chancellor of the Exchequer, and again on Churchill's American journey in 1931. The two men inspected Churchill's pistols, which had been taken out of their boxes during the summer, and repaired. That night Churchill slept soundly. But the news that greeted him on the following morning was ominous: an imminent German alliance with Russia, and on the following day, 24 August 1939, the *Daily Mirror* published an article in which Churchill wrote of how, as a result of the Sovet–German 'intrigue', and the advance of German military preparations it was impossible to see how war could be averted. That same day, Parliament was recalled. Waiting for Chamberlain to reach the Commons, a group of six men and women walked up and down the pavement carrying sandwhich boards with the word CHURCHILL in a blue circle.

The Nazi–Soviet pact was signed on 25 August 1939. Later that same day

Chamberlain announced the signature of a formal Treaty of Alliance with Poland, and all earlier efforts to persuade the Poles to make concessions to Germany were abandoned. Four days later, to make sure that no further pressure was being applied on Poland, Churchill telephoned the Polish Ambassador, Count Raczyński, who told him, in the presence of Duff Cooper and Brendan Bracken, that he was now 'completely satisfied with the support he was receiving from our Government'.

Churchill returned to Chartwell, and to the final chapters of his history. On 31 August 1939 he wrote to his publisher that a total of 530,000 words were now completed, and that he was concentrating every minute of his 'spare life and strength' in order to fulfil his contract.

That night Churchill worked once more on his book into the early hours of 1 September 1939. Then, while he slept, the German armies invaded Poland.

Churchill was woken on that fateful Sunday morning by a telephone call. It was the Polish Ambassador, Count Raczyński, to inform him that German bombs were at that very moment falling on Warsaw and German troops advancing into Poland. Churchill at once telephoned the news to General Ironside at Horse Guards Parade, and Ironside passed it on by telephone to the War Office, amazed to find that no one there had yet heard the news.

During the morning Churchill drove from Chartwell to London, for an emergency meeting of the House of Commons later in the day. At Chamberlain's request, he went first to 10 Downing Street, where Chamberlain asked him if he would be willing to join a special War Cabinet. As Chamberlain had already decided that the Ministers in charge of the Air Ministry, the Admiralty and the War Office should remain outside the War Cabinet, he offered Churchill a post without a Ministry. He would become a member of the War Cabinet, but with no specific departmental work.

'I agreed to his proposal without comment,' Churchill later recalled, 'and on this basis we had a long talk on men and measures.'

During their meeting on the morning of September 1 Chamberlain told Churchill 'the die is cast' and a message was sent to Berlin warning the Germans that unless they 'suspended all aggressive action against Poland' and were prepared to withdraw their forces from Polish soil, the British Government would fulfil their obligations to Poland 'without hesitation'.

In giving this message to the Germans, however, Sir Nevile Henderson was instructed to make clear that it was not an ultimatum, and despite the continuing German advance throughout the day, by midnight the British Government had still not acted on the basis of its warning, and had not declared war on Germany. Polish cities had been bombed continually throughout the day, and German forces had advanced steadily; but unkown to Churchill, the British Foreign Office and the French Government, encouraged to do so by Mussolini, were still trying to work out some formula for a compromise, and a conference.

During the morning of Saturday September 2, Churchill wrote to Chamberlain in some alarm about Britain's position. 'The Poles have now been under heavy attack for thirty hours', he wrote, 'and I am much concerned to hear that there is talk in Paris of a further note.' He told Chamberlain that he hoped the Joint Declaration of War would be announced, 'at *latest* when Parliament meets this afternoon.'

Churchill waited at Morpeth Mansions. 'I remain here at your disposal,' he had told Chamberlain in his letter; but Chamberlain did not ask for him. Kathleen Hill later recalled how, as the day drew on, 'he was pacing up and down like a lion in a cage'.

At 4.15 that afternoon, while Churchill was still waiting for the summons, the Cabinet met at 10 Downing Street. Halifax opened the discussion by explaining that negotiations were still in progress, at Italy's instigation, aimed at averting a wider war. He and Chamberlain were both agreed that the Germans should be asked to consider an armistice, followed by a conference. The main condition for such a conference was that 'German troops should first withdraw from Polish soil'. The conference should then take the form of 'direct negotiations between Germany and Poland'. But Britain was willing, if Poland and Germany desired it, 'to see other Powers associated in the discussions'.

Not an ultimatum to Germany, but 'consideration of a conference', was now the theme of British policy, as German troops struck deeper into Poland.

Sir Samuel Hoare was distressed that the warning of the previous day had not yet been acted upon. That communication, he said, 'had been generally regarded as in the nature of an ultimatum', and he warned his colleagues 'that he thought there would be tremendous risks in accepting any delay which might well have considerable reactions on public opinion'.

Leslie Hore-Belisha supported Hoare, telling the Cabinet, as the official and secret minutes recorded, that he was 'strongly opposed to further delay, which he thought might result in breaking the present unity in the country'. Public opinion, he added, 'was strongly against our yielding an inch'. An ultimatum should be sent at once, with midnight as its expiry time. If the Government were to hesitate now, he said, 'we might well find ourselves faced with war in a year's time'.

Sir Kingsley Wood supported the idea of a negotiated armistice, arguing that if Hitler agreed to a standstill, and to a withdrawal of his troops, 'it would mean a great loss of prestige, and might result in his downfall'.

Sir Thomas Inskip, like Hoare and Hore-Belisha, favoured an immediate ultimatum, and thought it was 'undesirable' to allow Hitler any longer than until midnight 'to make up his mind'. He was supported in this by Malcolm MacDonald, who pointed out that the Germans had been known to ask other people to make up their minds 'in a very short time'.

Chamberlain, having read out to the Cabinet an appeal by the Polish Government for the 'immediate fulfilment of British obligations to Poland', then stated his agreement with those in favour of a midnight ultimatum. The Cabinet then dispersed.

Two hours later, at 7.30 that Saturday evening, Chamberlain rose in the House of Commons, amid growing unease at the delay in the British response. To the amazement of his Cabinet colleagues on the front bench, he spoke, not of the ultimatum on which they had all agreed two hours before, but of the possibility of further negotiations. Chamberlain announced, in fact, as Hansard recorded, that: 'If the German Government should agree to withdraw their forces, then His Majesty's Government would be willing to regard the position as being the same as it was before the German forces crossed the Polish frontier.' Chamberlain went on to say that as soon as Germany withdrew its troops from Poland, 'the way would be open' to discussions between Poland and Germany, discussions with which the British Government would be willing to be associated.

The House of Commons was horrified. So too were most of Chamberlain's Cabinet colleagues. Immediately after Chamberlain's speech five Ministers, led by Sir John Simon and Leslie Hore-Belisha, hurried to Simon's room in the House of Commons. Soon they were joined by Malcolm MacDonald. All were agreed that the Cabinet's decision to deliver an ultimatum must be implemented at once. They then went to Chamberlain's room, where they put very strongly the case against further delay. Chamberlain promised to consider their view, then left for 10 Downing Street.

Unaware of this Cabinet revolt, the dissident Conservatives were in turmoil. Duff Cooper had gone to the Savoy Grill, where he found two Cabinet Ministers, both friends of his. One, when asked if he were still a member of the Government, made a gesture of 'shame and despair'. The other left a message that Chamberlain's announcement in the Commons had 'taken the whole Cabinet by surprise'.

Duff Cooper then went to see Churchill at Morpeth Mansions. Entering the flat, he found already there with Churchill, Anthony Eden, Bob Boothby and Brendan Bracken. 'We were all in a state of bewildered rage', Duff Cooper noted in his diary. Churchill at once explained to his friends that having agreed on the previous day to join the Government, he had not heard 'a word' from the Prime Minister. He had wanted to speak that night in the House, 'but feeling himself already almost a member of the Government had refrained from doing so'.

The conversation ranged over every possible contingency. Boothby was convinced, as Duff Cooper recorded, 'that Chamberlain had lost the Conservative Party forever and that it was in Winston's power to go to the House of Commons tomorrow and break him and take his place'. Boothby felt, and said, that Churchill should in no circumstances serve under Chamberlain, and that it was better 'to split the country' at such a moment of decision than to continue to 'bolster up Chamberlain'. Such, as they spoke, seemed the decision which Churchill might have to take.

But Churchill himself was, as Duff Cooper noted, 'very undecided, said that he had no wish to be Prime Minister, doubted his fitness for the position'. A telephone call was made to someone at the French Embassy, who said 'all was well – that we should see the situation from quite a different angle tomorrow', a message, Duff Cooper noted, 'which sounded very ominous to us'.

Bracken, Boothby and Duff Cooper then urged Churchill not to serve under Chamberlain unless Eden were included in the War Cabinet. Otherwise, they pointed out, Churchill would be forever in a minority of one. Eden added that he 'did not relish the prospect' of not being in the War Cabinet, but only Dominions Secretary outside it.

Churchill then went into another room to write a letter to Chamberlain. In this letter Churchill referred to his own total ignorance of the events of the day. 'I have not heard anything from you', he wrote, 'since our talks on Friday, when I understood that I was to serve as your colleague, and when you told me that this would be announced speedily.' Churchill went on to tell Chamberlain that he did not know what was happening but he felt that 'entirely different ideas' were governing Chamberlain's actions than those which Chamberlain had told Churchill about on Friday when he had said that 'the die was cast'.

'I feel entitled to ask you', Churchill added, 'to let me know how we stand, both publicly and privately, before the debate opens at noon.'

Churchill also told Chamberlain: 'There was a feeling tonight in the House that injury had been done to the spirit of national unity by the apparent weakening of our resolve.' Whatever difficulties there might be in coordinating Britain's action with France, if that was indeed the problem, decisions must now be taken 'independently', and a lead given to France.

Referring, without revealing his source, to Anthony Eden's unhappiness at being excluded from the War Cabinet, Churchill also pointed out to Chamberlain that the average age of the War Cabinet which Chamberlain had named to him on September 1 was sixty-five, but that if Chamberlain 'added Sinclair (49) and Eden (42) the average comes down to 57½'.

At 10 Downing Street, yet another drama was in progress: Lord Halifax, about to go out to dinner elsewhere, had been telephoned by Chamberlain and asked to go to Downing Street instead. In a record of their telephone conversation written two or three days later, Halifax wrote: 'The statement had gone very badly, he said, in the House of Commons, people misinterpreting the inability to give a time-limit to be the result of half-heartedness and hesitation on our part, with the result that there had been a very unpleasant scene in which much feeling had been shown. I had never heard the Prime Minister so disturbed.' Halifax had hurried to Downing Street, where Chamberlain gave him dinner. 'He told me', Halifax recorded, 'that the statement infuriated the House and that he did not believe, unless we could clear the position, that the Government would be able to maintain itself when it met Parliament the next day.'

At Morpeth Mansions, Churchill had completed his letter to Chamberlain, and now read it to his assembled friends. Outside, a violent storm had broken, with teeming rain striking the roof tops, and claps of thunder reverberating across St James's Park. Unknown to the group at Morpeth Mansions, the 'rebel' members of Chamberlain's Cabinet were at that very moment preparing to present the Prime Minister with an ultimatum. Walking through the rain from the House of Commons, the rebels had literally burst their way into 10 Downing Street, demanding to be heard. This bedraggled group, still led by Simon, but swelled to seven or eight, with Hore-Belisha and Malcolm Mac-Donald the most senior, found Chamberlain dining with Halifax. Sir Horace Wilson was also present. The rebels, as they saw themselves, then declared that they would not leave the room until Chamberlain promised to abandon all thoughts of negotiations such as he had outlined in the House of Commons, and return to the Cabinet's own earlier agreement of an immediate ultimatum.

It was almost midnight when Chamberlain agreed to the 'rebel' demands, and the ultimatum to Germany was set to expire at eleven o'clock on the following morning. The Cabinet dispersed.

At Morpeth Mansions Churchill, Eden, Duff Cooper, Boothby and Bracken were desperate to know what was happening. Eventually, as Duff Cooper recorded in his diary, 'Winston succeeded in getting through to someone whom he described as "a friend" who would be able to tell him what had taken place at the Cabinet. Unfortunately his secretary gave the show away by coming in and saying "Mr Hore-Belisha is on the telephone". Churchill was much annoyed. He came back with the information that after a very stormy Cabinet – stormy in every sense for it was attended by a terrific thunderstorm – it had been decided to deliver the ultimatum next morning.'

This altered the whole situation, Duff Cooper added. 'Our heated discussion cooled down. Winston said that he would send his letter to the Prime Minister none the less – and so in the small hours we wandered through the dark streets.'

On 3 September 1939 at nine o'clock in the morning, the British Government sent its ultimatum to Berlin. If Germany did not halt its attack on Poland within three hours Britain would be at war. When the Germans did not reply, Chamberlain broadcast that war with Germany had now begun.

Churchill recalled in his memoirs how he and Clementine had listened to the broadcast at their flat at Morpeth Mansions, and then, as the air-raid sirens sounded, had first gone to the roof where they had seen barrage balloons over London guarding the capital. 'We gave the Government a good mark for this evident sign of preparation.'

Churchill and his wife then hurried into the air-raid shelter, 'armed' with a bottle of brandy and other 'medical comforts'. The shelter, Churchill later wrote, 'consisted merely of an open basement, not even sand-bagged', and as Churchill 'gazed from the doorway along the empty street' he drew in his imagination 'pictures of ruin and carnage and vast explosions shaking the ground'.

After the 'all-clear' had sounded, Churchill went to the House of Commons to hear Chamberlain's account of the days leading up to Britain's ultimatum. Listening to this recital of events, Churchill later recalled in his memoirs, he was conscious of how 'a very strong sense of calm' began to grow in him, as the 'intense passions and excitements' of the days leading up to the ultimatum gave way to 'serenity of mind' and an 'uplifted detachment from human and personal affairs'.

Churchill added: 'The glory of old England, peace-loving and ill-prepared as she was but instant and fearless at the call of honour, thrilled my being and seemed to lift our fate to those spheres far removed from earthly fact and physical sensation.'

As Chamberlain spoke, he told the House of Commons that he hoped he might live 'to see the day when Hitlerism has been destroyed'. The Labour and Liberal leaders also spoke, followed by Churchill, who told his fellow MPs: 'In this solemn hour it is a consolation to recall and to dwell upon our repeated efforts for peace.' All these efforts had been 'ill-starred', but they had also 'been faithful and sincere'. That, he said, 'is of the highest moral value'. Outside, he said, 'the storms of war may blow and the lands may be lashed with the fury of its gales, but in our own hearts this Sunday morning there is peace. Our hands may be active, but our consciences are at rest.'

Churchill had been a backbencher, out of office, and out of favour for the past decade. But as he spoke, all those who listened to him recognized the voice of a man of stature, and of integrity. 'We must not underrate the gravity of the task which lies before us', he told the House of Commons, 'or the severity of the ordeal, to which we shall not be found unequal. We must expect many disappointments, and many unpleasant surprises, but we may be sure that the task which we have freely accepted is one not beyond the compass and the strength of the British Empire and the French Republic.' It was no longer a question, he said, of fighting for Danzig or of fighting for Poland. Britain was fighting 'to save the whole world from the pestilence of Nazi tyranny and in defence of all that is most sacred to man.' It was a war, Churchill declared, 'viewed in its inherent quality, to establish, on impregnable rocks, the rights of the individual, and it is a war to establish and revive the stature of man'.

In silence, Churchill drove with Clementine to 10 Downing Street. As she waited in the car, he went into No 10, emerging a few minutes later and hurrying back to his car. The door was opened and he called out to his wife, 'It's the Admiralty. That's a lot better than I thought.'

The wilderness years were over. But Churchill was never to shake off the bitter conviction that had other policies been followed, war could have been averted. During those ten years, those who recognized, and did not blind themselves to how near Britain was coming to destruction, were few in number, and most of them circumscribed by their official positions. Sir Robert Vansittart, Ralph Wigram and Sir Maurice Hankey had been among this small group. As civil servants, their job was to advise on policy, not to make it, nor to change it, and when their advice went unheeded, there was little they could do. Vansittart struggled on in ever more anguished tone until he was finally given a sinecure. Hankey adapted himself to his failure. Wigram, tragically, was likewise powerless, although he used unorthodox methods, including direct and secret contact with Churchill, in order to try to galvanize public opinion.

Only the politicians had the power; these politicians were led first by Ramsay MacDonald, then by Stanley Baldwin, and for the last two and a half years of peace, by Neville Chamberlain. At first, these three Prime Ministers, and a majority, but never every Member of their Cabinets, were reluctant to recognize that danger was near. Then, with each crisis, they were unable to contemplate the possibility of war because of Britain's weakness in defence, especially in the air. But after each crisis passed, they again convinced themselves that the danger was distant, and failed to take the measures that were being urged upon them, often by their own expert advisers. Theirs was a failure of leadership; a failure to educate the British people, to inform them and to arm them. Finally they brought the British people to the outbreak of war inadequately defended and with several of their potential allies already destroyed or isolated. Those few politicians, like Lord Swinton, Anthony Eden and Duff Cooper, who did see the dangers, were outnumbered and outmanoeuvred.

Before he died at the end of 1936, Ralph Wigram had tried to use Churchill's officially powerless but publicly recognized position as an elder Statesman to create greater understanding of what was happening in Europe, and to force Government action to try to prevent war. In this, he, as well as Churchill and Vansittart, failed, for as Churchill came to realize, only the terrible lesson of events would teach the British Government that Hitler would have to be resisted.

What Wigram, Churchill and Vansittart did achieve, however, was a gradual and total acceptance by the British people that Hitlerism was evil and would ultimately have to be resisted. They also established that Churchill himself was the man whose personal authority, knowledge and strength of character would be able to lead Britain through the most terrible and desperate war.

Shortly before he died, Ralph Wigram poured out his soul to his wife Ava. In doing so, he told the story of Churchill's wilderness years. 'I have failed', Wigram lamented, 'to make the people here realize what is at stake. I am not strong enough, I suppose. I have not been able to make the people here understand. Winston has always, always understood, and he is strong and will go on to the end.'

Sources

All letters to and from Churchill, and most of his articles and speeches, quoted in this book are from the Churchill papers (courtesy C&T Publications Limited, owners of the Churchill copyrights; and William Heinemann Limited, publishers of the Official Biography). All Parliamentary speeches are from *Hansard* (courtesy Her Majesty's Stationery Office). All other sources are listed below.

Individual recollections were given to the author by:
the late Torr Anderson, DFC, quoted on pages 172 and 177
Maurice Ashley, CBE, 52
Judge Brown, QC, 176–7
the late Randolph Churchill, MBE, 13
Sarah Churchill, Lady Audley, 13 (Lindemann story) and 164 (marriage)
the late Lord Coleraine (Richard Law) 234
the late Sir Colin Coote 233–4
Sir Michael Creswell 120
the late Sir Weldon Dalrymple-Champneys 51
Sir F. W. Deakin, DSO, 161–2 and 178
Sir Patrick Donner 65–66
the late Sir Reginald Dorman-Smith 264 and 265–6
Grace Hamblin, OBE, 178
Kathleen Hill, OBE, 254
the late Lachlan MacLean 177
the late Paul Maze, MM, 261
the late Sir Harold Nicolson 239
the late Sir Orme Sargent 234

Archival material cited in this book is from the following sources:
Amery papers (private possession): 15, 227–8
Baldwin papers (Cambridge University Library): 11, 12, 18, 31, 141, 146
Baruch papers (private possession): 253 (Bracken letter)
Beaverbrook papers (House of Lords Library): 18, 22, 29
Birla papers (private possession): 76–7
Boothby papers (private possession): 35
Camrose papers (private possession): 255–6
Austen Chamberlain papers (Birmingham University Library): 145
Neville Chamberlain papers (Birmingham University Library): 11, 141, 148, 150, 251, 252, 253, 255, 256–7
Randolph Churchill papers (private possession): 30, 32, 33, 142–3, 168
Duff Cooper papers (private possession): 234, 262, 264, 266
Cripps papers (private possession): 255
Derby papers (private possession): 69, 70

Dundee papers: (private possession): 14
P. J. Grigg papers (Churchill College, Cambridge): 215 (Wilson letter)
Halifax papers (Public Record Office, London): 265
Hankey papers (Churchill College, Cambridge): 28, 155, 184, 216
Harvey of Tasburgh papers (private possession): 256
Ironside papers (private possession): 257
Irwin papers (India Office Library): 11, 18, 26, 27, 29–30, 32, 32–3
Lord Lloyd papers (Churchill College, Cambridge): 150
Lloyd George papers (House of Lords Library): 24
Lothian papers (Scottish Record Office): 176 (Dawson letter)
Venetia Montagu papers (Bodleian Library, Oxford): 10 (Asquith to a friend)
Phipps papers (Churchill College, Cambridge): 216 (Hankey letter)
Sinclair papers (Churchill College, Cambridge): 23
Templewood Papers (Cambridge University Library): 39, 63, 64, 66, 66–7, 67–8, 69, 70, 73–4, 122, 146, 236
Ava, Viscountess of Waverley papers (private possession): 173

Official records cited here are taken from several archives, including:
Admiralty papers: 27
Cabinet papers: 16, 56, 66, 77, 78–9, 107, 113, 120, 130–1, 132, 142, 146, 147, 148–9, 150–1, 155, 157, 158, 165, 170, 175, 184, 211, 214–15, 215, 218–19, 219–20, 220–1, 226, 227, 228, 229, 230–1, 235, 241, 263
Foreign Office papers: 119–20, 122–3, 125, 127, 128, 129, 130, 131–2, 140, 140–1, 152–3, 184, 212–13, 219, 223, 249, 255, 256
German Foreign Ministry Archives: 36
India Office papers: 65
Premier papers: 117, 149, 160–1, 168, 241

The following newspapers and magazines have also been quoted:
Anglo-German Review 209; *Colliers* 45; *Daily Express* 217, 222; *Daily Herald* 246; *Daily Mail* 26, 41, 42, 49, 54, 141; *Daily Mirror* 206, 261; *Daily Telegraph* 132, 146, 221, 223, 225, 254, 255; *Edinburgh Evening News* 146; *Evening News* 68; *Evening Standard* 150, 152, 161, 181–2, 256; *Listener* 117; *Manchester Guardian* 258; *Morning Post* 28; *New Republic* 17; *News of the World* 145; *New Statesman and Nation* 246; *Picture Post* 247; *Strand* 140; *Sunday Graphic* 50; *Sunday Referee* 224; *Tatler* 96; *The Times* 116, 118, 124, 148, 250; *Yorkshire Post* 217.

Further quotations have been taken (courtesy the authors and publishers) from a number of published works, including:
Barbara Cartland, *The Isthmus Years* (London 1943): 258
Randolph S. Churchill, *Twenty-One Years* (London 1965): 23, 24, 46–7
Winston S. Churchill, *My Early Life* (London and New York 1930): 29
Winston S. Churchill, *The Gathering Storm* (London and Boston 1948): 128, 136, 147–8, 149, 150, 151, 173, 215–16, 217, 261, 262, 266–7, 268
Winston S. Churchill, *Into Battle* (London 1941): 258–9
Tom Driberg, *Guy Burgess* (London 1956): 235
Kay Halle, *Irrepressible Churchill* (Cleveland, Ohio, 1966): 44–5
Ernst Hanfstaengel, *Hitler – The Missing Years* (London 1957): 50–1
Robert Rhodes James, *Chips: The Diaries of Sir Henry Channon* (London 1967): 179

Sources

Robert Rhodes James, *John Colin Campbell Davidson* (London 1968): 171

Robert Rhodes James, *Victor Cazalet* (London 1976): 146

Thomas Jones, *A Diary with Letters* (Oxford 1954): 19–20, 148, 155, 209

V. G. Lawford, *Bound for Diplomacy* (London 1963): 118, 128, 149, 151

Harold Macmillan, *Winds of Change 1914–1939* (London and New York 1966): 250, 251–2

Harold Nicolson, *Diaries and Letters 1930–1939* (London 1966): 28, 166, 215, 218, 230, 231, 233, 251, 257

Cecil Roberts, *The Bright Twenties* (London 1970): 45

Cecil Roberts, *Sunshine and Shadow* (London 1972): 180

Vincent Sheean, *Between the Thunder and the Sun* (London 1943): 138

Lady Soames, *Clementine Churchill: the Biography of a Marriage* (London and Boston 1979): 31, 212

Major General Sir Edward Spears, *Assignment to Catastrophe* (London 1954): 260

W. H. Thompson, *Sixty Minutes with Winston Churchill* (London 1953): 267

Sir Colin Thornton-Kemsley, *Through Winds and Tides* (Montrose 1974): 248

Lord Vansittart, *The Mist Procession* (London 1958): 128

Arnold Wilson, *Walks and Talks Abroad* (London 1936): 110

Index

compiled by the author

Simpson, Mrs (later Duchess of Windsor): 169–72; photograph of, 190
Sinclair, Sir Archibald (later Viscount Thurso): 17, 23, 108, 116, 160, 222, 230, 233, 236, 256, 258
Snowden, Philip (later Viscount): 17, 39; dies, 178
Snowden, Viscountess: 178
Spears, Major-General (Sir) Edward Louis: 259–60
Stalin, Josef: 257
Stanhope, Earl: 231
Strakosch, Sir Henry: 46, 138, 222
Streat, (Sir) Raymond: 70, 74
Swaffer, Hannen: interviews Churchill, 246
Swinton, Earl of: and air policy, 135–6 147, 157, 157–8, 160, 161, 175, 184, 214, 220–1; resigns, 223

Thompson, W. H.: Churchill's detective, 40, 261
Thornton-Kemsley, (Sir) Colin: and opposition to Churchill in his constituency, 242–3, 248–9
Titulescu, Nicolae: 180
Treviranus, Dr: 180
Trotsky, Leon Davidovich: 163

Vansittart, Sir Robert (later Lord): 17; and German air potential, 107, 117–19, 127, 128, 129, 130, 133; and an approach to Churchill, 152–3; and German intentions, 157; and Ralph Wigram's death, 172–3; and Churchill's plans and writings, 180, 181; his 'pro-French bias' criticized, 209; removed from power, 212–13; and the Czechoslovak crisis (of 1938), 222, 223, 230; his struggle, 267–8; photograph of, 193
Victoria, Queen: 14

Villiers, (Sir) Francis: to combat 'the Winston propaganda', 66–7

Watson-Watt, (Sir) Robert: 157–8
Wells, H. G.: and the League of Nations, 106
Wenceslas, King: 61
Westminster, 2nd Duke of: 63
Wheldon, John: 254
Wigram, Ava (later Viscountess Waverley): 127, 128, 151, 172–3, 212
Wigram, Ralph: 118–20, 121, 122, 125–8; at Chartwell, 127–8; returns to Chartwell, 130; encourages Churchill, 131–2, 133; sends Churchill information, 132, 134, 138, 140–1, 142, 152; and the Rhineland crisis, 149–50, 151, 152; his death, 172–3; 'Winston . . . will go on to the end', 267–8; photograph of, 186
Willingdon, Viscount (later Earl, then Marquess): in India, 63, 65, 66–8, 182
Wilson, Sir Arnold: 110
Wilson, Sir Horace: 210, 214, 215; and Czechoslovakia, 228, 229, 230–1; and the Ministry of Supply, 241; and Anglo-German economic cooperation, 250; 'some hand which intervenes', 252–3; and Anglo-Soviet relations, 255; and fears of 'a second Munich', 256; and the coming of war, 266; photograph of, 201
Winterton, Earl: praises Churchill, 11; abuses Churchill, 67; cartoon of, 104
Wood, Sir Kingsley: 135, 147; as Secretary of State for Air, 223–4, 241, 249–50, 259; and the coming of war, 263; photographs of, 192, 199; cartoon of, 199

Young, G. M.: 254

Zetland, Marquess of: 214